Love and Rage

The Inner Worlds of Children

Love and Rage
The Inner Worlds of Children

Nupur D. Paiva

YODAPRESS

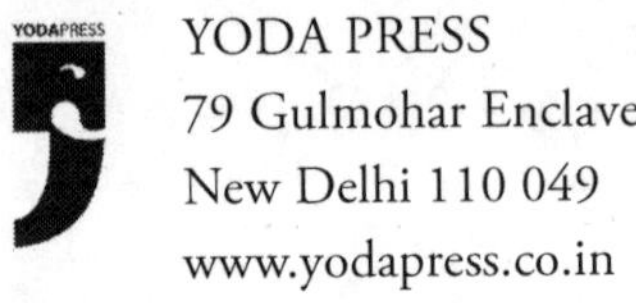

YODA PRESS
79 Gulmohar Enclave
New Delhi 110 049
www.yodapress.co.in

ISBN 978-93-82579-30-4

Editors in charge: Arpita Das
Typeset by Jojy Philip
Printed at Saurabh Printers Pvt. Ltd.
Published by Arpita Das for YODA PRESS, New Delhi

'Tell me one last thing', said Harry. 'Is this real? Or has this been happening inside my head?'

Dumbledore beamed at him, and his voice sounded loud and strong in Harry's ears even though the bright mist was descending again, obscuring his figure.

'Of course it is happening inside your head, Harry, but why on earth should that mean that it is not real?'

Harry Potter and the Deathly Hallows

J.K. Rowling, 2007

Acknowledgements

I can only take credit for putting these words on paper. The capacities, thoughts and feelings in here have emerged from many people and relationships over decades, where gratitude is long overdue.

To Anahita Lee, whose red-inked comments on my teenage essays made me think I could write. To Professor Ashok Nagpal, who deepened that belief in me, thank you for introducing me to Winnicott all those years ago.

To Gill Markless for changing my life with her presence, humour and wisdom during those cold and difficult years in London; for putting up with my barely cloaked maternal transference and for guiding me to find myself.

To my mother for just being her—a lot of my mind exists because of you.

To my sister, Divrina, for our shared childhood, I am grateful that we could find affection and togetherness after anger made us withdraw into silence for years. Thank you for your insistence and faith.

To Yun Pang and Lalit Sharma for gentle, affectionate constructive criticism and warmly egging me on.

To my friends: Rachana, for really understanding me and what I was on about, for reading between the lines, for knowing me so well. To Wrick, for repeatedly pulling me out of the dumps when I was really floundering. To Ashis, for putting the germ of this idea in my head to start with by saying 'this is your craft'. To Leila, for honest, unwavering support and clarity. To Nithya for her unrestrained affection and enthusiasm.

To Prerna Kapur for dependability, for teaching me and allowing us to learn together. To my students at AUD for taking me seriously and being truly present in class.

To Jon Frederickson, Elisabeth Henderson and Thomas Brod, for giving me the courage and skills to look both Love and Rage full in the face.

To Nilanjana Roy for adopting and mentoring me.

To my publisher and editor Arpita Das who really got the point of this book and practically yelled at me that we had to publish it. It would not have happened without you and your belief in me. You made it so easy because I did not need to convince you.

To all the young people and their families, for their trust in me, for letting me join them in the hardest parts of their journeys and for sharing their stories here. It is what makes this work worth publishing.

To Richard, Tara and Isabelle, for showing me the meaning of family. Thank you for making my life extraordinary and for giving me the opportunity to both love and work.

Contents

Note to Reader

This book has no particular order in which it needs or demands to be read. There are no chapter numbers, and your internal need can guide you. You can pick up a chapter for reasons you know best, something about the title that grabs you. The chapters are linked to each other, yet whole in themselves.

Moonwise

sometimes
you know
the moon
is not such a
perfect circle
and the master Painter
makes a passing
brush touch
with a cloud
don't worry
we've passed
the dark side
all you children
rest easy now
we are born
moonwise

—Jean 'Binta' Breeze

Preface
or
Why Write this Book

This is a book about children and about the child within all those of us who are chronologically adult.

By no means is this a new topic in the field of psychotherapy, psychoanalysis, psychology or emotional health. In fact, it forms the bedrock of some of the most influential theorizing in the field. Yet, like most simple truths, it seems to need reiteration, as if each society, perhaps each individual, needs to re-invent this wheel for itself. This book had to be written because through my work it became clear that the subject of small, vulnerable, dependent parts within our adult exteriors was extremely neglected in our society and because this neglect did not just die with us in our lifetimes; it passed on to our children, damaging succeeding generations and that the only way to stem the damage was through increased awareness of our inner worlds, by connecting up all the lonely bits.

Working as a psychotherapist is lonely work. Perhaps anywhere in the world but more so, I feel, in India. It is impossible to talk casually about our work anyway but the combination of being scanty on the ground as a profession and being cast into outer darkness by the public imagination makes it more so. At the best of times, no one wants to talk to a psychotherapist. At the worst of times, we are alone with someone's internal suffering.

After working for a decade for the National Health Service in the UK, I returned to India to find myself lonely; without colleagues or social sanction, so far back in the margins as a profession that I did not know where to start. When I began work as a child psychologist in Delhi, I refused to see individual adults, keeping my time and mind available for children and young people. 'If I fill up my appointment slots with individual adults, I will not have time to offer to a child who may come along' is what I told the few colleagues who would refer patients to me. Also, while I am trained as a clinical psychologist, I am not keen on cognitive assessments. There are plenty of well-trained people in the city who are able to do that and intervene effectively to help a child use strategies to manage their 'wiring' issues. There is a serious dearth however of professionals to help children and their parents attend to the emotional impact of life events—birth, weaning, food, sleep; going to school, making friends, losing loved ones, sharing parents with siblings; failure, anger, greed, envy. This is my work: the child's internal emotional world and the fundamental importance of the ordinary difficulties of growing up. There are still very few professionals in Delhi who understand what this means. Too few. This book is an attempt at reducing this loneliness.

Why do that? I ask myself. Why this need to build a community, link people and join minds?

I know a thing or two about loneliness, especially about the one created by external structures. There are different kinds of loneliness, I suspect. Moving countries as a 23-year-old student to focus on the development of my chronologically adult mind, leaving behind everyone I knew and loved, and more importantly who knew and loved me, I found myself in a huge, cosmopolitan, English-speaking city with a population of seven million and not acquainted with a single human being. Everyone I met, everywhere I went, was unfamiliar, including the vegetation, to the extent that the sight of a mango tree in the botanical gardens brought on waves of homesickness. There were streets of houses and parked cars but no people. Not even strangers. I found myself listening to the banter on the radio in the mornings just to have another conversational voice in the physical space I inhabited. Something to cut the thick silence, anything, even an unfamiliar accented voice about an unfamiliar aspect of pop culture or an unfamiliar climate. The morning weather report structured my wardrobe, my day and my mood. I could go for hours, perhaps days without speaking to anyone if I did not make the effort or a phone call. The Loneliness was palpable. At times, like when I put my headphones on and pretended I was in a film with a background score, I felt like a cliché. I knew this was unremarkable. Terribly ordinary. It was the experience of thousands of young people every year. Reams had been written and filmed about it both as fiction and academic research. I was not impressed by my own suffering.

At other times I knew I was struggling, barely keeping up with an emotional treadmill, running just to keep still. Years later, I look back on this phase and I have new respect for the manic defences—working hard to keep depression at bay. Then, what I had wanted was someone who had a background on me, someone who could link my past and present, not as events but as a relationship to a younger me. Keep in mind the child in me. The parts that also wanted to be fed familiar food or be hugged goodnight. The fact that no one knew anything about me could have been immensely freeing. I could have written my own script, been anyone; it could have been a reinvention. It wasn't.

I felt I was Unseen. Yet, I was seen in certain particular ways—my appearance and accent activated people's stereotypes and brought me face-to-face with a barely-cloaked racism, which was new to me. Coming from north India, sexism one had learnt to expect but the privilege of social class and caste had shielded me from other kinds of discrimination. Suddenly I had become Black, only because I was not White. The backdrop on the stage had changed behind me and I stood out. For the first time, I had to look at myself as female and Black, in addition to struggling South Asian student. If this does not bring about a need for a community, then what does?

This kind of ordinary, commonplace, life-changing awareness is the focus of much of psychotherapy and also of this book, the ordinary and other forces that shape us internally.

Another loneliness I know something about is partly a professional hazard and partly created by the response of social structures, which prefer status quo. Our deeply embedded social hierarchy demands compliance, and the quiet person, toeing the line, fulfilling their prescribed role, is good enough. We are wary of people's creativity and internal meaning-making worlds; of discovering who they are and what they think/feel. Mostly, status quo would prefer if young people did not discover themselves, their own thoughts, feelings and sexuality. There is therefore also the loneliness that we feel while living within our own homes and families, borne out of a lack of connection with others and validation from them. A family that eats together may stay together but eating meals together is not a sufficient condition. Communicating is. Families can be terribly lonely places too.

In large swathes of India, after the initial indulgences of infancy, children are often treated as things; precious things, but things nonetheless, whose inner world is overwhelmed by those in power on the outside. Our children's Innocence is constructed as an unseeing, unhearing and unaware state, as if untouched by the realities of the emotional and relational milieu that surrounds them. Young children's subjectivities—

their thinking, feeling, perceiving processes—are often denied as adults convince themselves that the children in their care remain oblivious to the swirl of unspoken emotions around them, to the life of the family and especially to conflict, be it in the marital relationship or between generations in a joint family. Many families seem to work hard to deny the child's experience and are overwhelmed by its expression.

Every so often, I find myself wishing that more conversations could be had about what actually happened in my consulting room. 'Do you sometimes wish that more people knew about what we *actually* did?' I ask my colleagues. We unanimously agree that we are tired of the caricature 'Tell me about your childhood' and 'hm….so you are angry with your mother'. I personally identify more with the 'How many psychotherapists does it take to change a light bulb?'*

We agree that we are also tired of the polite outward smiles we have to produce to cover the inner grimace when we meet the 'Oh! You are a psychologist? You can read my mind!' comment. 'Actually, no. I can't', I would want to reply. Occasionally I would want to add 'if that is an example of what is on your mind, I wouldn't want to read it', but I have never said that out loud. I have at times toyed with lying about what I do for a living though, wanting to come up with something commonplace or non-controversial, dull even, a real conversation-stopper—something the public imagination has relegated to the category of 'non-threatening'; something that would not raise eyebrows and therefore be effortless for me to respond to. Being honest about my profession in a social gathering then requires me to engage at an honest, genuine level; unfortunately, with parts that people are desperately trying to hide behind the alcohol, make-up and outfits, i.e., not really the time or place for depth.

---

* Just one. But the light-bulb has to want to change.

Perhaps this book could be that place.

My attempt is to underline the significance of ordinariness in our lives and how it often comes to define us, yet we work hard to minimise or deny its relevance. The novel, the unusual, the traumatic or dramatic grabs our attention, yet we forget to consider, or we un-see, the impact of how we live the everyday in an ordinary way.

The focus of my work and of the stories that follow is on children and young people; their relationships to their peers, their families, their bodies and their internal worlds; life transitions, the way that a new baby changes a family, both man and woman from the inside out—stuff that no one seems to acknowledge aloud. I find it is easy for parents, doctors and teachers to focus on children's capacities in their concreteness; in physical and mental terms—cognition, development, growth, height and weight— but not in emotional and relational terms. Their feelings toward themselves and their loved ones; their relationship to food, to their body, health, family, work and each other. This, in our country which has one of the highest rates of suicide amongst young people in the age range of 16–29. Where the burden of mental illness is the highest in the most productive ages between 16 and 44 and where the rates of suicide among homemakers is rising steadily (*Hindu Business Line BLink*, 2017). What is in the home that is so toxic that it makes both the youth and the caregiver want to die is a question we need to ask. There is so much work to be done that it is hard to focus without being distracted and overwhelmed by the sheer need for attention to emotional health in India today.

The writings that follow, previously published and elaborated upon or unpublished, are on topics which have stirred me deeply. They are all emotional, socio-cultural, historical, political and personal. They are also all true and entirely ordinary, generously shared by their owners. By sharing these stories I hope to start conversations in people's heads, between the child in them and the adult exterior and between generations in families, even if only as a silent conversation within one participant. Conversations that are too difficult, too sad, or too overwhelming to be had out loud because even a lot of love is hard to express. In our families, parents and children interact mainly through instruction, advice, expectation and obedience. We do not often share personal emotional histories in detail and depth; grandparents' lived lives are eons away from those of their grandchildren. We don't talk enough, tell enough stories or ask enough questions of our loved ones, mainly to protect each other from intense feelings and the fear of being overwhelmed. When my grandfather passed away I realised how little I knew him and of him; his growing up in the Punjab in a British-run boarding school, his losing his mother at the age of four and his father remarrying. His escaping the pogrom in a burning Rawalpindi with the clothes on his back and fear in his gut about his month-old infant and young wife. These constitute only the bare bones of a story of a life, of a history that is in some way also mine and that I know too little of. Why, I wonder, when we had 36 overlapping years of his 99? He was born in 1916, lived through two world wars, imperial rule, the partition of India and many decades after. The world wars and the partition have been documented and researched by social scientists of every hue but does anyone really know what it does to the atmosphere in a home or what is left of it? To the air the family breathes? I suspect that we do not realise quite how external events enter people's living rooms and bedrooms; as silences (so we can bear that-which-must-not-be-named) and unspoken imperatives (e.g., 'we must rebuild what we lost at any cost' or 'no amount of money is enough' or 'whatever you do, never marry a non-Hindu) and adds to the gap between generations. In my country, Punjab, Delhi and Bengal have no dearth of families with such painful experiences in their personal histories. It has become the stuff of the ordinary.

This book is about children; the children we once were, the child still in us or the children we may be looking after in one way or another. It is about mothers and fathers and caring freed from age and gender restrictions. It is a book about being aware of the seemingly small stuff—the anxieties, daydreams, feelings, fears and joy. Joy in the ordinariness. I hope I can encourage the reader to be thoughtful about our everyday, ordinary lives as adults in relationships where we care for others, dull and repetitive as they may seem at one level. It is also about the pain of losses, transitions, endings, the end of a day, the end of a marriage, the end of a life stage, the end of a life and the beginning of a new one. It is about the damage that we do to ourselves and to those in closest proximity to us—knowingly or unwittingly. It is about parts of ourselves that we are unaware of or have worked hard to become unaware of, but which are often significant forces beneath the surface of our consciously lived lives.

This book is about the love and rage in our seemingly ordinary lives and the extraordinary richness in their detail.

> 'Do not ask your children
> to strive for extraordinary lives.
> Such striving may seem admirable,
> but it is the way of foolishness.
> Help them instead to find the wonder
> and the marvel of an ordinary life.
> Show them the joy of tasting
> tomatoes, apples and pears.
> Show them how to cry
> when pets and people die.
> Show them the infinite pleasure
> in the touch of a hand.
> And make the ordinary come alive for them.
> The extraordinary will take care of itself.'

—William Martin, *The Parent's Tao Te Ching:
Ancient Advice for Modern Parents*

In what follows, I have brought all my various selves—the self I am at work and the one I am at home with my husband and two daughters; the person I am with my friends as well as my inner self that no one really hears about too often. The writing is therefore deeply situated in specifics: specific contexts, life stories and socio-cultural histories. They may not be generalizable at all. Single parents, children with special needs or disabilities, severe illness, trauma and poverty are not covered in this volume. On the other hand, since I do believe that the emotional needs of our children are similar, regardless of our contexts—safety, reliability, continuity, acknowledgement and learning to bear the coming together of opposites—perhaps there is some possibility of generalization. If any part of these chapters resonates with you as a reader, where it makes you wander off into your own personal history and begin reflecting on your feelings and relationships, my work is done.

Talking to others about matters related to feelings and personal relationships is difficult and people find it hard to approach professionals for help with emotional difficulties. The first few chapters look at the life situations when one might need to consider approaching a psychotherapist for a child or family. This is the subject of 'When to Talk to a Stranger' which also does a fairly detailed sweep of some of the key references I have looked at in my reading and practice, and in that sense acts as an Introduction to the chapters that follow. This Introduction and 'Being Kept in Mind, Not Mindreading', are about psychotherapy—what when and how.

'In the Beginning' looks at the significance of the early weeks and months of life and the bond between the baby and the world outside. The early feeding relationship is a crucial part of this introduction to the world and 'Breastfeeding' looks at this experience of the mother and baby in the context of present-day society.

'Baby, Don't Sing Me the Blues' is about the blues that a baby brings on, i.e., post-natal depression: its origins and impact on mother and baby. The chapter highlights how this is a neglected phenomenon and doubly neglected in the situation is the baby at the receiving end of her mother's blues.

'Play': Children are expected to play, and I do not mean video games, but do we really realise how valuable it is for their well-being? Play is making-sense-of-the-world, it is internal education, it is therapeutic, not just the manipulation of objects. A child who can play has a lot going for her.

Play hard and then rest. 'Bedtime' is about something fundamental, sleep. All through our lives, as children and forever to the child in us; both rejuvenating, helping to sort out the mess of the day and yet potentially full of conflict in the everyday.

'Nazar': A commonly used phrase in many families but rarely discussed in academic circles since it is terribly unscientific; the power of the gaze, especially the not-so-nice gaze is looked in the eye in this chapter.

'Fathers and their Absence' and 'On Why We Need Two Parents' are entwined and tricky subjects about us needing diversity in our lives and how that comes first from the difference between our parents. These chapters bring fathers into the scene in a significant way.

At the root of our capacity to learn is always something emotional, and things become interesting and meaningful to us only if they are 'Mindblowing'. 'First Day at School' is about negotiating the anxieties of going to school as a newbie and then as staying interested while it all becomes very dull around you.

The significance of our 'Siblings', whom we both love and

hate: the one relationship where we can acknowledge this ambivalence (usually) and the richness this brings to our lives.

'Anger: Beloved Demon'—perhaps the most difficult subject to address and a common theme in every psychotherapy consulting room.

'Childhood Desires'—the flipside of and intricately woven in with frustration, anger and pain, the desire for love, touch and closeness is our earliest lived experience, if we are lucky.

'The Air in the Home' looks at how children are remarkably, unnervingly perceptive and pick up minute events and details in the atmosphere, both particle and wave, of the home. Unstated emotional truths that we try to hide, and they know it is there, even if they don't know that they know.

'A Good Divorce' is possible. If you have children, you have a lot to keep in mind and share. Them. And you may even manage to make it a good one.

'Permission to Cry', is about the impact on children, on our vulnerable selves, of having our losses and sadness unaddressed; our grief unacknowledged or hidden in order to protect the feelings of others and to not overwhelm our loved ones. It is a gift of love from the child, to hide anger and grief and suffer within and the recipient may not even be aware of the sacrifice.

'Take Care of Yourself' is a simple instruction from our loved ones but is actually extremely difficult to do. What does it even entail? This chapter looks at the complexity behind this directive and the emotional roots of its success.

'Children and Emotions 101' busts some simple myths about children, in a somewhat satirical tone, in order to underline the power of our emotional lives, especially in childhood, to living healthy adaptive lives.

No Country for Children

March 2020 did many things for India. One of those was to make our children invisible; make them disappear.

For the initial weeks of the lockdown, the focus was on the horror of people leaving the cities in droves, along with their children. To the media, they were 'migrant workers'—a label that conveniently prioritised the economic and took the human out of the narrative. The fact that these were families leaving together was rarely focused on, but those were the stories that were drilled into my awareness at the time—Danish Siddiqui's photograph of the man walking with his child on his shoulders; the man who said he was lucky to have a cycle cart so he could put his children and meagre belongings on it because he had no work and no money to live in Delhi anymore; children who were walking along with their parents having been uprooted from what was familiar, from schools and local *gullis,* headed to uncertainty. The photographs of small children straggling behind their parents or straddling their shoulders were heart-piercing but not enough to make these children count, it seemed. After the television-owning-world in India watched the toddler trying to wake his dead mother on the railway platform, dead from starvation and misery, mainstream media did not keep up with that child (or for that matter, even the story). They have all disappeared from view.

In a parallel universe of those people who were privileged enough to retain their homes and screens to disappear into, we again forgot about the children. Apart from addressing the question of how not to interrupt the school curriculum, and hence, how to keep them occupied, we again made large parts of our children invisible. Or wished they would be. For over fifteen months now, the school corridors and playgrounds have been deserted, the after-school activity schedule has been blank and celebrations quiet. Have we paused to wonder where all that energy went? The energy that fuels daily learning, play, sport, competition, laughter, friendships, bullying, fist-fights and arguments with peers—it is not just lying dormant, it is actively eating away at our children from the inside, killing their motivation and aspirations, a phenomenon which is loosely being referred to as 'mental health problems'.

That is the more compassionate term. In many adult circles it is also being referred to as 'unmotivated' 'disinterested' and 'lazy'.

As a society, in 2020–21 we have repeatedly proven that we largely see our people as compliant capital. We are interested in what resource they will provide, without asking complex or inconvenient questions; ergo, the young need to be made pliable just as the workers need to work. In doing so, as policy makers and educators, certainly as politicians and sometimes even as parents, we forget that we live our lives from the inside. When we make our children's internal worlds invisible, we do so at our own peril because this will return to cost all society, all communities, in the form of aggression both outward and turned inward as rising hatred, violent and petty crime, as well as suicide. Much of this is already apparent. Year on year, statistics have been clear that India has the highest number of suicides among the youth.[1] More than 90,000 young adults killed themselves in 2019 alone, which is 67% of the total suicides that year.[2] This is a statistic which cannot reflect the number of young people who contemplated killing themselves or attempted to fatally hurt themselves but failed. It can never reflect the anguish of the people left behind, or hopelessness of the young person themselves. There is no way to reach the depth of distress in these young people. The work we do in the mental health field only touches the air above the surface.

When not attended to directly, the emotional world has a way to make its presence felt. Because our feelings are a force of nature, much like the wind or the rain; pretending they don't exist does not work. We cannot expect the sexuality and aggression of our youth, which fuels their creativity and desire to change/rebel against the world, to simply quieten down and comply. Distress accumulates; it pushes through and we are forced to notice it, if for no other reason than to make the young one be quiet and go back to sleep, or if they are older, to call in the police.

THE DISTRESS IN THE CLINIC

2020-21 has been revealing.[3] It has revealed so much of what lay hidden under the cover of productive activity, workplace objectives, targets and competition. The emotional world has made its presence felt.

Pre-COVID, our small-but-effective child and adolescent mental health team in New Delhi had a steady trickle of one new referral a week. Over the past months that has turned into a deluge, representing the increasing levels of anguish in families, led by the children, ensuring that our team had to return to work face-to-face, because emotional distress does not engage too well over a digital medium.[4] In many cases, the tides of children's emotional lives had numerous outlets in 'normal' times, and parents could get by thinking of them as merely niggling worries: the occasional scratch the child inflicted on themselves, the occasional nightmare, or the occasional sibling squabble. These could no longer be ignored when everyone was together at home for months. Strained relationships could no longer be avoided, resentments and rivalries could no longer be hidden, and 'teenage angst' could no longer be a dismissive depiction. After all, we are in lockdown with our feelings.

There is a pattern to the forms of distress we are seeing: a six-year-old fears earthquakes and is constantly anxious, unwilling to let a parent out of sight. A 9-year-old is afraid of death, troubled by events in other parts of the world where people have been killed. A 12-year-old fears losing loved ones; another is preoccupied with her appearance, smoothening her hair many times a day, scrutinizing her face for blemishes. Many moody, quiet, reclusive 13-year-olds are spending hours on a screen, their world reduced to 13 inches, supposedly at school but navigating to websites far-far-away. The boys' locker room incident that received so much public attention in the summer of 2020 could also be seen as an example of young people's sexuality and aggression emerging—through misogynistic, hateful talk. Hyperactive, angry children, unable to hear 'no', unable to sit still. Others who are smoking cannabis and using alcohol or pornographic material and gaming to tranquilize themselves.

We don't all experience or process distress in the same way. There are differences in how our children's distress shows up depending on their age, temperament, developmental life stage and previous history. In many cases we find that the current situation only exacerbated or unearthed an existing problem that the family was papering over. It would be foolishness to believe that 'the kids are alright'.

A 7-year-old boy was brought in by his parents saying he was being explosive. He was experiencing immense rage towards a loved aunt who was leaving to go back to her country of residence after the lockdown lifted but underneath that explosion was a massive fear of losing her, that she won't come back. This fear of loss was pushing out as explosions where he would shout, cry and throw things.

In many cases where parents are now working from home, the lines between office hours and family time have blurred. Activities like reading that were an integral part of bedtime routine pre-Covid, have fizzled out for 10-year-old Rahul, for instance, since everyone is home and 'spending time' together all the time. As far as Rahul is concerned, he has less quality time now with his parents. This makes him angry with them and brings on anxiety. Resumption of the bedtime routine of reading/pillow fights and having honest conversations around who misses what parts of their lives pre-pandemic/ acknowledging loss without masking it under 'we could have had it worse' has subsequently helped relieve Rahul's symptoms of screaming and crying.

For 6-year-old Ketan, on the other hand, the initial phases of lockdown proved to be a relief for some time wherein anxiety symptoms disappeared because now he knew he had his parents at home and they kept him close. This changed, however, as the world opened up somewhat in winter 2020 and his symptoms returned with greater intensity coupled with the fear of loss and death.

15-year-old Smriti was struggling to deal with the loss of school/peer relationships/post-school activities and being forced to be privy to familial dynamics. The change in situation came as a shock to her, almost as though she was getting to know her parents up close for the first time. Her parents too were meeting this adolescent rebellious teenager after years; it was as though they had skipped seeing the progression toward adolescence in their child because external forces such as work commitments, schoolwork and after-school activities had kept them busy.

7-year-old Mili's fears latched onto something concrete and identifiable: a monster she stumbled upon on YouTube. This made her afraid of the dark and so she ended up sleeping between her parents. She had experienced a series of losses during the pandemic—first her nanny had left abruptly to look after another child. Then Mili's best friend of six years changed neighbourhoods. From Mili's perspective, people she loved kept leaving. Her fear of the dark and ending up in her parent's bed was a great solution to the original problem of loss; now she could keep an eye on her parents and prevent them from also disappearing.

What we are seeing in the clinic is representative of what is happening in some measure in every family, in every socio-economic stratum, in every community—with greater or lesser intensity. Not even a miniscule percentage of that gets attended to. We are sitting on a colossal time bomb of emotional distress that will blow up in our faces; anxiety, depression, aggression and self-sabotage, perhaps even suicide, will be the main symptoms.

DISTRESS BY AGE

Children under the age of five are designed to be close to family members and have active fantasy lives, seen through imaginative play. Attachment bonds are formed and strengthened by this age and forms the bedrock for all future relationships. At this stage, social communication capacities are being built in small safe interactions with others who have been vetted by their carers. They are happy building tents under tables and talking to their dolls or dinosaurs. This is the easiest age group to manage at home with core attachment figures and without the social interaction that schools and playgrounds provide. Social skills cannot be learnt in isolation though, so how these children learn to interact with other children will remain to be seen. Their distress is easier to sooth by providing the safety of family and the familiar—hugs, favourite food, much loved stories, soothing music—interspersed with bouts of stimulation—outdoor play, finger painting, digging in the grass, chasing a ball. It is easier than handling the distress of older children but it is by no means easy on the parent. As a 12-year-old explained to me recently, 'adults expect us to behave like adults but treat us like children'. I understood that to mean that adults expect older children to soothe their own distress, regulate themselves, find ways to occupy themselves when it is convenient for the adult, but dismiss their views and opinions, refusing to take them seriously when it poses a challenge to the adult.

Children between the ages of six years and puberty are designed to learn and to move and certainly to learn by moving. When we shut this age group of children indoors, away from peer networks, outlets for creativity and energy, away from learning by fighting, falling, failing, we are shutting down a force of nature. Much like trying to shut down the wind, it will push back with force. When this development-design is interrupted, one of two things can happen. The urge to learn and move can either shut down and adapt (the quiet, listless, depressed child), or it can push back (the agitated, hyperactive, angry child). A 10-year-old may not be able to come up to you and say 'I am aware that it is not possible to meet my friends but I really miss them and I miss playing in the park'; they may instead go quiet and lose their appetite. Or be stuck to a device, gaming. Or develop a habit of touching their genitals, wetting the bed or waking up with nightmares. Or they may be agitated, get aggressive and become difficult to calm. No one likes the aggressive child but the latter has more hope. Though it is not easy for the grown-ups who have to juggle work, virtual-school (which has huge problems of its own), home, attention-to-child, financial stress and COVID-anxiety at this time, this push-back is in fact a display of the child's resilience. It is demanding an outlet for its age-appropriate energy. From the perspective of the psychotherapist, the child who can be aggressive and protest has hope.[5] The quiet children are the ones we worry about the most.

This is usually the age group of under-14, for which we continue to get the maximum referrals in 2021. The first problem we face as a team with regard to this age group is that it is almost impossible to work effectively with them and have a trusting relationship built on a virtual platform. Nine-year-old Anamika is busy watching YouTube videos during our session, her eyes fixed on some other tab on the screen, while she insists she is talking to me. 13-year-old Tarini is clearly playing Fortnite or Roblox while she multitasks and chatters away to me at top speed but about everything irrelevant and inane. This is not how therapy works. This inattention is not how any relationship works.

We all need a flesh-and-blood presence in order to connect to the reality of the other. On the screen, I am a two-dimensional presence, not a real person; no different from the YouTube videos or cartoons they watch. My attention on them, my questions, my curiosity, my concern—is all hypothetical. A 14-year-old summed it up for me when he said he preferred to have our sessions 'In Real Life'—as opposed to what, I wondered—imaginary? Fantasy? Because when the zoom call is over, when the screen is closed, what happens to the person? What happens to the relationship when we have not breathed in the same room or experienced the other person's emotions as a bodily reality in front of us? Is there even a relationship between us?

Then there is our adolescent population; designed to disagree with adults and to bond with peers, but since the latter have now become virtual entities, there is more of the first, less of the latter. Or we see symptoms of high anxiety. Adolescents are in the process of making relationships outside of their family and domestic arrangements. In addition, they are starting out on the toughest parts of human development—emotionally separating from parental figures and discovering their own selves. This process, technically called Identity Development (a phrase which unfortunately glosses over the emotional turmoil inherent in it) is difficult enough without the added burden of uncertainty of the future that older adolescents have to now face with the shadow of COVID. Leaving home and moving to another part of the country or to another continent was never easy, but now it comes with extra guilt and fear attached. 16-to-18-year-olds are struggling; unable to focus, suffering brain-fog, suicidal ideation, heart palpitations, insomnia, they are overwhelmed by the sheer weight of not-knowing and sometimes by rage. No wonder the tranquilizer or a gaming device or a joint, or even cutting themselves to let out blood, brings some calm.

When an adolescent knows what is at the base of their distress, our work is made easier. That rarely happens. Many of the 18-19 year old's who have approached us do not link any of their distress to COVID. They disconnect it from external reality. Their distress is often minimized as their 'inability to be motivated' or 'everyone is handling it better than I am' or 'my friend has it harder so how can I admit to struggling'. There is also a hyperawareness of news, political upheaval and fight for rights in the external world (right to privacy, the farmers' protests, issues of citizenship and belonging, rights of the minority groups in India) with a jarring lack of compassion for the internal fight for rights. Then these young people do not know how to respond to our compassion toward them. It seems like an alien experience which they both want and reject.

More often than not, adolescents come in apathetic and detached, therefore not really bothered or troubled by anything. They tend to be referred by a parent who can see the sabotage and self-harm. This apathy is rarely a problem to the teenager themselves since it is an effective solution to whatever distress they were originally feeling. 15-year-old Ashish sat in front of me, slumped over, no muscle tone in his body, not making eye contact and responded with 'I don't know' to my question of what emotional difficulty he needed help with. After 20 minutes he could say that he often considered dying but he was not sure it was a problem he wanted help with. When I responded that it was certainly a problem for his family, who wanted him to be happy, he laughed a cynical, mirthless laugh and said 'What does that even mean?' Eventually we could reach the awareness that there was a part of him that did not want to die. It is not completely clear if that means he wants to live. We are still working on it.

16–18-year-olds have come in, not making the link between their anxiety, low mood and the reality of having had their lives in lockdown. They minimize the impact of their losses by saying they are 'unmotivated' or 'just being lazy'. Between this minimization and judgement, our young people are expected to 'get on with it' and be productive, reach goals that have no meaning anymore to some (such as finishing grade 11). They are not even permitted to acknowledge that their life has come to a standstill.

WHAT YOU CAN DO AS A CARE-PROVIDER

In this year when our children have suffered multiple losses— of people, spaces, relationships and familiarity—it is not possible to move on to a conversation about gratitude without also acknowledging the losses, tempting as it may seem. Many of us are plagued by not being permitted to mourn because there is always someone else who has it worse, or 'we have so much to be grateful for' and 'we are really so blessed'. While this may also be true, 2020-2021 has also been the year of frozen dreams, especially for young people. Can we not make grief into a competitive sport? If we acknowledge individual, personal meaning, perhaps we can have permission to also mourn everything, everyone and every dream that died in 2020. Sticking to either/or thinking only shrinks us and makes for emotional poverty.

The list of what you can do for yourself and the children you interact with:

1. Don't lie about reality: Whether it is sadness, death or loss of some other kind, be honest about what is happening. Children have an incredibly sensitive radar, they are superbly in tune with the emotions of the adults they are close to. If you are going through something difficult, your child knows. They don't know what it is, but they know something is not ok. More often than not, they will blame themselves for your difficulty. Adults find this difficult to believe but it is a part of every under-12's cognitive operation; the world is only comprehended from their perspective.[6] If something is going wrong in the family or someone is sick, sad or angry it is somehow their fault. Somehow, they have to be responsible for it. It takes us months or years to unravel this in therapy. You can help by letting your child gently know about reality: for example, that Nani is ill, that is why she cannot play with Ketan, not because he did something wrong. You may have to be honest with little Ketan that Nani is very ill and may not get better. If she has a terminal illness like cancer, please don't make false promises that she will get better soon or by next week. She will not and Ketan will blame himself for it.

7-year-old Mandakini's father died of Covid after three weeks in hospital and no one told her that he was never coming back. She saw her mother withering away in front of her, losing her to grief as well and still no one told her. She continued to play her games on the floor with her toys. She said nothing and so adults assumed she was fine. She and her mother moved into her Masi's home, away from her familiar space, away from photographs of her father with her and still no one told her.

When a member of Mandakini's family contacted me for advice, they were extremely reluctant to take it because I said 'tell her the truth.' The truth will give her a chance to adapt to reality, which is the basis for emotional health. Keeping her in the dark is not healthy. If you hide the truth from her, you don't give her a chance to mourn, to express her sadness and her love for her father, to keep his photograph under her pillow or hug his kurta.

In the clinic we regularly see the amount of damage unexpressed grief and guilt can cause, for years at times, and it is far worse than death.

2. Have some honest conversations in your family gatherings: Sit down together and say out loud what the last 18 months have done to you, both as a family and as individual people, of all ages. From the little ones who no longer go to nursery school, to the young people waiting for their colleges to open; the carers who get no time for themselves; the families where proximity may have brought tensions to the fore but perhaps greater closeness as well. We need to acknowledge to ourselves and to each other what we have lost—whether it is work, relationships, money, opportunities or meaning. We need to have conversations about what gives us meaning in our lives now. What we wake up for in the morning.

When I tried this at home, I found I could not finish my sentence without first having to stop to weep. My husband held back tears too because for both of us closing our workspace, which was also our mental and creative play-space, has been the most painful part of this lockdown. Our children had lost friends and mentors, and we had had to let staff go—specially chosen, dependable, hardworking, creative, energetic young people. We used to see over 40 children in-person at our centre every week for individual psychotherapy, and more than that number in The Art of Sport groups. Now it is an empty space; the toys in the playrooms wait, gathering dust.

Until this point in the lockdown, which was somewhere around July 2020, the children's experience and COVID-anxiety had taken precedence. The abrupt loss of peer contact; missing the comforting regularity of meeting the same children on the school bus; and the loss of their reality. One offspring had buried herself in books and Lego, the other in learning to play a new song on the guitar. The song was called 'Memories' by Maroon 5. It is a song about losing someone you love and it has been the soundtrack to 2020.

3.   Keep up with the emotional graph: because it keeps changing:

Are they very quiet? Are they more aggressive than usual? Are they lethargic? Are they on the screen a lot? Are they eating a lot of junk or not eating? What is going on with the children today, last week, next month?

Keeping up with the emotional changes in our own children, makes me and their father aware of just how much work parents have to do now. It is not just that we have had teaching duties for the last 18 months that we did not sign up for (I have often confessed to my children that on some days they would go to school so I could get six hours of quiet. That is no longer possible); it is also that we are the only available adults to receive everything from—be it instruction, concern, containing, encouragement or boundaries. We found that the lethargy of moving from bed to sofa to chair was making our otherwise physically active children extremely sluggish and jammed even in their internal states. We initiated (actually I think the children did) having regular pillow fights, playing table-tennis at the dining table and catch-the-ball-without-dropping competitions, putting many items in the house at great risk of damage, but the children cheered up.

When schools still did not open, one year of virtual school headed into a second, 2020 became 2021, their father took matters into his hands, scheduling daily physical play for them. Structured exercise, runs in the park, cycling round the block, even running up and down the stairs of the building—a variety of physical movements to get them going. It worked because both children were full of irritation at their father for having done this but after every sweaty workout, they were happier, laughing more, getting along better as siblings and more able to put their feelings into words. Our 13-year-old now tells us that 'the quality of life is seriously declining'—a combination of sarcasm, humour and the truth—sounding a lot like 6-year-old Calvin from Bill Waterson's comic strip Calvin & Hobbes. I am sure soon I will also be told that my ratings as a parent are dropping.

4.   Physical movement, art, literature, music, imaginary play: These are not just hobbies. These are simultaneously life-giving, energizing and a calming balm. Children whose lives do not include these, struggle with an internal poverty that leaves them starving but also wrecked by anxiety.

12-year-old Anamika was a good student and sometimes played badminton. She loved school for the social interactions she had. At home, an only child, she was doted over which she both enjoyed and demanded. However, it had given her no sense of herself, no experience of her own capabilities. When lockdown hit her, she found herself overly anxious and unable to verbalize why. Her mind found reasons that had to do with her health and with COVID but the truth went deeper; she had many feelings, including sexual ones, that accompany puberty, and all of this internal drama had no outlet because she did not read, draw, paint, dance, play, run or make crafts. She did nothing other than study and look at a screen.

The truth is that much like in physics where matter cannot be destroyed but can turn into energy, in human beings, emotions are that matter. It cannot be destroyed and it regularly changes form into energy, including creative energy. Help your children find an outlet. You might have to join them initially and not expect them to be superbly motivated, creative or grateful to you. In fact, it is guaranteed that they will be irritated and rejecting, sulky and resentful. It's okay. It is a change from listless and detached. After all, anger is the most powerful emotion and it generates both potential and kinetic energy.

If our children trust us, we parents will be at the receiving end of every single emotion they experience. We will be smothered by hugs and told that they love us so much they want to eat us up. They will yell at us telling us they don't need us and they hate us. That wave of emotion coming in our direction is a complement to our parenting, it is a measure of their trust in us, of the security of the attachment bond. It means you are a safety figure. It means you did your job well. After all, as parents that is our first job—to provide safety, then our second job is to not collapse or retaliate[7] when the real child shows up with their anger, tantrum, demands.

This is the main reason I said earlier that it is the quiet children who we worry about. A quiet child is protecting the adult, the quiet child does not trust that the adult can handle their feelings, or help with a struggle. A child who is keeping an eye on the parent's reaction and not on their own internal landscape. The detached apathetic teenagers who are cutting their arms and thighs, lying in bed and not attending school, these teenagers are protecting their parents from worse things.

It is true that currently frustration, anger and sadness predominate and when this comes our way, it does not feel like a compliment at all. At these times, remember that family bonds are the foundation to mental health and it builds resilience in the everyday interactions in the home. Mental health, emotional wellbeing always takes work, persistence and patience. In the current scenario, emotional and mental health is a full-time task.

NOTES

1. "Suicides in India Chapter – 2 - NCRB." Accessed November 8, 2021. https://ncrb.gov.in/sites/default/files/Suicidal%20Part.pdf.

2. Rampal, Nikhil. "More than 90,000 Young Adults Died by Suicide in 2019 in India: NCRB Report." India Today. India Today, September 4, 2020. https://www.indiatoday.in/diu/story/ncrb-report-data-india-young-adults-suicide-2019-india-1717887-2020-09-02.

3. Natasha Badhwar. Phone conversation. I am grateful to Natasha Bhadwar for this comment that really struck a note with me.

4. Though some young people have used this medium to connect very effectively. Paiva, Nupur Dhingra. "Psychotherapy with No Body in the Room." *Journal of Child Psychotherapy* 46, no. 3 (2020): 355–61. https://doi.org/10.1080/007541 7x.2021.1900331

5. Winnicott, D.W. 1986/1990. Delinquency as a sign of hope. In Home is Where we Start From: Essays by a Psychoanalyst. Norton: New York pg 90

6. J. Piaget. 1971. 'The Theory of Stages in Cognitive Development'. In D.R. Green, M.P. Ford, & G.B. Flamer. *Measurement and Piaget*. New York: McGraw-Hill.

7. Winnicott, D.W. 1991. Needs of the Under Fives. The Child, the Family and the Outside World. London: Penguin.

Introduction
When to Talk to a Stranger[*]

Armaan and his parents lived many hours' journey away and were in town for a few days when they came to see me. My first impression of Armaan was of a slight child with his shoulders hunched over, as if weighed down by something significant. He was clearly burdened and this was before his parents had said anything about their shared distress. His mother explained that he routinely told his parents that they did not love him; that he wanted to run away from the house, shoot himself, etc. This had gone on for a couple of months, if not more. He was described as a sensitive and affectionate child, giving many kisses and hugs to his parents and sister. However, the statements about no one loving him had become frequent enough to worry his parents and they thought he needed to have a chat with someone other than them.

Five-year-old Armaan met me, the stranger, for an hour and a half just the one time. I got Armaan's mother to read him a story about a child who hid his feelings in his socks and within a few moments, having followed this fictitious child's

[*] This chapter is a modified version of a chapter by me in Reena Nath (ed.): *The Healing Room*, New Delhi: HarperCollins India, 2017.

travails, Armaan treated us to a commentary and depiction of an encounter between two dinosaurs, one fiercer than the other and attacking with fury. As his story progressed, getting bloodier by the minute, I wondered how such violence could find place and be acknowledged in his family. Was Armaan also hiding his feelings in his socks? It was plain to see that the first-born child of these mild-mannered, high-functioning, high-achieving, emotionally super-intelligent, liberal-minded, intellectual parents was struggling with a raw conflict between love and hate. He was furious with his parents for having 'borned' another child and he did not know what to do with that fury. He was enraged and because he also adored his parents, in order to protect them, he turned that rage onto himself.

His violence onto himself was a gift of love.

Later in the hour, Armaan's father joined us in the room, forming a small circle on the floor, and listened to our conversation, where I spoke as-if to his parents, but in truth I was addressing Armaan and his inner world. As I mentioned his conflict—his little baby self within the five-year-old high functioning child who went to school, his love for his family and his rage at having been displaced; his enormous sadness at having lost his father's attention to his little sister—he let me know that it felt true to him. Slowly, he crawled into his father's lap and curled up there like a little prawn, very much the baby he wanted to be and also the boy who wanted his father's company, his father's attention and the joy of playing with him.

Because Armaan essentially had wonderfully empathic parents, this made sense to them. It was hard to bear but emotionally straightforward. No intellectual hoops were involved. At the end of our session, he ran out of the room with a smile. A few weeks later his mother wrote saying he had been lighter, less weighed down since then. He started going to karate with his father in a miniature version of the white martial arts uniform. Three months later I heard that Armaan had not once mentioned wanting to shoot himself or run away from home since. A year later, I met a chatty, smiling six-year-old who proudly showed me the karate moves he had learnt.

This had been a good time to talk to a stranger.

A child psychologist or psychotherapist, put simply, is someone who is trained to understand children and their unspoken feelings; what is of greatest import to them; the conflicts that weigh the most. The internal dramas we need to help unfold rather than deny because they help to develop a richness of personality because to have it all happy is not the road to building inner strength or character. There are some painful experiences that we need to have and to bear.

Ordinary life could do with psychotherapy—for both children and their parents. Nothing terribly traumatic needs to happen before we attend to our feelings about something. Ordinary living is full of difficult transitions and emotional upheavals and we gloss over them in an (often ineffectual) attempt to cope with them. Glossing over is ineffectual because our emotional lives are a force of nature. You cannot bottle it up or shut it down any more than you can bottle the wind or push down an ocean wave; there will be repercussions.

For a child and parent the need for psychotherapy may begin before birth, as pregnancy can in itself be stressful, especially for parents who have already had difficult experiences such as losing a baby or repeated miscarriages. The early days with a baby can be difficult on all the family and sometimes feelings about babies can be complicated and not always positive. It is extremely difficult to unconditionally care for another if our own experience has been mixed.

As children grow and have to share their parents with siblings or careers, family life can be full of difficult feelings and it is common for psychotherapists to see families that are struggling to get on with toddlers and young children.

Learning, social and attention problems can become more apparent as children approach school age. At school other difficulties can occur, such as anxiety, social difficulties, as well as more difficult behaviour such as anger and aggression, non-compliance and behaviour disorders.

With approaching adolescence, further difficulties can emerge, such as eating disorders, gender identity problems and depression. Occasionally children can start to show signs of more serious psychotic illness such as becoming very withdrawn, getting serious obsessions and displaying 'odd' behaviour. As young people enter adulthood, relationship, drug and alcohol problems can emerge as well.

None of these problems come out of nowhere. The most common reason for children to have emotional difficulties is problems in the family. Negative communications, high expectations, constant criticism or punishments, parental ill health, depression, divorce, violence, unemployment, losing a loved one or the fear of losing one—are the most common reasons behind children's difficulties.

Seeing a psychotherapist for emotional difficulties is not very common in India, despite the fact that mental health disorders account for nearly a sixth of all health-related disorders. This means that 65 out of 1,000 persons are at some point of time in their life in need of psychological care for a mental illness. Yet we have just 0.4 psychiatrists and 0.02 psychologists per 100,000 people, and 0.25 mental health beds per 10,000 people. While 65 million Indians suffer from mental illnesses (Ministry of Health and Family Welfare, 2009), India spends just 0.83 per cent of its total health budget on mental health (WHO 2001a). There is a severe shortage of mental health professionals—psychiatrists, psychologists, psychotherapists and psychiatric social workers in urban and rural India. Compare this with the UK government which came under severe criticism in 2016 for cutting its spending on mental health and it is still at 10 per cent of its health budget (fullfact. org).

These figures are for an adult population, and children's emotional worlds are far from being included under 'mental health'. The burden of mental disorders, especially in urban India, is highest among young adults aged 15 to adults of 44 years. This means that students in schools, colleges and universities are especially vulnerable to major psychological upheavals and these don't emerge in a vacuum. They may become manifest in early adulthood in the form of depression, drug addiction, identity crises, conflicts in families, disturbances in the arena of sexuality and the body, aggressive and destructive urges, self-harm and/or suicide, but their roots lie in early life experiences.

Just because it is easier to communicate in words with a young person about their emotional state (er… actually it isn't that easy. Anyone tried talking to a teenager lately?), and it is easier to identify mental distress, does not suggest that younger children are free from emotional difficulties or that difficulties only begin in the teenage years. If freed from the coating of stigma (which is asking for a lot), parents are usually the first to feel that there is something 'not right' with their child and they can be the best mental health radar (Acquarone, 2004). Asking for attention to be paid to their baby's or older child's communications is the beginning of an important process, one where the parent's concerns are often validated.

INFANCY: EARLY EMOTIONAL STORMS

Concerns may begin as early as in the first six months of life. Communication difficulties between parent and baby may be picked up very early and identified by the parent in themselves or the child. These could be in many forms: parents may be finding it difficult to enjoy interacting with their child; no attraction in the baby for mother's face; interest in objects rather than people; lack of babbling and imitation; avoiding eye contact; dislike of being picked up or held; lack of curiosity; extremely stiff muscles that don't allow the baby to mould to the mother's arms—are a few early signs of concern that parents may notice (Acquarone, 2004).

No one is in tune with their baby 100 per cent of the time; it is simply not humanly possible. Parents and children are always moving between disruptions and being in tune (Stern, 1985). The aim in parent-child relationships is not complete understanding or full attunement but *to move toward attunement after a disruption.* Simply put, this means making up after a disagreement. *This builds a capacity to communicate difficult feelings and also builds trust that it is safe to communicate them.* A sensitive baby can be extremely difficult to be attuned to and look after, and is usually misunderstood. If very sensitive to light, touch or sound, a baby may be irritable or crying a lot of the time which makes it difficult for the mother to be around this baby. A sensitive child could turn out to have enhanced abilities in the fields of music, art or academics in the future but in the present, the baby may be very difficult to understand and live with.

In the early weeks and months (and perhaps forever), our physical and the emotional needs are not separated from each other. To have our physical needs satisfied, at the right time, in a gentle, responsive way is love. To be fed when hungry, is care. To be held with warmth when upset brings people emotionally closer. Mothers know that to feed a baby when he is hungry is fulfilling at many levels, for both baby and mother. They know, or soon learn, that babies like to be fed in quiet surroundings with little distraction so they can focus on the breast or bottle and on their mother. Yet, many babies have feeding or sleeping difficulties; some parents experience their babies as crying too much or needing to be held all the time and they struggle with negative feelings toward their babies. These are all ordinary experiences in all families but that does not mean they are easy or can be ignored. These are communications from the baby about their physical and emotional experiences, not manipulations or actions especially designed by the baby to destroy their mother. By paying attention to them, parents and professionals can consider deeper underlying issues in the baby or the family.

Crying is how babies communicate their need for attention. What else can they do? Their crying is what keeps them alive by ensuring that people respond to them. They specialise in it; it is their job description, they have nuanced capacities in this area, so it is no surprise that there are different kinds of cries and anyone looking after a baby will be able to differentiate between the cry of hunger, anger, sadness or boredom (Winnicott, 1991a, p. 58). A lot of the psychotherapeutic work in such situations is to help the parent to observe, understand and then respond to the baby's needs without becoming caught in their own feeling of being manipulated by the baby, angry with the baby or hopeless about their own capacities. Many parents have had difficult relationships with their own parents, many have experiences of loss, trauma or rejection or are depressed. Depression in parents in the early years of a child have been shown to have long-term and wide-ranging negative impact on the child in areas of learning, emotional growth, capacity to make rewarding relationships and to deal with their own feelings (Gerhardt, 2004; Hay, 2001). There are parents who, after the birth of a child, may have feelings toward their baby or toward each other that are not positive. Babies are extremely demanding and leave little time or energy for other activities or relationships. The couple relationship goes through a difficult transition when a baby enters the mix; time for each other and energy for sex is often out of the window and it may not be easy for a new mother or father. A depressed mother or father may feel hopeless, angry or overwhelmed about being demanded by their new baby in this intense, 24/7 way. They may find it difficult to notice their baby's needs or attend to them (Murray, 1996); they may feel unable to attend to their baby or feel envious that their baby should get something they did not. Life circumstances may be difficult for some families, when time with a parent, affection and thoughtfulness may feel like luxuries which are unnecessary for learning to live in the world. Yet it is these very early experiences that form the foundation for future capacities to make relationships (Gerhardt, 2004). Shaky foundations make for shaky futures.

Depression follows childbirth in 10–15 per cent of cases (O'Hara, 1996) and often goes unnoticed (Dennis, 2004). Feelings of hopelessness, helplessness, crying, low mood or high anxiety before or after a birth are legitimate experiences that need to be taken seriously and attended to (Milgrom, 2008). The current non-personalised, modern medical assembly-line approach to childbirth is a big contributor to post-natal emotional difficulties in new mothers (Marchant, 2016). All the current research suggests that the thing that makes the biggest difference for women giving birth, 'reliably reduces pain, distress and the risk of complications and interventions during labour' is not high-tech hospitals or a new drug, it is simply 'having the same caregiver stay with you throughout a birth' (Marchant, 2016, p. 136; Hodnett, 2012) In other words, a caring, attentive relationship is more comforting than any medical intervention. It is therefore no surprise that psychotherapy has been shown to be one of the more effective ways of addressing post-natal difficulties (Milgrom, 2005) primarily because of the acknowledgement of the emotional support it provides.

TRANSITIONS: POINTS OF WEAKNESS AND POTENTIAL

All parents know that children change very quickly: be it their height, shoe size, food preferences, favourite story or best friend. Parents also know that they tend to be a step behind their children; quick to learn, if they are attentive, but rarely able to pre-empt an upcoming change. However, even the most attentive parent may struggle to know how to adapt to the changing needs of their child, because what a child needs their parent to provide keeps changing subtly throughout their relationship and life stages. The particular kind of attention a new-born baby needs is different from the quality of attention a teenager needs, no one will dispute that. Yet is it not easy to adapt to these in-between stages. We may struggle to understand how our affectionate, easy-going one-year-old changed into a screaming, adamant three-year-old who refuses to eat a sandwich because it is cut the wrong way. Another parent may not realise that it may be easier to negotiate with a 10-year-old than to expect unquestioned obedience by threatening him with punishment or withdrawal of affection, ridiculing him or being sarcastic. Interaction patterns and expectations between parents and children tend to be formed early on and can become stagnant, so what was adaptive in a particular life-stage, becomes less useful in the next one.

Most of us want our children to be confident without being arrogant. However, most parents remain unaware that they play a significant part in the development of these qualities. They may notice that their six-year-old is very keen to make drawings but may not notice that their child is as eager to learn to do the math sum on their own, regardless of the end result, tie their own shoelaces, eat their own meals, or help in a household task like sweeping the floor. Being industrious is linked to achievement and growing self-confidence, yet it may not be easy to notice that one could hold back from tying those shoelaces, show the child how it is done, encourage independence in this small capacity because it has the potential to produce an 'I can do it!' moment. In the anxiety that their child will fall and get hurt, parents can end up keeping the support wheels on the bicycle a lot longer than it may be necessary.

Whether they are transitions of life-stages or circumstances, all changes are potentially challenging because they require us to be different from what we have become used to. Some common but important transitions in children's lives are:

a)   Starting day care or nursery
b)   Change of nanny/carer
c)   New sibling
d)   Starting school
e)   Moving from junior to senior school.
f)   Moving homes, neighbourhoods, towns or countries
g)   Puberty
h)   Changes in family living arrangement—nuclear family, joint family; grandparent moving in or out.

These are ordinary changes that we expect ourselves and our children and families to adapt to. Is it possible for us to accept that there will also be a period of struggle? Difficulties with separations such as refusing to go to school, or the birth of a new sibling are also significant transitions.

For adults as well, moving from being single to living as a couple or part of a joint family, to becoming parents are huge transitions that most of us adapt to, kind of, more or less. However, if the struggle becomes too intense, too elongated or causes too much of a disruption, it may need attention in order to understand what has come in the way of the ordinary course of adapting and settling down.

EARLY PUBERTY

Puberty may be seen as a significant life transition but it deserves a special mention because it is also a transition many parents do not prepare their sons and daughters for. It is a shared, expected and an ordinary part of life and yet in most families it stays under wraps. It is not an unexpected event; certainly not a shock for anyone but the child concerned, and absolutely not a disease. Yet, most north Indian girls say that when they started their period, they thought they were going to die. Millions of young girls become ashamed of their bodies and therefore of being female, which then affects how they live. It affects how they look after their health, their relationship to food as well as to other people. These are emotions that have significant impact well into adulthood and affect a young person's experience of their sexuality (Kaltiala-Heino et al., 2013).

Many young girls are now starting their menstrual cycles earlier than the previously expected average of between 10 and 13 years of age. This has been attributed to changes in food habits and lifestyle (Kaplowitz et al., 2001; Herman-Giddens et al., 1997), specifically the presence of the hormone oxytocin in industrially produced milk and poultry (*Times of India*, April 2012). For these reasons, parents of girls may need to consider having the conversation about puberty sooner than they had previously imagined.

For boys, puberty marks the entire period of adolescence. The obvious physiological changes have covert psychological repercussions and the latter are usually left to the boy as though he is equipped to deal with them by himself. Along with greater awareness of one's sexuality and of the other gender, the young boy feels a sharp distinction between the sexes. It is a crucial stage where the relationship with one's own feelings and those of others may be accepted or harshly rejected; a stage where sexuality can take on a sensitive or a more ruthless turn (as pornography) depending on how the young person's peer-group and others around engage with it. Because parental views are being challenged and/or replaced with ideas from a peer-group, an ongoing conversation between parents and children can be the crucial glue that keeps them in touch with each other.

Anger

This is perhaps the most common reason for families to seek professional support for emotional difficulties (the other being anxiety and depression), when a child is difficult to manage because of the levels of displayed aggression.

Ten-year-old Krish's mild-mannered parents came in to meet me very distressed, describing Krish as constantly contrary and argumentative, bossy towards his sibling, attention-seeking and always bored. They were struggling to manage him and his mother was barely able to control her own anger toward him. Six-year-old Milind's parents described him as out-of-control when he did not get his way. With a child who often refused to go to school, was violent to his mother and cousin, and very loud, they said they were embarrassed to take him out since they did not know when he would fly off the handle in social gatherings.

Anger is a difficult emotion for everyone. Whether we observe anger in another or experience it within ourselves, be at the receiving end of it or want to avoid receiving it, it is difficult. Usually this is because many of us have been schooled in how to either avoid feeling anger or avoid expressing it because one is powerless in a particular relationship. As a result, we tend to be afraid of anger itself, afraid of its power, afraid that if we allow ourselves to feel truly angry, we may cause some serious damage, that things will catch fire, relationships will be destroyed, people may be hurt or killed. With such fantasies about what our anger could do, most of us allow ourselves little experience in how to regulate anger or to experience its full strength. Children often learn not to display anger in front of other more angry people—teachers and parents. They save it for smaller, powerless others: younger siblings, servants or neighbours, small animals or inanimate objects and in the future, for their own children or junior colleagues.

However, anger can also be a very useful emotion because it tells us that something is not right for us, something that we would have liked to be different. Anger is, in its origin, a protective mechanism. By ignoring our feelings of anger or by expressing them in hurtful ways, we often make anger into a destructive monster, thereby also losing its transformative potential.

Anger, fear of hurt or loss, guilt at having harmed another and the desire to make things better are all emotions that live very close to each other and often come as a package deal. A little exploration of emotional states will show that it is possible for different, sometimes conflicting, feelings to be present simultaneously but that only anger gets presented to the outside world. Therefore, an angry child is trying to communicate something about their needs to the adults around and the code needs deciphering. With Krish, his parents were supported to first notice any instance when Krish was anything other than argumentative. They said it was when he was reading. He read voraciously and was very quiet when he did. They also described a phase when his behaviour was worse than usual but they later discovered he was worried about his mother's health in the early stages of a new pregnancy. Talking to a psychotherapist helped the parents to see that Krish needed help to understand his own emotions. Sadness and anxiety felt unbearable to him and he could only express it by shouting it out, which was experienced by his mild parents, as anger.

ANXIETY AND FEARS

Anxiety is a response to a perceived threat; this may be an actual external event or an internal one, a fantasy or a feeling. Anxiety in children is an expected part of their emotional place. After all, a child is dependent on others for all her needs and it becomes important for the child to keep an eye on the powerful people in her life, to understand them, to monitor their emotions and behaviour especially if they are unpredictable and liable to become aggressive and to know when it is okay to be oneself.

Anxiety in childhood is a given. Some of these moments are in conscious public awareness, such as separation anxiety or stranger anxiety, both of which are to do with children worrying about their safety, as they should. But children also become anxious if they perceive a threat to the love or approval they receive from a loved one. Unwittingly, many parents play into this or enhance this with simple, unheeded statements. Consider the following interaction:

Mother (to child who is in the playground): 'Come on, let's go.'
Child: *no response*
Mother: 'Come on!! We are getting late.'
Child: 'No! I want to play.'
Mother: 'Ok. I am leaving. You can stay here.'

Immediately the child gets up, abandons the play and follows his mother.

What has she achieved, apart from the evident compliance? She managed to make him feel anxious about being left behind in the park and that she may abandon him if he did not obey. (Chances are that she won't try this if he is in his friend's home because he may say 'ok. You go. I'll stay.') Perhaps she could have worded it differently. Perhaps she could have communicated her strength in their relationship rather than his weakness/smallness. Perhaps something like 'I know you want to play but we need to leave now and you are coming with me' (and starts walking). There is power that comes from being the person-in-charge out of love and there is power that comes from being the person-in-charge who instils fear. Qualitatively, they create different relationships with our children.

There are particular mental capacities we develop as we reach early adolescence that are not available to us in childhood. These capacities help us to see the world from the perspective of another. Before this, children can only see the world from their own viewpoint. As a result, pre-adolescent children tend to blame themselves for any difficult family circumstance or loss. These can range from a parent losing a job, parental divorce, marital violence, to the illness or death of a parent. Anxiety is also a result of feelings in the child that are judged as unacceptable by the child themselves and by those around him; for instance, feelings of rage or of sexual arousal are the most commonly censured, both ready and available very early in life. There are numerous other daily events that may create anxiety in children and one important role of parenting is to make that anxiety easier to bear.

An important role of psychotherapy in working with anxious children is to help them acknowledge their intense feelings and view these as a part of the normal range of human emotions. Accepting the strong negative emotions one may feel toward loved ones is often the key to reducing anxiety. If not attended to early, anxiety can become entrenched in the personality and become the basis for serious mental illness in adolescence or adulthood.

ADOPTION

This is a family arrangement that is full of potential. On the one hand, there is a rejection. It is *because* someone did not want them that these children wear the tag of having been adopted. On the other hand, lies a potential to re-frame this view: that someone else *does* want them, which is why they wear the tag of having been adopted. However, adopted children tend to focus on the rejection for a long time and may want answers to many questions which are about their inherent worth to others and therefore to themselves.

Living with one's biological children is challenging in itself. In cases of adoption, the potential for difficulties is often very high because a parent may not be aware of or prepared for the impact of the child's early experiences on them; things that happened in another family arrangement but now affect the new family. Essentially, in cases of adoption, one may be dealing with difficult attachments, with anxiety, anger, depression or acting out the difficulties, such as by running away, through violence, use of drugs, alcohol, etc.

Psychotherapy can play an important role in the following areas:

1. The child's pre-adoption experience: what circumstances and negative experiences led to the child being put up for adoption? Trauma, neglect, deaths, criticism and violence, consciously remembered or not, is a common reason. These form the child's emotional background and, depending on the child's age, the expectations they have from the world.

2. Within-family adoptions may not have these underlying reasons for the eventual arrangement of who-parents-whom, but there may be unexplored questions of 'why?' and 'how?'

3. Both within-family adoptions and formal institution-

arranged adoptions may reach a point where the child wants an explanation for why this happened. These can be complex situations in families, especially if the adoptive parents have not given this subject considerable thought, have lied to the child in the past thinking it was a way to protect the child from the truth or worry about losing the child's affections.

There are many children adopted as tiny babies with no verbal memory of their early life experiences and only know one set of parents. There may be children whose adoptive parents intend to never let them know of their status. There may be children living in the new family with other children who are biological children of their now shared parents; none or all of them may experience difficult emotions at some point when they know of their adopted status, sometimes as young adults, and can be helped by psychotherapy.

BEHAVIOUR DIFFICULTIES

Because the list of behaviours that may be seen as difficult by a parent or school is potentially endless, these have not been addressed as such. A psychotherapist is likely to see 'bad' behaviour as meaningful, as a communication, and the work will be about trying to get to the emotional difficulties underlying them. With Milind, it turned out that he was refusing to go to school because he was worried that his mother would be sad at home when he was at school. His behaviour was designed to protect his mother, since there was a lot of strife in the joint-family arrangement that they were part of. Some of his violence stemmed from the fact that both his parents used physical violence with each other and with him when they were angry. Seen in context, Milind's behaviour was not unreasonable.

What Psychotherapists Do

A psychotherapist focuses on the child's lived experience, close relationships and emotional world, which are seen as being at the base of the capacity to learn and interact socially, with peers, adults in authority and younger people. Close early relationships are seen as the soil from which the child's inner world grows.

A psychotherapist working with children has particular knowledge about children's emotional lives and the skills to draw these out, understand them and resolve issues. What a parent usually needs from a trained child specialist worker such as a psychotherapist is not advice or instruction on how to do something but an understanding of the underlying causes of their child's emotional situation (Winnicott 1991b, p. 186). Most parents are then able to respond appropriately to their child's emotional needs, unless they have emotional difficulties or mental health problems of their own, which is not uncommon. Most issues are resolved by responding appropriately and sensitively to the child's emotional and developmental needs at a particular life-stage.

A psychotherapist working with children provides a space for the child to have a say, without the fear of losing love. The aim is to give the child a voice and space to be able to think in a non-judgemental space. This is an important part of working with children, to see children as 'experiencing', not just as reacting and obeying. Because psychotherapists are not teachers, they do not instruct. Therefore, parents need not be concerned that their children are being given ideas or values that are different from that of the family. Children have their own feelings and views that they may not be able to share in words with parents or teachers. The role of the psychotherapist is to listen to a child without judgement and help them to think about how to communicate important issues and feelings to their family.

Psychotherapists help children in the following ways:

a) To notice that they have feelings and thoughts: Eleven-year-old Nitin kept running away from home. Once he was helped to locate his deep feelings of loss at the birth of a new sibling, the death of his beloved grandfather and moving home from his village to a large city, sad feelings that were so unbearable that he had to physically run away, he stopped running away.

b) To experience themselves, i.e.,that it is okay to have these feelings and thoughts. Nitin was helped to 'normalise' his feelings. That it was okay to feel sad because these were difficult transitions and losses.

c) To think about themselves, i.e., to have a 'story' about their thoughts and feelings.

d) To communicate between different parts of themselves, i.e., how their body feels, what their thoughts are and that they can have different thoughts and feelings at the same time such as sadness and confusion; anger and guilt (Britton, 1992, pp. 102–13). Fifteen-year-old Matthew was traumatised after having been robbed at knife-point at a bus stop. He was now scared but also ashamed for what he saw as his weakness, as if he had let himself be attacked. He was losing weight, not bathing, not going to school because he was struggling to face himself and his peers. He was not very good at expressing his feelings in words and they came out in frightening visions involving blood and metal. Psychotherapy helped him to see his visions as his feelings of fear of being attacked, which helped him normalise his experience.

e) To communicate with members of the family and significant others. Thirteen-year-old Rahul's parents were getting divorced after more than 20 years of being married. He wanted his parents to know that he did not want to have to choose between them, that he loved and needed them both, even if they did not love each other. Psychotherapy helped him to become clear about his feelings enough for him to say this not only to his parents but to the judge at the family court.

WHAT TO EXPECT

Walking into a child psychotherapist's office, you may notice a variety of seating for different sizes of people, play materials, sand, water, art materials and an attitude in the professional that helps to reduce the anxiety of the newcomer. This is important, since a parent is in the process of choosing a professional to work with their child or the family. People working with children are trained to use simple language, have informal-looking methods of gathering important information about people's emotional states, and in using play to initiate conversation, all of which is essential when working with children.

When you make an appointment with a psychotherapist, expect the first meeting to be at least 45 minutes long, though initial meetings may go up to 90 minutes. The professional will expect you to have given some thought to what emotional support your family is looking for; why now, at this time and who is most concerned about the difficulty. Who is it a bigger problem for—the child, parent or teacher? What has happened that has propelled you to reach out to get support from a professional? The initial meeting explores how the difficulties have come to be the way they are, followed by the history of the child in the particular family from birth onwards in order to understand the current difficulties. Unlike a visit to a medical professional, a single session of psychotherapy is not enough. Usually a series of sessions are required, on a weekly basis, depending on the difficulty.

This process, what professionals call an 'assessment', can

take a significant amount of time in the beginning. Because psychotherapists need to take into account all aspects of a child's life, they may be talking to parents and significant others, school teachers, grandparents and siblings. There may be a school observation or a home observation as well. The initial process of making sense of the particular difficulties, and their meaning to the child and family, may take a few weeks. There may be meetings with the parents, children and parents together, child by themselves, school teacher and parents, school teacher and child together or everyone together. This will help to decide the particular form of intervention best suited for the child.

Sometimes, the children being brought to a psychotherapist are not the real problem. Their difficulties may be the expression of a bigger problem in the family. A behaviour problem or eating disorder in a child may be the symptom of a conflict between the parents. In such situations, the psychotherapist may suggest working with the parents and the extended family and not with the child. It is not uncommon for child psychotherapists to suggest that the marital couple or a particular parent consider therapy for their own difficulties simultaneous to the child being in therapy. At times children are offered time on their own in order to explore their own feelings in a safe, non-judgemental environment.

THE BEGINNING... OF THE REST OF YOUR LIFE

Parents may worry that approaching a professional for help reflects poorly on them, that it may be seen as a failure of their parenting. While it is true that parents are the biggest influences on their children's lives, it is also true that children do not come with instruction manuals. Parents learn how to be a mother or a father to a particular child while they are on the job and it takes time as well as constant adaptation.

Psychotherapists work with emotional difficulties and the aim is to help a person toward health, which really is the task of a lifetime. Therefore, psychotherapists are not judging what emotional difficulty you have come with; they are interested in where *you* would like to *get to*.

REFERENCES

Acquarone, S. 2004. 'Early Signs of Alarm for Communication Disorders: Parent-Infant Psychotherapy Training', Lecture, London, 22 October.

Bowlby, J. 1988. *A Secure Base. Parent-child Attachment and Healthy Human Relationships*. London: Routledge.

Bion, W. R. 1988. *A Theory of Thinking*. London: Routledge.

Britton, R. 1992. 'Keeping Things in Mind'. In R. Anderson (ed.), *Clinical Lectures on Klein and Bion*. London: Routledge.

Cohn, J.F., Campbell, S.B., Matias, R. and Hopkins, J. 1990. 'Face-to-face Interactions of Postpartum Depressed and Non-depressed Mother-infant Pairs at 2 months', *Developmental Psychology*, 1(26), pp. 15–23.

Cross, D. 2013. *Pastoral Care*. Available at http://isca.edu.au/wp-content/uploads/2012/08/Donna-Cross1.pdf. Accessed 26 June 2014.

Dennis, C. L. 2004. 'Treatment of Postpartum Depression, Part 2: A Critical Review of Nonbiological Interventions', *The Journal of Clinical Psychiatry*, 65(9), pp. 1252–65.

Fonagy, P., Steele, M., Steele, H., Moran, G. S. & Higgitt, A. C. 1991. 'The Capacity for Understanding Mental States: The Reflective Self in Parent and Child and its Significance for Security of Attachment', *Infant Mental Health Journal*, 12(3), pp. 201–18.

Fullfact.org (2016) https://fullfact.org/health/spending-mental-health-services/ Accessed 5 September 2017

Gerhardt, S. 2004. *Why Love Matters*. New York: Routledge.

Hay, D Hay, D.F., Asten, P., Mills, A., Kumar, R., Pawlby, S. and Sharp, D., 2001. 'Intellectual Problems Shown by 11-year-old Children whose Mothers had Postnatal Depression', *Journal of Child Psychology and Psychiatry*, 42(7), pp. 871–89.

Herman-Giddens, Marcia E., Slora, E.J., Wasserman, R.C., Bourdony, C.J., Bhapkar, M.V., Koch, G.G. and Hasemeier, C.M., 1997. 'Secondary Sexual Characteristics and Menses in Young Girls seen in Office Practice: A Study from the Pediatric Research in Office Settings Network', *Pediatrics* 99.4, pp. 505–12.

Hesse, E. 1999. 'The Adult Attachment Interview'. *Handbook of Attachment: Theory, Research, and Clinical Applications*, pp. 395–433.

Hindu Business Line Blink (2017) SOS from the Homemaker. http://www.thehindubusinessline.com/blink/cover/sos-from-the-homemaker/article9587743.ece Accessed March 17, 2017.

Kaltiala-Heino, Riittakerttu, Marttunen, M., Rantanen, P. and Rimpelä, M., 2013. 'Early Puberty is Associated with Mental Health Problems in Middle Adolescence', *Social Science & Medicine* 57.6, 1055–64.

Kaplowitz, P. B., Slora, E. J., Wasserman, R. C., Pedlow, S. E. & Herman-Giddens, M. E. 2001. 'Earlier Onset of Puberty in Girls: Relation to Increased Body Mass Index and Race', *Pediatrics*, 108(2), 347–53.

Kumar, M. &. Fonagy, P. 2012. 'Conceptualizing Attachment Trauma: Exploring Emotional Vulnerabilities among Disaster-affected Children of Gujarat', *Psychological Studies*, 57(1), pp. 9–21.

Milgrom, J., Gemmill, A.W., Bilszta, J.L., Hayes, B., Barnett, B., Brooks, J., Ericksen, J., Ellwood, D. and Buist, A. 2008. 'Antenatal Risk Factors for Postnatal Depression: A Large Prospective Study', *Journal of Affective Disorders*, 108(1), pp. 147–57.

Milgrom, J., Negri, L.M., Gemmill, A.W., McNeil, M. and Martin, P.R. 2005. 'A Randomized Controlled Trial of Psychological

Interventions for Postnatal Depression', *British Journal of Clinical Psychology*, 44(4), pp. 529–42.

Murray, L., Fiori-Cowley, A., Hooper, R. and Cooper, P. 1996. The Impact of Postnatal Depression and Associated Adversity on Early Mother-Infant Interactions and Later Infant Outcome. *Child Development*, 67(5), pp. 2 512–26.

O'Hara, M.W. and Swain, A.M. 1996. 'Rates and Risk of Postpartum Depression: A Meta-Analysis', *International Review of Psychiatry*, 8(1), pp. 37–54.

Stern, D. 1985. *The Interpersonal World of the Infant*. New York: Basic Books.

Tavistock and Portman NHS Foundation Trust, 2013. *How We Can Help: Your Child* Available at: http://www.tavistockandportman. nhs.uk/yourchild Accessed 4 March 2014.

Times of India. 2012 'Oxytocin Triggers Early Puberty among Girls', 17 April.

Winnicott, D.W. 1991(a). 'Why Do Babies Cry?' *The Child, the Family and the Outside World*. London: Penguin, 1991.

Winnicott, D. W. 1991(b). Needs of the Under Fives. *The Child, the Family and the Outside World*. London: Penguin.

Being Kept in Mind. Not Mindreading

He had come in huge and limping. It was hard to believe that he was 17 years old. He was too big and yet when I looked closely at his face, hiding behind too-big glasses, it looked like it did not fit the body. His face looked like he was 12. His body was much older, like that of a middle-aged man with the gait of a toddler.

To my standard opening question of 'What is the internal emotional difficulty you would like help with', he answered, 'I am very disconnected from my emotions. I can't feel anything for very long. It goes away. Even happiness.'

Aside from the fact that he had not answered my question directly, I wondered whose words those were. It sounded more like stating a professional opinion rather than a struggle. I made a mental note to bring this up later.

He gave me an example: he had come back home from his economics exam and was unhappy with his performance. He was angry with himself, he said. I noticed that he interrupted himself several times; it was very difficult for him to tell me this one story.

A few questions later, I asked him—'You say you are struggling to hang on to your feelings. Do you want to be able to feel them? Is focusing on your feelings something you want to do?'

Somewhat emphatically, he said 'Yes! I don't want to feel anything! I want to be numb. I want to be stable.'

So that was it. Not feeling his emotions was not actually a problem for him. It was his aim.

The contradiction did not escape me. I found myself becoming agitated, irritated, angry even during that session. It started as a heat inside and it was out, sarcasm and all, before I could edit it to make it more palatable.

'I see. So, I can focus on your feelings and you can focus on being numb. This is going to be a great therapeutic relationship.'

You may wonder as you read this: this therapist's feelings are intruding on the session. Is it allowed? The answer to that is not straightforward. It is both yes and no. This hour is about him and his feelings and especially about his internal tussle over them. My feelings are mine and an important guide to me about what is going on in the room.

The fact is that all human beings have feelings and psychotherapists are no different. Of all the helping professions, psychotherapy may be the only one that openly acknowledges that the professional is not neutral. We all have our own experiences, views and feelings. The training we undergo, which includes being in therapy ourselves as a central part of it, teaches us to separate our own feelings from the client's. A first step in this is to be aware of our feelings as they happen. It is an invaluable tool in the therapeutic process.

My sense during the session described above was that this therapeutic relationship was going to be terribly stilted from the very start if my 17-year-old client was going to abdicate his role in the process. The prospect of lugging him along, with him resisting and kicking and screaming to be let go, much like a toddler throwing a tantrum, made me extremely uncomfortable. This is not how psychotherapy works.

That I became aware of my discomfort in the instant it emerged and responded to it, made it possible for me to be honest with this young man. It cleared the way for him to form a partnership, without which I would just be another adult giving him advice on how to live his life.

As the words came out of my mouth, I wondered if I had blown it or just saved myself hours of misdirected rescue effort, psychotherapeutic imperialism (much like international development organisations who come in to 'rescue' the victims of a disaster in a less developed part of the world, convinced that they know what the victims need to improve their lives.)

The effect of this was startling. For both of us I think. I almost held my breath at my own reaction. He looked shocked and somewhat sheepish, as if I had caught him at his game. He sat back in the chair and very slowly said, 'I never saw it like that.'

One would imagine that he could have seen it. After all he knew psychotherapists, he had seen his previous therapist for over six years. Perhaps this ruse had worked before. To be fair to him, he had started therapy when he was a young boy and he really would have needed pointers and guidance, perhaps even rescuing. Something different needed to happen now.

I repeated myself, more elaborately, less sarcastically this time. I explained that he had come in saying he wanted to feel his feelings, yet there was clearly a part of him that wanted to be numb. To be a rock. To feel nothing. 'So, you want me to do the work but you don't want to feel.'

Yes, he said, everything that I do is to distract myself from my feelings.

So, whose words were the previous ones?

'My mother's, my therapists', he said.

So, your mother thinks you should be in therapy.

'Yes. But so do I. I asked for this meeting.'

And what is the internal emotional difficultly that *you* would like help with?

We were back at the beginning.

Over the next hour we looked at the various ways in which this young man tried to numb himself: alcohol, marijuana, tobacco, sugar, food, music. Insufficient sleep. The neglect to his body was only too obvious. Carrying 125kg, he was overweight even for his six-feet-tall frame, with an unhealthy, diabetes-inviting waist of 54 inches. His thyroid gland was colluding with his intra-psychic state by not making sufficient thyroxin, slowing him down further and he regularly forgot/ neglected to take his medication. Bones broke and muscles tore under the strain of carrying him around and I wondered about the effect on his heart muscles. An intelligent young man; intellectually he could see that the neglect and abuse he was unleashing on his body was damaging him, but he could not stop. He could not stop eating 20 spoons of sugar a day. He could not allow himself to sleep when he was tired at night. The motivation to harm himself clearly had deep roots, deep emotional roots extending back to childhood but now buried in adolescent rebellion, foul language and an ungainly appearance.

The emotional neglect was less obvious but available for me to see as soon as we got past the surface. As he spoke about himself, he was consistently discouraging, minimising, rejecting and critical. It was obvious that he did not like himself very much. He was lonely, isolated, helpless and powerless and there was no way that I or any other psychotherapist could change that if he did not want to make the changes. Much like the lightbulb.

***

This happens so often. Therapist and patient end up working at cross-purposes. It is especially easy to do this with an adolescent in the chair across the room. They are designed to disagree and rebel while the adults around them are designed to reason, attack, argue, cajole, badger. He would have turned me into yet another person in his life whom he had little use for; defeated me in my rescue attempts as the other adults in his life had been. I really did not want to fall into that hole and be part of a pattern.

One of the difficulties that enter the room at the same time as the patient and which had already been made evident with this young man was his resistance to change. The powerless 12-year-old, perhaps younger, child I saw behind the large glasses was basically telling me to do something, everything. That it was all up to me. That he had no power except the power to stay small and stuck.

It is a very compelling position to be placed in. Irresistible, seductive even. He was making me the powerful professional who could rescue him or the maternal figure who could look after the child in him and the me of a few years ago would have found it hard to resist. Yet there was another part in him, one that did not believe he deserved care or rescuing. This would ensure he rejected my efforts; the part that wanted to be a rock, since rocks have no needs and need no care. This is where the resistance lay and we could go around in circles endlessly until it was addressed.

***

That is perhaps the essence of what happens in psychotherapy. Somebody, a complete stranger, agrees to keep us in mind. Slowly, that begins the process of us being able to keep ourselves in mind.

There is a lot more to it of course, many techniques and theories, nuances and years of training. But it would amount to nothing if one were unable to keep the other in mind.

It is not easy though, to believe and trust that another can keep us in mind, and building that trust takes time. How long it takes us depends to a large extent on the quality of feeling 'kept in mind' as a child, in our earliest relationships.

I had been seeing Sheila for over a year, twice a week. Our session time and days had been fixed and rarely changed. Yet often she would send me a message, usually in the early hours of the morning before the session wanting to confirm if we were meeting a little later in the day. I often wondered what was going on. Was she finding it hard to keep in mind that we had a fixed time and day or was she reminding me? Did she not trust me or did she not trust herself?

One year into our work, I had to cancel three sessions in a row because I was out of the city. We had talked about the effect of a break in continuity on our relationship and on her anger toward me for being absent, which she covered up with a 'I don't really need her'. I fully expected a message asking me to confirm our next session. There was none. In that morning's session, she spoke of how she feels infuriated with her mother because she feels her mother can only communicate with her when she is physically present. She felt her mother could not keep her in mind from a distance. Now, whether this is real or not I cannot confirm, but it is real for Sheila that she felt dropped from her mother's mind if she was not present in concrete form. She was also letting me know that she felt convinced that I (her mother, in the session) would forget about her if she was not physically present in the room with me. In that one instant, her need to confirm our session time and again began to make sense. She could not trust that I would keep her in mind if she did not make her presence felt. Yet, the fact that we had not met for two weeks and she had not needed to confirm suggested to me that our relationship may now begin turning a corner. Perhaps trust would begin to creep in.

We are all afraid of our feelings. More accurately, we are afraid of our intense feelings. This begins in early childhood when we experience our feelings as very powerful—in fantasy, love wants to eat you up and rage will destroy everything beyond repair. Feelings are always intense in young children. We learn to put dampers on them as we get older and when they overwhelm the adults who look after us. The importance of a caring adult being there to understand these feelings and help them become more digestible cannot be overemphasised. It is central to our emotional development and at times parents need help with learning how to 'hold' their children's intense feelings and not label them as 'good' and 'bad'.

More accurately still, we are afraid of being judged for our intense feelings. All of them. Even the ones labelled 'positive'. In fact, as it turns out, our biggest anxiety is often about loving too much; of wanting to devour the one we love[1]; of wanting to be close to people but being afraid of it. Entering psychotherapy, therefore, is always hard work. It is an emotional commitment to yourself and to your feelings. It is an act of faith, that our feelings will be understood, held, contained.[2] It is a commitment to *feeling*; a commitment to experiencing them all, in their entirety and their intensity: anger, grief, love, sexual attraction, acknowledging them, experiencing them, not just acting on them or throwing them out onto another. Therein lies the difference.

Yet, our work is a privilege, an honour and a rare opportunity to be witness to another life in a way that we do not get to do in our other relationships. Even in families, parents and children interact mainly through instruction, expectation and obedience. We do not often share personal emotional histories in detail and depth; grandparents' lived lives are eons away from those of their grandchildren. We don't talk enough, tell enough stories or ask enough questions of our loved ones, mainly to protect each other from intense feelings and the fear of being overwhelmed.

Psychotherapy is not easy nor does it promise to make you happy. The process invites people to be honest to and of themselves. It pushes people to make a commitment to their emotional growth and to take responsibility for changes in their lives and in their internal worlds. It does promise to make you, your relationships and expectations, from self and other, real. It makes you accept the meaning of being human. Often, I wonder, whether that is part of the reason for psychotherapy being in the margins. It is not easy to accept ordinary human fallibility. In our Indian cultures, with our emphasis on the other-worldly, being human and imperfect may sometimes just not be good enough.[3]

We are all damaged to some extent; we are all somewhat dysfunctional; self-sabotaging, self-punishing, depressed, anxious, defensive, isolating ourselves or intruding on others or somewhere in between. This is not my original thought, having been voiced with greater passion and daring over decades.

What we call 'normal' is a product of repression, denial, splitting, projection, introjection and other forms of destructive action on experience. It is radically estranged from the structure of being. The more one sees this, the more senseless it is to continue with generalised descriptions of supposedly specifically schizoid, schizophrenic, hysterical 'mechanisms.' There are forms of alienation that are relatively strange to statistically 'normal' forms of alienation. The 'normally' alienated person, by reason of the fact that he acts more or less like everyone else, is taken to be sane. Other forms of alienation that are out of step with the prevailing state of alienation are those that are labelled by the 'formal' majority as bad or mad. [4]

'So, do we all need psychotherapy?' I was asked by, one no less erudite and hard-to-mess-with than, my own mother. 'Is it not normal to be this way? We have all been at the receiving end of failures, disappointments, careless comments by friends, parents or loved ones that have hurt us and that we have coped with so is this not just what happens in life?'

It is absolutely.

All of this is undeniably, completely ordinary.

It is also undeniably painful.

Whether one wants to take a closer look at it, at ourselves, our lives and how it connects to others, is a matter of choice. And of degree. A lot depends on what we make of the too much or the too little we got.

It is always a matter of degree. How dysfunctional? How depressed? How anxious? The point at which that underlying pain becomes actively distressing or damaging to other relationships is the point at which people usually look for help. Why have you come to see a psychotherapist? in one form or another is a standard first question in a first psychotherapy session. That, followed by 'why now?'

Regularly my colleagues and I are confronted with the following question in its various versions:

'But do I *really* need therapy?'

Or

'Do I really *need* therapy?'

Or

'Do I really need *therapy*?'

Are we really aware of what *all* we need to nourish the different parts of our selves? For many of us, becoming aware of what our own needs are is a challenge in itself. Attending to them, yet another. The truth is that therapy can help us discover what we need, from our lives and loves. Therefore, there is always an internal struggle about therapy and whether it is really needed. It is portrayed as an indulgence, which one could do without or a betrayal of some other dearly held self-belief, world-view or worse, of a person. It is not my role to talk someone into psychotherapy or to force change. My work is to help young people become aware of their inner voices; to be able to differentiate their own from those of others they hold dear.

We could all use psychotherapy in some form or another. It makes us feel heard, validated, attended to; more aware of ourselves and our personal needs. Better observers of how and why we are the way we are. It may make some things clearer but that may also make things more painful. So we often choose to not know; to not change; to stay with the pain we know than to risk the unknown. There is, after all, some bliss in ignorance and it works well for some of us.

One year or 54 sessions of regular psychotherapy later, the now 18-year-old young man weighs an impressive 84 kg and wears a smart 34-inch waist trouser. He has more energy and ambition than ever before, having discovered what inspires him (math) and what his pitfalls are (a tendency to doubt and attack himself, in the face of conflict with close family). In his 54th session, having driven himself (he got a driver's licence a few months ago) through two hours of bumper-to-bumper traffic to reach his session on time, he did something remarkable. He looked back at the younger boy he had been and said,

> 'I feel bad that I completely piled so much shit on top of myself for years... unknowingly... I feel... many times I just want to go back to 2008, 2007 and give myself a hug.

And pull myself into this world, 2016; basically just protect myself.'

His hands moved up and down vigorously as he spoke and from that activation I gathered that these were not just words, these were intense feelings.

I asked him what feelings came up for that little boy: 'When you want to give him a hug. What is the feeling coming up for that little boy?'

'Overwhelming feeling of protection, making him feel secure. Making him feel not so abandoned and exposed and hurt.'

'You want to protect him from all of that', I said, underlining the main point, since protecting himself, taking care of himself had been so difficult for him.

'Yeah. I want to protect him from nana-nani, I want to protect him from school.'

Since I was helping him consolidate his strengths I wanted to ask him what capacities he felt he had to be able to do that now, but it seemed he was thinking along similar lines because he interrupted me and asked me 'To do all those things?'

I nodded.

'Capacities to understand that whatever I do …what happens to me, I can deal with it. I am not going to have an existential crisis about that!' he practically shouted.

'Like, if I got shouted at by anyone, if I got into a fight or something… anything I always started to feel like "Why do I exist? Oh God!" …I just wanted to die honestly. I just felt like my world had just come crumbling down or something but that is just how I was made to feel my whole life, that any small bump on the road is a boulder or something. Or a crater.'

He did not feel that way any more.

'I can't imagine honestly living in my old skin anymore. Living with my old mindset. Living that. Just being this free, mentally free of bullshit is so liberating. It is so fulfilling to be able to use my mind in my everyday life, not just dealing with past shit that was piled up on top of me.'

He was still an 18-year-old with his life ahead of him and undoubtedly, more 'shit' would come his way, as it always does (inspiring the learned phrase 'Shit Happens') but now he was no longer piling it onto himself.

He was now ready to have a life.

Another year later, now 19 years old, this smart, good-looking young man is finishing school, having lost two years to severe depression and self-sabotage. He is taking standardised entrance tests for admission to an American university, is motivated to have meaningful friendships and to discover what makes him tick and turns him on. In other words, he wants to feel alive.

The lightbulb had wanted to change.

Notes

1. Think of how often we hear people say, usually about babies 'so cute! I could eat it!' or 'so cute! I could bite her cheeks'.
2. N. Coltart, 1993. *How to Survive as a Psychotherapist*. New Jersey: Jason Aronson.
3. Even though our myths and epics urge us to see our elders as human. They are replete with stories of errors of judgement on the part of revered figures.
4. R.D. Laing. 1990. *The Politics of Experience and the Bird of Paradise*. Penguin UK.

In the Beginning

Where is the beginning? Is it at birth? Is it at conception? Or is it in the mind of the woman, or better still, of the couple, when the wish or hope or the imagination of a baby arises?

A baby that is desired, hoped for and wanted has a very different life from one who is not. Keeping aside neglect and abuse, there continue to be many different ways of being treated by the family one is born into. Attention lies on a continuum.

In the beginning, we attend to this bundle that is, at first, a body. A responsive, alert, warm vulnerable body that needs to be gradually helped to live in air (as opposed to in liquid) We attend to the taking in and pushing out of stuff—air, milk, urine, faeces, vomit. The quality of this attention is love.

There is little else more dramatic than the entry of a baby into the life of a couple. It certainly is for the mother, who laboured first to grow the baby and then push it out, after much anxiety, sweat, blood and guts or had it pulled out, hammer and tongs, with even more anxiety, blood and guts. It is dramatic for the father too, who is on the outside—both terrified and relieved about his supposed mimimal involvement in the birth process, possibly watching the birth, perhaps not, and either way being wrung out of shape inside. An invisible labour.[1]

And for the baby too, from the first moment of being outside the amniotic fluid and onward, there is a lot to get used to. First there is air, on the skin and in the lungs. It is so different, it changes temperature, it rattles about in the lungs and it moves on the skin (no baby enjoys this change of experience; most let us know). Then there is milk, nourishment that has to go in through the mouth and not via the umbilical cord. For both air and food, the baby now has to get used to putting her own muscles to work, till the breathing becomes involuntary and sucking kicks in as a reflex. Before now, neither was necessary.

Nothing moves and rattles on the inside more than food. The milk that goes in is at first an entirely alien substance which each of us is pre-programmed to search for, take in and process. It is better in its natural form and when not made in a factory because it makes for smoother passage. However, the quality of this passage is determined equally, if not more, not by the what but by the how—*how* we are fed, *how* we are held, *how* we are introduced to the business and pleasure of taking in and pushing out. It begins from the first few hours of birth and continues for the first few years. It creates our relationship with food and with our bodies—to control, to where we house anxiety and pleasure; to desire, to holding on and letting go and to our needs both for sustenance as food and as people. Its imprint remains with us all our lives. It is what neuroscientists now call 'unrememberable and unforgettable'.[2] We cannot recall what happened with us at infancy, in words or as images and episodes because the parts of the brain that house these capacities are still forming, but our early interactions with people and through them, with satisfaction and love, become our neuronal wiring. It becomes our experience.[3]

It is not a small matter that so much of the distress and tension between mothers and their babies arises out of this issue of what goes in and what comes out. In children, doubts about food, issues of greed or inhibition—too much or not enough—are usually conflicts about love being played out through their control over the one thing they can control, i.e., what goes into their body.[4]

Milk/food and toilet/toilette—these become the concrete markers of how we assert our sense of control or mastery over our world and in our relationships. When these seemingly simple, repetitive experiences are provided to the baby while keeping her in mind, she can thrive. If done mechanically, she will remain alive, even grow but may experience a neglect of a form that is hard to describe because it hits at her very sense of 'being in the world', of feeling real. Many experiences of depression in children, adolescents and adults come from this place, of having been kept alive without really having been attended to. Without having been seen.

Nineteen-day-old Jaya, was being prepared for a massage and a bath, as all babies are. The only trouble for her was that she was sleepy and that the 'massage-wali' insisted that Jaya pee into a sink first, not into the nappy. She kept carrying her to the bathroom to get her to do so but Jaya, the baby, who cried throughout, would not, could not (as if this process is under conscious motor control at this age anyway). She was brought back to the bed and eventually peed in the nappy. After this she was fed.

After the feed, the baby continued working her mouth and stuck her tongue out. As she lay, she turned on her side and started to fall asleep. The mother said that she had started to sleep on her side and she put her on her back again. The baby again began to cry and the mother put her on her side and patted her, but she kept crying. The mother lifted the baby again and she became quiet. Earlier during the feed, the baby had started to fall asleep and the mother had gently prodded her cheeks and said to the baby, 'You can't sleep right now.' As the nanny returned, the mother gave the baby to her and asked her to make her pee again. The nanny took the baby into the bathroom and she was now crying more loudly. The nanny brought her back, talking to her softly saying, 'There is no need to cry when you are peeing.' The mother took her and the nanny then asked if she should massage her now.

Through the massage the baby cried continuously and the nanny lifted her several times to soothe her. Both the mother and the nanny commented on how her sleep had been disturbed, that was why she was crying. Every time she calmed down, the baby closed her eyes, opened them and looked about her. She looked sleepy. During the massage the baby defecated and was wiped clean. Three to four times during the massage, mother put something sweet in the baby's mouth to quiet her down, but the baby did not really become quiet. Once the massage was over, the baby was wrapped in a blanket and handed to mother, who held her while the nanny prepared the bath. Both the mother and the nanny commented again on how sleepy the baby was. As the nanny took her for a bath, the baby was crying again.[5]

Each time, the adults notice the baby's needs but proceed with the 'hygiene' requirements instead. They notice but do not respond to the experience of this tiny barely three-week-old. This was just one recorded instance. What would such a repeated acknowledgement-yet-dismissal of Jaya's physical discomfort and sleepiness, the fact that she was not allowed to have 'a completed experience',[6] have on her sense of bodily needs? At such an early stage, to have the environment impinge regularly and have a carer be blind to the link between the psychological and the physical—what will the result be? In India these are the early beginnings of the processes that make women split psyche and soma, mind and body, privileging the latter, blind to the travails of the former.[7]

There is a time and place for the external world to be acknowledged, and that time is not at the beginning. In the early months, when the bedrock of the relationship to the outside is being formed, the world need only enter in small doses.[8]

On any given day we tend to veer somewhere on the continuum between veneration and dismissiveness towards babies, their needs and their inner worlds. On the one hand, babies are perceived as valuable, divine blessings that need to be looked after and have all their needs met.[9] On the other hand babies (often infant girls in India) are neglected, barely fed, barely held as if they won't really notice what is going on. Neither pole is conducive for the growth of a person.

Every society has their own theory about babies, what they are about, and how best to look after them in order to turn them into a useful member of that particular community (remember that undemanding, neglected, unaware-of-their-plight-girls are very valuable in maintaining social and familial status quo in many communities across the world). However, in some of the most detailed studies on babies from the 1960s onward (see Winnicott, Stern, Spitz, Bowlby)[10], views emerge (unfortunately for us) mostly from middle-class western white society, that the emotional needs of babies are inherent and unchanging regardless of who you are and where you are born. We may know this fact but we tend to forget it.

Now we come to the inner world.

Human babies have ideas, fantasies, a pre programming if you will. An imagination of what would be good to receive just at a particular moment; a life force propelling us from within. Something warm and satisfying to suck on, something solid that will envelop and make for safety. Simultaneously, emotional drama is ever present for the baby because when needs present themselves, let's say hunger, the internal experience is perhaps something akin to wild animals tearing up everything.[11]

Mothers know this because they are tuned into their babies and feel the urgency, the pain and rush to be present; they hate to delay the feed and if they make it in time, their baby rewards them with eagerness followed by satisfaction. But if the feed does not make it in time, or the mother does not notice, or the bottle is too hot or the buttons get stuck on the way to getting the breast out, the baby's experience may tip over into where things get spoilt. Many hungry babies are then angry and some may then even turn away from the very food that they desperately wanted a minute before.

Babies let us know that they have things going on inside them. If we watch carefully and if we want to engage, we can make the causal links between external visible events (kicks, poo, puke, smiles, snoozes, calm) and what was happening just before.

The one person who is likely to have the most educated guesses as to how to look after this particular baby is the baby's mother. Beyond the physics of how to hold the baby to breastfeed, hold her safely in the bath or the mechanics of nappy tying, i.e., those which can be taught, she knows this baby's temperament and preferences, i.e., that which cannot be taught. It can only be gleaned through an ongoing emotional engagement and responsiveness. The mother literally *feels* the baby and she has, unknowingly, been developing this capacity over the months she was carrying the baby and through her own state of vulnerability after the birth. She and the baby are more similar than those on the outside may realise. The traditions that emphasise *Jappa* and the 40-day confinement may know what they are on about. Here the mother is 'babied' as well. There is great care taken about her diet so that she does not suffer gastric distress, just like great pains are taken to help the baby avoid colic (more common if the baby is bottle- and formula-fed). She is massaged regularly, just the way the baby is and her visitors are limited so she can rest, recover her strength and can focus on the baby. A medicalised pregnancy and birth can severely hamper this process.[12] And so does anxiety.

All this, because a baby needs focus, a baby needs the outside world, represented by the mother or any other caregiver who spends a lot of time engaging with the baby, to keep her in mind. This changes everything since it is the difference between a neglected baby and one who is not. And this experience of being kept in mind in fact helps the baby's own mind to come into existence.[13] 'Acts of human reliability make a communication long before speech means anything— the way the mother fits in when rocking the child, the sound and tone of her voice, all communicate long before speech is understood.'[14]

Cut to a few months later, maybe just nine or twelve and this is a different baby who is much more directly expressive. Depending on how the first year has gone, much has been established and can now be considered almost safe enough to challenge, to take for granted and to push against. And this is when the real drama begins: when frustration enters. It begins with weaning; 'a quest for new resources, and the freedom of having new, more various needs. When weaning works it opens up the world'.[15] When it doesn't, it can become a wound that resurfaces at every new experience of separation, forever.

Malini calls me struggling with feelings of rage towards her eldest child, all of eight years old, saying they are always in some state of conflict. She has two younger children as well. They are fine, they listen to her, but her older one does not and that is the root of all the problems. This is her analysis.

Of course it is. It would be wonderful, and it was perhaps for both mother and child when they were fused as one for the first three years of the child's life as baby and Malini's life as mother, if things had stayed the same. But then things changed. As they do.

The baby changed from tiny to age three. A second baby was born. The root of it all is that stuff happens and we change. The root of it all is that at age eight, Malini's first-born spends more than half her day at school away from her mother, using her own mind and drawing on her internal resources (much of which her mother worked hard to help her develop). Because she has to. And when she returns and her mother wants her to turn her mind off and just comply, she won't.

The trouble (for Malini) is that her child now knows that she has her own mind and knows she can use it. The trouble (for Malini) is that she is unable to accept that there is more than one mind in the room now. After an argument when her daughter reacts with 'leave me alone!' Malini is devastated, shocked even. She cannot imagine that her daughter would push her away, having spent so many years feeling clawed at for attention. When we looked at her complex, painful feelings toward her daughter, Malini realised that she felt rejected and could only think of polar opposites; that she could either be the way she has been or she can 'leave her be', i.e., alone. Malini was struggling to notice that her daughter (and her other children) will continue to need her as a parent, but in different ways over the years. As their capacities developed, they will challenge her, push her to change along with them. Can she bear to see them as separate human beings with their own will?

And what is the trouble for her daughter? All of it is. Sharing her mother with her siblings is a problem, having her mother's mind completely focused on her demanding compliance is a problem. Having her mother 'leave her be' is also a problem. Fusion and separation are both unbearable and some third place needs to be found. She continues to need her mother but not the way she did when she was a baby. And they can only solve this riddle together.

Fusion and Separation

Seeking this balance is our lifelong work, in all our relationships. And for mothers, this is the most heart-wrenching one. Keeping the baby alive, safe and loved depends on fusion. Letting the baby grow into a person with her own mind, is the work of separation. And how is one person supposed to be able to achieve both successfully? How is one person supposed to always be able to gauge what this baby needs and get it right? She cannot do it unless she is able to feel this baby's feelings. Yet, the same person has also to allow this baby to disagree with her (on everything!) and display its own mind a few years later and learn to negotiate rather than impose.

This is 'one of the sources of all conflict, the moment when and mother and a child realize their insufficiency as a unit, echoed in adulthood when lovers discover that they can't be everything for each other and they need'[16] something or somebody else.

Mothering. It is the hardest, unseen, most ordinary, ubiquitous work of all.

I think it is right to say that babies and little children do not remember when things went well, they remember when things went wrong, because they remember that suddenly the continuity of their life was snapped…. If things went well, they never say 'thank you', because they did not know it went well. In families there is this great area of unacknowledged debt which is no debt. There is nothing owing, but anybody who reaches stable adulthood could not have done it if somebody at the beginning had not taken him or her through the early stages.[17]

Notes

1. Ayushi Madan, MPhil Psychoanaltyic Psychotherapy candidate, 2017 personal communication.

2. D. Watt, 2001. 'Emotion and Consciousness: Implications of Affective Neuroscience for Extended Reticular Thalamic Activating System Theories of Consciousness'. www.phil.vt.edu/ASSC/watt/defaulthtml.

3. S. Gerhardt, 2004. *Why Love Matters*. London: Routledge, p. 66.

4. A. Phillips. 2010. *On Balance*. New York: Farrar, Straus and Giroux, p. 17

5. U. Agarwal & N.D. Paiva. 2014. 'The Uncomfortable Subject: Observing the Indian Girl Child'. *Infant Observation*, *17*(2), pp. 151–66.

6. D.W. Winnicott. 1964. *The Child, the Family and the Outside World*. London: Penguin. p. 77.

7. Agarwal & Paiva. 'The Uncomfortable Subject'. 'It is not entirely far-fetched to link Winnicott's (1960) idea of the false self to such impingement, where the developing psyche must constantly adapt to external stimuli and not be allowed to connect to, or, at this early stage, even come upon its inner experience.'

8. D. W. Winnicott. 1964. 'The World in Small Doses'. In *The Child, the Family and the Outside World*, p. 69.

9. P. Uberoi. 2009. *Freedom and Destiny: Gender, family, and Popular Culture in India*. Oxford University Press.

10. D.N. Stern. 2009. *The First Relationship*. Harvard University Press.
D.N. Stern. 1971. 'A Micro-Analysis of Mother-infant Interaction: Behavior Regulating Social Contact between a Mother and her 3 1/2-month-old Twins'. *Journal of the American Academy of Child Psychiatry*, *10*(3), pp. 501–17.
R.A. Spitz. 1950. 'Anxiety in Infancy: A Study of its Manifestations in the First Year of Life'. *The International Journal of Psycho-Analysis*, *31*, p. 138.
R.A. Spitz and K.M. Wolf. 1946. 'Anaclitic Depression: An Inquiry into the Genesis of Psychiatric Conditions in Early Childhood, II'. *The Psychoanalytic Study of the Child*, *2*(1), pp. 313–42.

J. Bowlby. 1958. 'The Nature of the Child's Tie to his Mother'. *The International Journal of Psycho-analysis, 39,* p. 350.

J. Bowlby. 2012. *The Making and Breaking of Affectional Bonds.* Routledge.

11. D.W. Winnicott. 1964. *The Child, the Family and the Outside World.*

12. J. Marchant. 2016. *Cure: A Journey into the Science of Mind Over Body.* London: Canongate, pp. 134–36

13. W.R. Bion. 1962. *A Theory of Thinking.* London: Routledge, p. 110.

14. D.W. Winnicott. 1986. 'Children Learning'. In *Home is Where we Start from.* Compiled and edited by C. Winnicott, R. Shepherd & M. Davis. London: Penguin, p. 147.

15. A. Phillips. 2010. *On Balance,* p. 293.

16. Ibid.

17. D.W. Winnicott. 1986. 'Children Learning', p. 146.

Breastfeeding

Breastfeeding. 'It is a bit like sex' I thought to myself, early one morning.

a)   It does not ever happen the way they show it in the movies,
b)   You can't really learn by watching others do it and
c)   You really don't know what it is going to be like until you do it.

Further,

1.   It involves your body and one other person, so intimately attached to you, whose body you will be acquainted with in great detail.
2.   It takes practice to get to be good at it and every baby is different, just like every lover, so there is the matter of fit though breastfeeding ends up getting (and also needs) more frequent practice, which often means that skin gets chaffed and it hurts. There can be infections and it can hurt a lot.

So really, it is a lot like sex for the first few times.

It is not everyone's cup of tea though, this attaching and feeding another person from your body. I suspect there are people who feel similarly about sex but one does not get to hear about it as much, or at all, in fact.

One new mother confided in me that while feeding her infant son, being skin to skin, with scarcely a breath to part them, she became acutely aware of how intimate their relationship was. That she understood his communication through his movements and sounds, through his body, at a level of detail that would never be possible in any relationship other than a sexual one, if we were lucky. It would also cease to be this way once he was weaned off the breast; that from weaning onward they would only get more and more distanced from each other; that one day he will have a relationship with someone else, one she will not participate in. I thought I saw her eyes mist over at considering the prospect of losing this intimacy with her son, illogical as it may seem from where they were currently placed, still breastfeeding. She valued this stage of their togetherness such that the impending loss was acutely felt.

Not so far removed from feelings in a romantic relationship, I thought—the fear of loss, the gnawing envy, the anxiety of being neglected are so familiar. And yet, she is not crazy. Just honest. She is putting into words what many mothers experience and know to be true.[1] Silently.

Taking your clothes off, or intimacy regardless of one's state of undress, requires one to be vulnerable and who to be vulnerable with is a large part of the comfort or discomfort. As a matter of fact, there are few emotional states more vulnerable than a new first-time mother. That is, except her newborn baby. The little baby is definitely more at risk but then again, this is not a competition. Mothers are terribly delicate in the first few weeks after birth, both physically and emotionally, and a large part of this state of mind is useful because it helps her to identify with the baby, to imagine, even experience what it feels like to be small and needing a lot of care and responsiveness. It does not make it easy for her though.[2] The pregnancy itself brings up so many feelings and memories from the past about significant relationships and feelings towards loved ones—losses, abandonments. It is as if the new baby inside you makes you a conduit for feelings across generations. Your relationship with your father and mother come swooping in through you; in your day-dreams and night-dreams you are assaulted sometimes by memories you did not know you had stored away somewhere. It is as if the baby growing inside needs to become connected to the internal theatre of the mother and all the rest of the cast. The memories and feelings link grandparents, dead or alive, to this new baby, through the mother of course. This internal drama is most evident to the mother and because it is accompanied by changes in her physical body and her mood, she has the choice to dismiss it as 'just hormonal' or attend to it as a valuable reality. A reality less tangible but no less powerful; a reality that underpins the feelings with which a baby is received into the world; how the prospect of labour is made bearable and hope overcomes the inevitable anxiety of death that accompanies every pregnancy.

So here we have two vulnerable people, one of whom has to get their act together enough to be adult at the same time; to envelope a tiny thing in her arms, despite pain and oozing blood; while trying to not be overwhelmed by a multitude of opinionated onlookers, contort herself into awkward positions to peer at her chest for hours every day, try and try again to give this baby something she is told is invaluable.

Not really like sex anymore.

But why get into all this to begin with? Why spend all this word-count on this subject of breastfeeding, I asked myself. Something in my dream or in the conversation the previous night or from the depths of my unconscious had woken me early one summer morning with the thought that 'breastfeeding is a lot like sex'. As I stumbled to my computer, thinking 'maybe

I'm onto something here and I had better write it down before I forget', the grey Delhi dawn felt only too familiar, too similar to the grey dawn outside my window when I would be awake feeding my own babies. I noted that there had been just the two of us. No one in the world would have been aware of what went on for us had I not told them. And yet, what went on between my baby and me was beyond words. Before words. It could only be felt, not said.

My husband, who never abandoned us for the comfort of another room and an uninterrupted night's sleep, would often try to wake up with me and I was grateful for his company. It meant there was a witness to our experience. While I was sitting up, calming a small person and putting her needs before my own, his presence made me feel less lonely. From being something the baby and I experienced in isolation, almost in secret, we became a family. (This, despite my practical mind being aware that two under-slept, groggy adults did not make for very efficient bread-earning, housekeeping or childrearing.) I would be torn between patting him back to sleep and prodding him with my toes to keep him awake. There was a warmth in being kept in mind, to have him be aware that he was part of something important going on. For this reason, beyond the science of nutrition, immunity-building and cognition, for the emphasis on the relationships being formed and being re-formed, I place this emphasis on breastfeeding. Because it needs to be kept in mind—every mother and what she does, in the most ordinary and neglected of experiences that helps to form the fundamental building blocks for our capacities for relating to others, needs to be kept in mind.

Depending on where in the world one is located, whether rules of protecting the mother-baby pair from *nazar*[3] operate or not, the multiple onlookers can include the near family, female neighbours as well as nurses and doctors if one is in a hospital. Their frequent peeping suggests that as soon as you have pushed a person out from between your legs, all the rules of social decency are out of the window. These onlookers come complete with opinions, of which there are plenty too, on everything from what to eat and what massage oil to use, to how to get the baby to feed or sleep, which keep changing (which is really annoying as well and hard to keep up with). They have changed their tune towards breastfeeding too. It was perfectly okay to use a powder that came out of a box to feed your baby some decades ago but then the World Health Organization said 'no actually it's not', so now if a woman is not a calm Perfect Mother who breastfeeds till her child is going to nursery school, she is liable to be judged by her peers and suffer pangs of guilt and inadequacy.

For me, this does not come from a 'grapes are sour' perspective. I was very keen on breastfeeding and did not think there was much to it. How wrong I was! I underestimated how powerless and 'un-able' the combination of physical pain, blood loss, hormonal whirlwind and emotional rough-and-tumble would make me feel. And of course, I had forgotten to take into account the fact that my baby would have an opinion too. She did. She was pissed off that the milk did not flow immediately as soon as she sucked and would scream and yell, shredding my already stretched nerves. My valiant husband, without whom I would never have coped, would pick her up, walk around the room with her and sing to calm her down and pass her back to me so we could try latching on again. (Years later I see how these responses are actually quite typical of our respective personalities, all three of us. But that is a different story.) This went on for three days, every couple of hours, day and night, where a tiny person of barely three kilograms in weight had four adults spinning with anxiety. I was miserable, our baby was probably hungry and we were both exhausted. The midwife who was visiting us at home tried to help us get the latch right by shoving the baby's head onto my breast.

Of course, it did not work: shoving is no good, for sex or for breastfeeding. After trying this for five minutes each on two successive mornings, she declared that breastfeeding was very difficult anyway, she had not been able to do it either and in any case my nipples looked like they were the wrong shape so I should probably give up and give the baby a bottle since she was losing weight.

Perhaps she was trying to be kind to me and perhaps if I had been less eager to breastfeed I may have jumped at the thinly veiled permission she offered. But I was not. I was hurt and offended at the suggestion that there was something wrong with the 'shape' of my nipples. I was angry that she was useless at her job and I wanted to get rid of her. I could do neither; instead, I cried a lot. My adult, professional brain had become defunct and I just could not gather the strength; in fact it did not occur to me that I had any strength. After the midwife left I called (and possibly blubbered to) a friend for help and either because I knew and trusted her or because she was not jaded, opinionated and rough (and shoving), I felt relaxed in her presence. Watching me hold the baby ready to latch her on to my left breast, mid-conversation, my friend very gently, almost imperceptibly, tilted the baby's head a tiny bit back from the position I was attempting so that instead of being parallel to the breast her face was ever so slightly turned upward. That was all it took, a subtle change of position. My frustrated, hungry four-day-old latched on and had her first proper feed. I could tell the difference in the way her mouth felt on me, I could feel fluid stinging and flowing inside me and it became immediately obvious that we had had it wrong all along. We were off! I eventually breastfed her till she was a one-year-old without incident.

Misshapen nipples. As if!

It got worse before it got better though because the morbid midwife arrived the next day, with a student in tow, not having asked me if it was okay to increase the number of strangers staring at my apparently misshapen nipples and non-milk-letting breasts and made further dire declarations. This time it was about the baby having lost too much birth weight and needing to be taken to hospital, but that is another ghastly story we don't need here. And yet, it is a ghastly story that is only too common and one that does no favours to the developing breastfeeding relationship.[4] Having a newborn baby in a Neo-Natal Intensive Care Unit, being prodded with needles and a feeding tube through the nose, you can perhaps imagine the soul-battering wrench it creates for a mother and new baby. Nine years later I still shudder at the memory.

On the other hand, if rules of *nazar* do operate, then it is unusual to get near enough to the mother-baby feeding pair long enough, quietly enough and unselfconsciously enough to actually be able to observe what is going on (though the ruckus created in the 'multiple onlookers' scenario is not conducive to quiet reflective observation either). On the rare occasion when I have been privileged enough to be invited to quietly observe a baby feeding, I am struck by the extraordinary capacity a tiny baby and new mother have to communicate with each other wordlessly. Baby Aman's mother was comfortable enough with me to have me in the room while feeding him. At five months, Aman had clearly had enough experience of joy and satisfaction at the breast such that when his mother picked him up to feed him, he gurgled and giggled with the excitement of anticipation. Somewhere between a cry, a laugh and a song, he seemed to smile with nervous anticipation. Perhaps nervous in case it did not actually materialise. But when it did, he latched on to the breast with such practised ease, that I realised a five month old is a veteran at this business of working for his supper. Sucking hard for the first few minutes, he broke off from the nipple to look directly and intensely at his mother. She looked back at him, nodded as if to unhurriedly, gently ask him 'what?' and letting him take his time, smiled at him. They were communicating in that silence.[5] There was deep love in that silent gaze.

When he had filled himself with the sight of her, he returned to the feed.

There is no one right answer that works for everyone. One truth is that breastfeeding is also a bit like learning to ride a bicycle or swim. Once you get it, you can't forget. But it is also true that you need help to get it right (just like riding a bicycle, swimming or sex) and many women don't have the right kind of help especially in urban settings if they have not been around other breastfeeding mothers very often. Once you can do it comfortably (which takes a few weeks of practice the first time), most women find it very convenient. It is certainly less fiddly than bottles: nothing needs to be sterilised, it is always at the right temperature, available at all times so there is no wandering about in the dark between bedroom and kitchen for the 3 am feed; it is created by biofeedback so there is no worry about 'how many ml should my baby be drinking at this age', etc., and no wastage. Baby starts, baby stops for burps and has some more. Mother relaxes and trusts the baby. All good.

There is always the other side of course. Breastmilk is perfect food so it is used up very quickly, which is a pain-in-the-you-know-where for mother because the three-four feed schedule means zilch. It is a huge commitment to being present. It also needs you to take your top off or expose yourself somewhat and that, in urban India, is not very easy or comfort-creating. The baby has to be with you all the time because you never know when they need you or you need them or you will start to overflow and leak if you two have been away from each other too long. It is best done if there is little else that needs your attention for the first six months, which sounds ridiculous said out loud because there is rarely such a thing.

What I am referring to here is less about social discomfort and more about an internal one. A lot of it has to do with closeness and distance. How close is intimate and when does it become intrusive? How close is suffocating and makes me want to recoil? As a new mother, am I ready to change my life around completely and devote it to another person, even if they are tiny and need me for survival? Or do I need my own space sometimes so that I can remember what it used to be like to be me?

It is exceedingly and distressingly common for a baby to be unable to feed at the breast in the early days. Often it is not because of an inherent inability in the baby or mother but an outcome of the baby's struggle to meet his mother's attitude to feeding. Many things interfere with the mother's capacity to adapt to the baby's needs. Many things, potentially, as we see above, but mainly self-doubt, medicalisation, anxiety, depression or illness or feeling not-looked-after and there is nothing more destructive to breastfeeding and latching on than anxiety in the mother. Many emotional/mental health relationship issues are a matter of degree—how anxious? How depressed? How ill?

Ironically, for a first-time mother, anxiety is a given. Most of us are overwhelmed and uncertain about our own capacities, at least some of the time. Perseverance and a kind assistant can really help, all the latest research says exactly this.[6] At other times, advice to persevere with breastfeeding is disastrous. A transfer to the bottle can be a big relief for both and can actually rescue their relationship. Maitreyi lost her own mother at the age of eleven and always cherished a desire to be a 'very good mother' to her own children. Breastfeeding them was part of that ideal but getting her baby to latch on was excruciatingly difficult, painful and frustrating. Her breasts were engorged, the nipples were not ready, the baby was hungry and her nerves were stretched. At the age of three days when her baby was put in Intensive care to attend to her rising bilirubin levels causing infantile jaundice, the little reserves Maitreyi had were shattered. She could not eat, sleep or be looked after herself, stuff a new mother needs to be able to make breastmilk. The anxiety in her, the distress in the baby all compounded to make her more uncertain of her capacities to provide for her infant. 'No one was putting pressure on me, my husband was so encouraging, telling me to try again and again but the baby was hungry, no one was able to sleep, the milk was not enough and Anya was not latching on because my nipples were not formed properly.' Being a medical doctor herself made no difference to how vulnerable, anxious, exhausted and uncertain she felt.

She recognises the self-blame, the pressure on herself to be a particular kind of mother, her feelings of having failed her baby. Eight years later, as she recounts her ordeal, her eyes mist over and I find a tear rolling down the side of my face as I listen to her. Even as she tells me how her husband's voice was a reality check—that she can be a perfectly good mother with a bottle full of formula, that there is more to their relationship than milk—a part of her is still in pain.

Plenty of first-time mothers, usually years later, have confessed how they hated the breastfeeding experience. Some gritted their teeth and endured it, some expressed milk, one courageous woman I knew expressed every single feed for six whole months; others gave up after the first few weeks and were relieved. Breastfeeding made one woman so unhappy and depressed that her doctor suggested she stop. She was much happier after that, finding that her relationship with her child improved vastly.

The early feeding relationship is the template for later ones, especially to one's own needs, body and capacity to trust the outside world.[7] Success at breastfeeding does not mean that all problems are solved but it does mean that the baby will be introduced to a more intense and rich experience in human relationships.[8] Something very powerful happens between two human beings during feeding and has an immense impact on the child's developing capacity for deep intense relationships, which are laid down in us as our wiring, at the level of connections between neurons. However, and this is the crucial part: a lot of problems are created between mother and baby in the feeding experience because we take the words 'breastfeeding' literally.

In psychological writing, the term breastfeeding means 'the kind of care that goes with personal attention from the mother. Actual breast milk is not necessary, the mother can bring up her infant perfectly well without it. Everything depends on *her way of doing it* (italics mine)'[9]. 'Being lovingly held is the greatest spur to development, more so even than breastfeeding.'[10]

Breast or bottle, if done mechanically, without being in tune with the baby's *need*, without responsiveness to frequency, quantity, speed, discomfort and closeness, harms the relationship the baby has with food, with nurturance and eventually with love. This means, only a mother, or other person looking after the baby, *who is in tune* with the baby can decipher the code of whether a particular cry is about hunger, a need for holding, pain, anger or boredom. The vast majority of feeding difficulties in babies and children have to do with the immense problem that every mother has in adapting to the needs of a new baby. She has to do this on her own because no two babies are alike, and in any case no two mothers are alike and one mother is never the same with each child. The mother cannot learn how to do what is needed of her, either from books, or from nurses or from doctors…. The main things that a mother does with the baby cannot be done through words.[11]

If breastfeeding is love, fantasy and satisfaction, then weaning is where rage enters, along with grief. The first true separation and the quality of it, the gains and losses from this first big upheaval, form the template for responses to future separations. Aman, at the age of 14 months is down to three breastfeeds in 24 hours. He is being weaned from the breast and steadily engaging with solid food that helps him join the social gatherings at the dining table. He has a few teeth and loves pasta, pumpkin, chapati, rice, stewed fruit and many other foods. He has started walking, is deeply interested in exploring the room, the house and the worlds that he now has access to from his full height of just over two feet. Yet, his mother reports that when he sees her he will stop his exploration and look at her with sadness and reach out for the breast. She is very aware that she too is sad because feeding Aman used to be such a special, uninterrupted time for them together. And now they have less of it.

No one can tell her when and how to wean. 'The wish to wean must come from the mother'.[12] Only she, in interaction with her child, knows what else he is ready for in the outside world and how changes have to come in a bit at a time, to make it manageable, because 'a weaning from is also a weaning to'.[13] She provides a stable setting for this process, avoiding travel, change of nanny or moving and focuses on that which she knows is hard for Aman but one on which he will grow and extend himself. Of course, he is not growing forward at all times. By the time the day is over and he is tired, he is a tiny baby again, wanting to be held and carried and nursed to sleep. Growing up would be unbearable if we could not go backward every so often and be cared for as if we were truly very little.

By the time a baby is nine months old, he/she has had more than a thousand feeds at the breast and has a trusting relationship with it, as a representation of the world, that provides satisfaction, survives anger, greed and destruction (let's face it, babies are often fierce in their demands at the breast as if they would devour it. In imagination, they perhaps do so every day). This is a huge achievement for the mother-baby pair and a relationship to the world that starts well has a good chance of going on well. If the feeding itself has gone well then there is something worth being weaned from. All good things come to an end and *that* is what keeps them good in memory.

We all carry the traces of being cared for in a particular way somewhere in our minds and in our bodies and that is what we dredge up when we feed our own children. If a mother can bear the anxiety generated by onlookers' judgements, competitiveness about the baby's weight and rate of growth and just trust herself and her baby's communication, about feeding, they will be the richer for it.

It is only possible to be maternal (which includes the man's capacity to be caring) by a high degree of identification with the baby, while maintaining one's adult status and remembering that what is required is not perfection but an ordinary, repetitive, good-enough responsiveness, complete with human failings. Good Enough. Just that.

NOTES

1. S. Kakar. 1978. *Inner World: A Psychoanalytic Study of Childhood and Society in India.* New Delhi: Oxford University Press, pp. 90–91.

2. Societies that follow the 40-day ritual period of post-natal confinement where the focus is on the exclusivity of mother and baby, have an enormous amount of good sense. The oil massage for mother and baby, the uninterrupted time to breastfeed, the limited visitors, the absence of sexual contact and housework, the special diet to aid lactation—is the closest the mother gets to being 'babied' herself.

3.   Loosely translated as 'the gaze' but it is always the gaze of the evil eye, usually also the envious gaze. See N.D. Paiva. 2014. 'Who Observes Whom? Infant Observation Observed: An Experience of Setting up an Infant Observation Skills Training in India'. *Infant Observation*, *17*(1), pp. 5–19.

4.   J. Marchant. 2016. *Cure: A Journey into the Science of Mind Over Body*. London: Canongate, pp. 134–36.

5.   S. Kakar, *Inner World*, p. 54.

6.   J. Marchant. 2016. *Cure*, pp. 136–37 citing Hodnett, E.D. et al. 2002. *Journal of the American Medical Association*, 288, 1373–1381.

7.   S. Kakar. *Inner World*, p. 52.

8.   D.W. Winnicott. 1964. 'Breastfeeding'. In *The Child, the Family and the Outside World*. London: Penguin, p. 52.

9.   D.W. Winnicott. 1957. 'Adopted Children in Adolescence'. In *Thinking About Children*. London: Karnac, p. 147.

10.   S. Gerhardt. 2004. *Why Love Matters*. London: Routledge, p. 40.

11.. D.W. Winnicott. 1967. 'The Bearing of Emotional Development on Feeding Problems'. In *Thinking About Children*, p. 40.

12.   D.W. Winnicott. 1964. 'Weaning'. In *The Child, the family and the Outside World*, p. 82.

13.   Asha Phillips. 2008. *Saying No*. London: Faber and Faber, p. 90.

Baby, Don't Sing Me the Blues

The phone rings. It is the editor from a newspaper that publishes some of my writings and she wants my opinion on a topic she is writing a piece on. I am flattered and happy to help. Then I hear what it is about—she wants my thoughts on why the census data has found that the number of 'suicides among homemakers' is steadily rising.[1] I am now completely hooked and my mind is whirring at top speed. How do I explain to her that her question taps straight into a reservoir of thought, reading and experience that has weighed on me for over a decade? How do I remain professional and informative, useful to her and not get overexcited, even somewhat hysterical? Because women and depression is central to my work; because for every successful suicide there are hundreds, perhaps thousands of women who are depressed, suffering, somatising and ill and because, most central to me, at the receiving end of a woman's depression there is usually a child.

I start off calm. I tell her that from the 1970s with Brown and Harris' research[2] in the USA it was found that women who lived in poverty, did not have employment outside of home, had more than one child under the age of 14 (Huh? Is that not most of us), had lost their own mothers before the age of 11, and did not have a confiding relationship[3] were at the greatest risk of depression. That in my mind equals homemaker. The group she is wondering about.

But suicide. That is not depression, you may say. Yes it is not. It is the end point of one. It is the violent, extreme concrete destruction of a body because sometimes that is the only way in which a woman can be taken seriously. Because the destruction of a woman's mind or internal world does not really bother people, even people in her own family, since it is uncommon for women to be attributed a mind or an internal world to begin with.

I am reminded of 11-year-old Yogesh's mother who came in saying he was clawing at her and she could not bear it. That she was desperate to get away and not feel guilty about it; that she wanted to walk away from her son and a husband who adored her. She fantasised about her son dying and the relief that would follow if she did not have him around. This fantasy in turn would be followed by extreme self-punishment in which she was 'killed' while still alive. She sacrificed her vigour in order to keep her son alive. In the complex description that followed, what was extremely painful was the context in which Yogesh had entered the world. Hers was not a planned pregnancy. Nothing of what followed was planned either. The plans had been around her own growth and developing her own career in medicine, all of which had to be shelved because she could not get support from her parents and her husband to terminate this pregnancy in the first six months of their marriage. They never had any other children and she did not return to work for the next 10 years.

Yogesh. Born into his mother's grey cloud, had not even begun to find his own mind yet. At the age of 11, he worked diligently to keep his eye on his mother's mood, trying desperately to keep her happy. To enliven her. His entire character structure up to this point was designed in response to his mother's depression.[4]

'Mothers are people who have no future'.[5]

Can I say this out loud? The most revered role of women in our country, the most valuable role a human being plays in the existence of our species and I am saying they have no future?

When mothering works well, when she does in fact move from looking after the child to looking out for his growth, pleasure and freedom, then the child moves on and the woman's role as mother is over. As a person, if she clings to that role, she only comes in the way of her child's freedom. However, if she can continue to be her own person, beyond being a mother, she continues. It is this lack of a future for women beyond their identities as mothers, which is at the base of some of the feelings of depression.

As a woman, can I give myself permission to acknowledge that I am not entirely deliriously happy with my acquired motherhood? Does our society, especially the media, give a woman, from any socio-economic class, the permission to have mixed feelings, which include unhappiness, about becoming a mother? (Yes. There is one clause under which you may get such permission—if you have given birth to a series of daughters, i.e., more than one.) And since this is not an acknowledged or valid emotional state, no one will believe that you can possibly feel this way. Not your mother, not your gynaecologist or child's paediatrician, not your husband. Mixed feelings about motherhood simply do not exist in India. Apparently. Therefore, no psychiatric category can exist for this experience and one cannot be diagnosed with postnatal depression.

'You are alive, you have a child. That, as a combination, is more than what most women have. What do you have to be upset about?'—is the theme of what one can expect. A friend of mine was told by her child's neo-natologist 'You have had a son! How can you be upset?'

So what do you tell the 15 per cent of women who are likely to experience post-natal depression? This would be 15 per cent of non-Indian women. After all we deny the very experience, so there is no question of quantifying it. A bit like marital rape, postnatal depression 'does not exist in our culture'.

So what is this alien state of post-natal depression that 15 per cent of women can expect to experience after the birth of a child? 'Post-partum depression is very real!' Maitreyi tells me, gesticulating wildly with her hands 'Your body is a mess, you have not slept, everything is yucky.' Calming down a little she says 'My rational mind knew she was fine, but I was so upset, each time she fell ill I felt it was my fault, that I had not breastfed her and not given her immunity… .At other times I would be so fed up. I would look at the baby and think *"yeh kahan se aa gayi; kya musibat hai"*. Maitreyi only began to feel better when she went back to work and started to forgive herself.

Some of postnatal depression is because babies are in fact a huge *musibat*. They stretch us beyond anything we can imagine. That is inevitable and mothers can only stretch this way[6] because in their own emotional history, their mother did it for them. If a mother's own early emotional history has been less-than-optimal, depression at the birth of her own child is almost a given. While poverty is more likely to limit opportunities and bring along humiliations and frustrations, low income and multiple problems by themselves do not cause depression. 'What does is the context of a life history of poor regulation, rooted in their own childhood experiences. What mattered most was whether or not they had a good relationship with their own mother in childhood.'[7] It is emotional poverty that is the most damaging, across generations.

Some of the feelings of depression come from the inevitable anxiety of death. From the moment the baby is conceived, this anxiety makes its appearance. The anxiety, at first not really perceptible, then more palpable as worries about haemoglobin levels, folic acid and iron supplements emerge with regard to the well-being of the foetus, and about our own capacity to take this pregnancy to the end. Manifest in our worries about the right diet, the right emotional atmosphere, the right exercise, it really is a worry about whether this baby will be okay inside. The honest truth is that the baby will never be safer anywhere else. The outside world will always feel more threatening—with germs on unwashed hands and unsterilised bottles, viruses, strangers and whatever else have you, including the mother's own ambivalence.

Then there is the birth; also replete with the anxiety of death but once you have survived the terror of childbirth, whether by pushing and shoving or by being slit open, the haze of pain recedes as the baby, hopefully with 10 fingers and 10 toes intact, is brought closer to your chest. One way or another, the baby you have longed to hold is finally in your arms. You are overwhelmed, perhaps crying and laughing at the same time, for this is the beginning, as we know it, of the anxiety of looking after a tiny, fragile life and creating it into a halfway decent human being. If you are lucky.

Postnatal depression is also about losses—of other parts of our lives as women, of other parts of our identities, as they become swamped by and subsumed under the one title of 'mother'. It is a continuous, often lonely (because women don't talk to each other enough about the things that really matter most, the internal struggles), personal battle to reclaim the lost parts—the friendships, the career, the sexual life and most immediately, the body. Every woman who has given birth and not had a 'tummy tuck' simultaneously, knows that she still looks about six months pregnant even though the baby is out. Only now it is a hanging bag of loose muscle, terribly unattractive yet unavoidable. My male friends expressed horror at my leftover pregnant body, saying 'Why is your stomach still like this?' Your body has not been your own since you went into labour and will not be for the next many months. A friend of mine told me she felt like she was a cow since her main work was to eat right and produce milk. Luckily she got on with the task at hand and her body took care of its shape after a few months. To be honest, even your mind is not your own. It has probably become a conduit for intense feelings from the past, your own personal past, the present and anxieties about the future. Any lurking depressed feelings from adolescence and early adulthood are probably going to resurface now and create an inexplicable low mood, hopelessness and weepiness. Add to that incessant infant-caring advice from in-laws, parents and every passing neighbour, and you have a recipe for internal chaos.

For a decade I worked in UK in a multidisciplinary mental health team that included midwives and children's nurses and my job description specifically included working with families with postnatal depression. Mind you, families. Not just mothers. It is possible for the father to experience difficult feelings after the birth of his child, girl or boy, but we cannot address this here. Let's just deal with one bit of denial at a time.

I recall young women abandoned by their boyfriends after an unplanned pregnancy; couples lonely and drifting away from each other by the entry of a baby they thought they were looking forward to. I recall terribly homesick, young, immigrant first-time mothers who yearned to be looked after by their own families but instead were in an alien country with incessant grey dripping skies, hearing a foreign tongue, surrounded by unfamiliar food and child-rearing advice. It is enough to depress anyone.

When I returned to Delhi, I was not surprised to find that no one spoke of depression and motherhood in the same sentence; however, I was surprised that even medical doctors dismissed it. Meeting a college friend after 10 years, we spoke of our experience as working mothers and the combination of feelings that it created. She is a successful businesswoman and shared with me how she was terribly unprepared for the complete and utter takeover of her life by her newborn son. She was exhausted all the time and could not keep up with work, yet her business was her 'baby' too. She had set it up from scratch and could not let it wither and die. It was an important part of her identity. She felt trapped, stuck and resentful at her husband, who was working in another city, for her loneliness. Upset at herself for feeling upset, she went looking for someone who would hear her out—her gynaecologist told her to go away; the psychiatrist told her that she could not possibly be upset after giving birth to a son and prescribed anti-depressants to make the feeling go away; her mother denied that such a feeling could be possible. Eventually, my friend found a psychotherapist, people of my ilk, who at least believed in her experience, that she could be overwhelmed with love for her child, panic and loneliness at the same time. A few months worth of regular appointments and she could forgive herself for her feelings, acknowledge that it was normal to have a range of feelings and move on. She continues to be a wonderful mother, a successful businesswoman, and a woman generous enough to share her story.

My own story is not too different. The postnatal midwife watched me struggle to breastfeed by first-born and instead of helping to adjust the latch, told me that my nipples were the wrong shape and that I should probably give up and give her formula. My daughter was three days old and here I was, a first-time mother, being told that I was fundamentally 'wrong' and could not do this right and I needed to depend on Nestle's invention to keep my child alive. I was so vulnerable, anxious and in pain that I was devastated, even as my rational mind refused to believe it. It did not occur to me to throw her out of my house but luckily it did occur to my husband, who did exactly that. A friend who was also a trained midwife came over, helped me hold my baby the right way and we figured it out.

I breastfed my daughter successfully for a year and turned into one of those annoying, smug mothers who never used a bottle and whose child went from breast to cup. There was nothing 'wrong' with me but I saw how callous, insensitive handling of the postnatal mother, an over-mechanised, medicalised birthing experience, complications in the mother and baby's health also lead to postnatal depression.

However, what did tip me into feeling depressed were the fatigue, loneliness and the sheer repetitiveness of caring for an infant. Six months later when my baby woke incessantly at night and I had not had even four hours of unbroken sleep for a month, I found myself crying in the day, easily overwhelmed by every small demand, lonely at home with a baby while everyone else had resumed their pre-baby life. I had not had an uninterrupted meal, nap, bath, night or conversation ever since she was born. I could not read or concentrate on any adult conversation, let alone on intelligent adult conversation about society, politics or my non-existent career. I could not focus on anything, not even the baby. I felt myself slipping away and my husband would tell me I did not speak or listen to him. I felt trapped and angry toward my six-month-old baby (Oops! Did I just say that out loud?) for being so demanding. Yet, anger was not all I felt. There was a lot of love and a deep desire to be able to fulfil everything this baby may ever need, perhaps even before she expressed it. That last idea was perhaps at the root of my difficulties; it was hard for me to accept that I also needed help, that the baby would be fine with an occasional change in carers, that 'imperfect' care would not harm her. I was overdoing it.

Eventually, it was my mother who rescued me by taking the baby away so I could sleep for a while. I had clearly needed mothering. I needed to be kind to myself. And this is not a surprise. The care a woman receives for her own vulnerabilities is central to keeping her sane at a time when she is in the thick of the most specialised of tasks—'primary maternal preoccupation'. (It is an official term. I am not making it up.)[8]

Self-doubt and neglect of the mother's needs is often a large part of postnatal depression and these needs continue to exist even after the first 40 days.

Conversations (with my therapist) where we acknowledged how I felt—that this was an extremely demanding and important task, creating the foundation for health in another human—and sufficient sleep did help me feel better and I started enjoying my baby again. A routine that included meeting other like-minded mothers with small babies, some physical exercise and a few breaks from the baby also helped. Did I just say that out loud again? Breaks from the baby made me feel better. That is part of what I needed. If I wanted to look after my baby to the best of my ability, I needed to look after myself.

So what happens to the baby who has a depressed mother? What happens when the mother feels helpless, not knowing what to do, how to get the baby to stop crying, or to sleep through the night, wanting the baby to grow up fast and not need so much attention?

Since postnatal depression is 'not in our culture', we have no depressed mothers, so no one has looked at the baby at the receiving end of this either.

It is very easy to blame, and all the blame lands on the mother, whether in theory, clinical practice, society or emotional fantasies because she is emotionally so central. But she is also human and often powerless in the wider social context.

The impact of a mother not being able to keep her baby in mind, not being able to convert the sensory and somatic into something more mental is that it gives the baby the experience that the world does not want to know it and the world does not want to be known.[9] The impact of this experience, when it is something the baby is repeatedly confronted with, is one that tells in its relationship to itself and its curiosity about the world. When a child grows up with the experience that the world does not want to know or be known, it affects his capacity to learn, both at school and from his own experience. How can we learn to trust in our own capacities to negotiate the world when this world has been disinterested in us?

'Babies come into the world with a need for social interaction to help develop and organise their brains. If they don't get enough empathic, attuned attention'[10] from a parent who is interested in them and reacting positively to them, then important parts of their brains simply will not develop as well. They will have a lifelong battle with managing stress.

This is one reason to take a woman's depression seriously—because it is not just her life where the lights have dimmed for whatever reason, from her past colliding with her present, but also her children's lives, and their relationship to the world and its people.

NOTES

1. P. Anima. *SOS from the Homemaker*. Published 17 March 2017 in http://m.thehindubusinessline.com/blink/cover/sos-from-the-homemaker/article9587743.ece

2. G. Brown & T. Harris. 1978. *Social Origins of Depression*. London: Tavistock.

3. Ibid. There are also protective factors—especially a close relationship with your husband. http://spmoodle23.aisgz.org/pluginfile.php/63643/mod_resource/content/0/Brown%20and%20Harris.pdf

4. D.W. Winnicott. 1948. 'Reparation in Respect of Mother's Organized Defence against Depression'. In *Through Paediatrics*

to Psycho-analysis: Collected Papers. London: Tavistock. Reprinted 1984, London: Karnac.

5. Adam Phillips. 2011. *On Balance*. London: Penguin, p. 293.

6. It is not random that in the animation film *The Incredibles*, Mrs. Incredible's superpower is to be able to stretch endlessly. She also has three incredible children.

7. S. Gerhardt. 2004. *Why Love Matters*. London: Routledge, p. 125.
    K. Lyons-Ruth. 1992. Maternal Depressive Symptoms, Disorganized Infant-Mother Attachments And Hostile-Aggressive Behaviour in the Preschool Classroom: A Prospective Longitudinal View From Infancy To Age Five. Rochester Symposium on Developmental Psychopathology 4, 131–71.

8. D.W. Winnicott. 1956. Primary Maternal Preoccupation in *Through Paediatrics to Psycho-analysis*.

9. Ronald Britton. 1992. 'Keeping Things in Mind'. In *Clinical Lectures on Klein and Bion*. Edited by Robin Anderson. London: Routledge, p. 107.

10. S. Gerhardt. 2004. *Why Love Matters,* p. 126.

Play: Better than Words

Three-year-old Tanya is on the floor of her living room, engrossed in putting yellow plastic ducks into her pink t-shirt. Her face is partially obscured by her mop of dark curls but there is a sombre mood about her movements and I imagine that her forehead is frowning in concentration. As she puts in the twelfth and last duck, she stands up and they all slide out from the bottom of her t-shirt. She peeps into her t-shirt, somewhat incredulous, as if checking to see what happened. Her father, who is recording this on video so that I could see it, seems to know that this is a grave matter because he does not interrupt, speak or go in to help. He quietly watches her as she figures out the solution since only she knows what she is trying to do. She proceeds to tuck the bottom of her t-shirt into her pyjamas and puts the ducks back in. This time as she stands up, the ducks form a pile in her t-shirt and she circles it with her arms and smiles. 'I have *choti behen* in my tummy' she says with evident satisfaction.

Her mother has given birth to a baby girl four days ago.

Three-year-old Naina was gradually being settled into a crèche. Her mother spent some days sitting at the playgroup along with the new (as in, new to Naina) teacher and other children. Gradually she started to leave Naina at the crèche, 20 minutes at a time, to give her time to experience it by herself. She told Naina that she was going to the shop to buy bread and salad and would be back in 20 minutes. The first day, the teacher reported, Naina was upset and crying at first but then quietened down. She did not play or interact with anyone; instead she sat on the side of the room, very still and slowly fell asleep.

The next day, for the second instalment of 20 minutes, Naina stayed awake and gradually joined another child on the floor, playing with plastic food. After that day, Naina did not protest to her mother by crying; instead she took to playing it out. When her mother would come to collect her, she would stop outside the main door of the building and say 'Ok. Now I am mumma. I am going to leave you in kindergarten. Now you cry; I am going to buy bread; now you cry.' These were the instructions, leaving little doubt as to what was happening. When her mother would cry at having been left in kindergarten, she would be kind and say 'I am coming back soon. I will get you a lollypop.' This scene was played out each time for weeks, sometimes with variations, where mumma departed on a tricycle or where she went to buy something other than bread.

> Another little girl aged 18 months, whose mother left her in the care of a friend while she went shopping, sat and wept for a little. She then picked herself up, put a piece of string over her left wrist as if it were a shopping bag handle, and began to trot in and out of the kitchen door repeatedly, waving her right hand and calling in a reassuring tone 'Boo-bye, boo-bye', as if she were mummy leaving and the babysitter were the baby left behind.
>
> By becoming the mummy who is friendly and loving as she leaves her little girl, it is easier to return to reality, to recognising that she is the little girl. Play can be a bridge to the acceptance of reality, by enabling feelings to be expressed

and seen from different points of view, and in a controlled way.[1]

Children's need for repetition in play has a significant emotional role. When interactions with parents and siblings feel worrying, or sad, they are better assimilated by being replayed again and again, but with crucial changes in the cast: who is the person in power and who is the one feeling bad. A child who is able to play it out is probably coping better than the one who is not.[2]

Children need to play. Nowadays, we are all obsessed with our children developing motor and cognitive abilities through play but my pitch here is different. Children need to play to make sense of their internal and external worlds. For children, play is not just recreation or leisure, which implies that it is an indulgence, but important and serious work. It is pleasurable and engrossing precisely because it is emotional. Otherwise it would merely be the handling of objects.

If you wish to understand your child you need to understand his/her play because it is through play that children express themselves, conveying what they cannot express in words. What a child chooses to play at betrays 'his inner processes, desires, problems and anxieties'.[3] It is how children make sense of difficult feelings—jealously, anger, guilt and hatred are enacted between dolls and monsters—which makes it easier to handle it in real relationships. In play, the little child can escape from the impact of a situation that is too painful for him to accept as it stands. He can escape for a little while by pretending that he is someone else.

In her real life, eight-year-old Tina was at the receiving end of many instructions from many teachers—for sport, music, art, theatre, schoolwork, dance—all of which she (at least partially) strongly resented. In her play with me, she made herself the teacher who gave the children endless instructions. She talked non-stop for 40 minutes, entirely disinterested in the other. She would ask 'Is that okay?' of the children (i.e., me) but never wait for the response. It was just lip service to democracy or consensus. It was clear to both of us that this was a totalitarian regime with one person in charge. Keeping in mind that in our fantasy lives we tend to be excessive,[4] I wondered whether she was communicating that she wanted to have her voice heard, to be negotiated with rather than be infantalised. She wanted to be taken seriously, not just indulged.

Left to themselves, children will play with anything: empty cardboard boxes become houses, curtains become tents, dolls and stuffed animals talk to each other; kitchen odds and ends become a drum-set or an imaginary playing house. It is not the objects, therefore, that are as important as the fantasies that accompany it. Children have ideas about what they are doing; a kind of storytelling, sometimes consciously expressed and easy to understand if we are paying attention, but also with unconscious undertones, less obvious to see.

Watch a young child playing (where they are free from instruction, anxiety or targets of outcome); for example, jumping off the sofa again and again: this is one kind of play—to achieve mastery over something, build skill and lose the fear of being hurt. Then there is acting out active destruction: building towers with blocks only to enjoy toppling them over, or displaying complex emotions in imaginary play—death and destruction, anger, loss, magical strength and resurrections as well as persecution, care and affection.

Every evening in the garden of her home, four-year-old Anya would play at being jailed by the evil policeman, dragged to the tree and tied up. What was being played out is difficult to know exactly since no one really paid much attention, though her mother recalls that they were going through a difficult phase together where Anya was frequently angry and defiant with her. Clearly something was going on for Anya that, according to her internal justice system, deserved punishment. Eventually the theme ran out of steam. The same theme is repeated over and over with little variation (or children want to hear the same story day after day, in exactly the same way) because it means something to the child. Repetition does many things—it makes things feel bearable, less frightening, more consolidated. It is like leaving feelings to marinate so they truly sink in or pushing down on them so they sediment and become more substantial.

Games where there are emergencies, rescues, doctors, blood, thunderstorms, evil jailors, robbers or death are a child's way of destroying and repairing relationships in fantasy. When a three-year-old pretends to be Chota Bheem, beating up Mangal Singh, who has captured his friend Raju, there is a lot going on beyond depicting what the child may have watched on television. Power, anger and making things better are some of the processes at play here. Being small yet powerful, is an important part of why *Chotta Bheem* and his friends appeal to children.[5]

Most parents/carers/child workers are aware of the importance of the make-believe world because when invited to join in and play a role, many do so willingly. One can see parents pretending to hide from the rain, or be shot at by bullets and be grievously injured or fall dead, only to be magically revived by the doctor/child. By playing the role well, parents are doing something significant. They are making the experience emotionally real for the child and not ruining it by bringing in reality.

Something similar happens when a child is 'helping' in the kitchen or home. Parents may know that the child's presence actually creates more work for them, that it takes more effort and creativity to keep the child engaged in mixing the batter, more serenity in overlooking the mess they make by spilling water, yet they allow their child to feel that the cake would not have been so tasty had it not been for the raisins he put in or that his assistance in the garage was crucial to getting the car clean.

After all, external facts are not the only truth.

Coming back to the kind of development that today's market-driven educational systems are interested in—even here children's play is the valuable nugget from which wonderful things happen. Intellectual growth, motor abilities yes, but also perseverance, which is so essential to all learning. 'To learn that we rarely succeed at a thing as easily or promptly as we might wish is best learned at an early age when habits are formed and when the lesson can be assimilated fairly painlessly.'[6] A child learns, if she can bear it (and to help her bear it is where her parents come in), that she need not give up in despair if a block does not balance neatly on another block the first time around. She learns to try and try again. But she will not learn this if her parents are interested only in success, if they praise her only for the end result. A child will only learn perseverance if she is praised for tenacity and effort,[7] for hanging in there while under fire.

It is well-known that play releases aggression—not literally by throwing and bashing things, but yes, that as well. As children get older, the component of physical play and sports increases and imaginary play tends to decrease. Nevertheless, it cannot be overestimated how much good it does to children, both boys and girls of all ages, to use their limbs as a way to release pent-up anxiety, aggression and destructive urges. A 14-year-old explained how playing tennis focuses her mind on winning and it calms her down. She said 'It is not that I am imagining the ball is someone I am angry with and I am whacking. I feel less angry after I have played. I feel relaxed. It comes out of me.' Competitive sports, especially team sports, iron out many interpersonal and internal conflicts, wordlessly. Self-control, taking responsibility for your actions, extending yourself for yourself or your team, gaining respect and a sense of belonging, all come easily through playing a sport, and are useful in any classroom or social situation. Physical play has the added advantage of creating satisfaction in the effectiveness of our limbs and the use of our musculature. In short, using our body feels good.

Parents are pressured to buy toys that hide under the guise of being educational and to believe that play is not much point if there is no clear learning outcome. This is disastrous. When we push our children to learn what a manufacturer designed for a toy to teach or do what we think ought to happen rather than what our child wants to learn, we kill both play and learning. And this is an epidemic: craft activities becoming about the end product; children attending after-school activities or a structured sport. Many children have hectic social lives with play-dates. Between all this and screens, solitary free play is dying.

There are screens everywhere—on smartphones, on tablets and in televisions. Screens may give parents some peace but there is such a thing as too much and at what cost. It is less about the content of what children watch on screens but the frequency of their use. Screens are ways in which we avoid our feelings, especially of hatred, sadness and loneliness. Screens don't help children work out how to spend time with themselves and by themselves. Screens kill the imagination that is truly their own and that which reflects their inner reality. And, what's worse, screens don't listen or respond. We are growing a generation of children who demand to be entertained, whose experience is that being alone is either a punishment or space and time that must be filled because we don't know how to bear it. It is a generation that is easily bored because they may have little experience on how to be alone with their inner selves, where being bored is shorthand for not wanting to engage with anything in a meaningful way.

Most of all, screens interfere with children being able to develop the capacity to be alone.

To be able to enjoy our own company, our internal reality, find pleasure in solitude is a useful skill and a sign of emotional maturity. It is a tyranny to always need the company of others, even if the others are only on a television screen. This capacity to be alone begins with the baby or small child who can be alone in the presence of someone.[8] In other words, who can be permitted and even encouraged to have a satisfied, peaceful time without having to be in response-mode to the outside world and its people, but in the presence of someone reliable. There has to be someone present, but without making demands so that the child has the possibility to safely drift off into themselves. In this context when an internal impulse, desire or sensation arises, it will feel real and an authentic personal experience.

This is the basis for the capacity to play and the basis for knowing ourselves.

NOTES

1. M. Harris. 2011. *Thinking about Infants and Young Children.* London: Karnac, p. 99.

2. E.H. Erikson. 1950. *Toys and Reasons. In Childhood and Society.* New York: Norton.

3. B. Bettelheim, 1987. 'The Importance of Play'. *The Atlantic, 259*(3), pp. 35–46.

4. A. Phillips. 2010. *On Balance.* New York: Farrar, Straus and Giroux, p. 11.

5. This is a universal theme, well-known and used by authors of the most compelling fiction, from J.R.R. Tolkien (*The Lord*

of the Rings) and Enid Blyton (all the series with children as detectives), to Phillip Pullman (*Northern Lights*) and J.K. Rowling (the Harry Potter series).

6. B. Bettelheim. 1987. 'The Importance of Play'.

7. C.M. Muller & C.S. Dweck. 1998. 'Praise for Intelligence can Undermine Children's Motivation And Performance'. *Journal of Personality and Social Psychology*, 75, pp. 33–52.
W.U. Meyer. 1992. 'Paradoxical Effects of Praise and Criticism on Perceived Ability'. In W. Stroebe & M. Hewstone (eds), *European Review of Social Psychology*. Chichester: Wiley, pp. 259–83.

8. D.W. Winnicott. 1958. 'The Capacity to Be Alone'. In *Maturational Processes and the Facilitating Environment*. London: Karnac, p. 36.

Bedtime

A preparation for the close of the day; a preparation for, an acceptance of separation, perhaps loss, even death—for when we sleep who knows where we go. Who knows what visits us. Whether we will return from our travels and most significantly, whether the ones we love, and leave during sleep will be there upon our return.

Sleep can be time travel, anti-gravity, circular, illogical, rejuvenating or exhausting; losing ourselves and finding ourselves; being here and not being here. It is an 'experience of an absence that is not a form of waiting'... since 'once we are asleep we are not waiting for anything.'[1]

'Sleep, after all, is by far the most time-consuming of our earliest desires; and, of course, the only one of those desires that cannot be satisfied by another person (the parent can create the conditions for sleep, but cannot give the child something called sleep).'[2] For all these reasons and more, the child, every child, at some point, has a struggle with it.

This is where the child in each of us can use a bedtime ritual. The bedtime ritual becomes a symbol of the constancy, the continuity of life, love, relationships; of day and night. Of togetherness and letting go. In other words, it communicates human reliability and if this is the pattern of childcare, it builds up into confidence in the environment,[3] which when it goes well means we don't have to worry about it.

Bath, toilette, dinner. Milk, water, prayer, stories. Being patted, being tucked in, being held or sung to; holding a hand, a lock of hair, a toy, a blanket, a pillow. Lights dimmed, shadows in the room, hushed whispers: parents, siblings, grandparents and other caregivers the world over, know and use all of this in some form, some combination, whether they ascribe meaning to it or not. They are taught, if they are open to it, by the child they are looking after, the significance of the right cadence, the right pitch of the song, the correct rhythm of the sway, the speed of rocking, the nth repetition of the same story.

A calming bedtime ritual allows for daytime storms and resentment between parents and children to be patted down and contained so they can arise another, usually the next, day. Forgiveness or at least acceptance that there is a relationship that is not damaged by our anger or by separation, is reassuring to the extent that it forms a template for future relationships. Perhaps, 'don't let the sun go down on your anger' comes from here. What better way to draw it to a close than to reinforce it with loved ones. To be reassured that the arguments, scraps and disagreements, tantrums, disappointments and slights of the day can be laid to rest. That as we part, we are together, with no gaps to separate us. This is best reinforced through the concreteness of sleeping together and the world over there are communities where children never, ever sleep alone. And not for want of space but from an acknowledgement that the young need the physical presence and warmth, both literal and metaphorical, of caring adults.[4]

Any parent used to a bedtime ritual knows that it is the moment their child will pick to discuss what is uppermost on their minds, whether it is a dilemma, a conflict, an anxiety or an event. Urban, nuclear, double-income families struggle with bedtime because fatigue and the tasks of today and tomorrow come in the way of parents and children. Between school mornings and homework, preparations and completions, there is often little time to attend to the child's need for consolidating the day.

Grandparents often help. Somehow they are good with bedtime rituals and children know that. Some children can only sleep with their mothers. Others want to but paradoxically can't seem to relax enough with them. Almost as if it is too hard to let them go and she must be kept an eye on in case she runs off to some other activity or person. Some want a grandparent or a nanny; often fathers are a calming influence. Babies find it easier to fall asleep with a person who does not smell of breastmilk, which can be too exciting, familiar and enticing a memory to allow for the separation of sleep. Other babies need an external focal point to keep their eye or ear on—a light, a song, a voice or the physical sensation of a lap, rocking and providing a concreteness, an anchor that can counter the twilight zone of sleep so that it may feel safe to relax the muscles and the mind.

A bedtime ritual gives safety. The sameness counters fears and uncertainties that darkness makes us all prone to, no matter how old we are chronologically. As we age our rituals change, but unless sex, drugs and alcohol are used too frequently to avoid feeling and as a crutch for inviting or allowing sleep, the themes remain similar—a reliable bed, the same bed; the glass of water, the bedtime story/book; bath, dinner, toilette, prayer and if we are lucky, someone to hold and be held by. The same someone.

NOTES

1. A. Phillips. 2010. *On Balance*. New York: Farrar, Straus and Giroux, p. 82.
2. Ibid., p. 83.

3.	D.W. Winnicott. 1986. 'Children Learning'. In *Home is Where we Start From: Essays by a Psychoanalyst.* London: Penguin, p. 146.
4..	R.A. Shweder, L.A. Jensen and W.M. Goldstein. 1995. 'Who Sleeps by whom Revisited: A Method for Extracting the Moral Goods Implicit in Practice'. *New Directions for Child and Adolescent Development*, 1995(67), pp. 21–39.

Nazar

*N*azar. Literally, according to Google Translate and other platforms, it means vision; eyesight. But if you grew up in India, you and I know that there is more to it than that. To be fair so do the people at Google because it detects *nazar* as 'Turkish language', not Hindi, and in Turkish, *nazar* means evil eye.

So, word travels. More importantly, feelings travel.

Nazar. The gaze. To look, watch, observe, all of which seem innocuous enough. But then there is *buri nazar* and *nazar lagna,* which hold the potential for things to turn altogether sinister. A look, a gaze, can be potent, full of intent and meaning. A gaze can bode ill; a look can 'stick' on to that which is gazed upon. The eyes are windows to the soul and that makes them very powerful, a direct conduit to internal wishes, concealed designs and negative feelings. A gaze can become highly suspect because of the assumption that the intent behind it is of scrutiny. Judgement laced with a desire to acquire, harm or spoil.

Nazar as the 'evil eye' is envy. The angry feeling that another person possesses and enjoys something desirable—the envious impulse being to take it away or to spoil it.[1] Envy is destructive to that which the gaze falls upon and whether we think about it consciously or not, we acknowledge it in various ways. The black face painted on an earthen pot tied onto a new building; '*buri nazar wale tera muh kala*' written behind trucks, and *kala tikas* on babies. In the 1980s an advertisement for a brand of televisions used it to their advantage. In a short but effective sound clip, all the viewer heard was a sound of breaking glass and the voiceover saying, 'neighbour's envy, owner's pride'.

Beyond anger, the envious one hates the other but is also discontented with oneself. When one's self esteem is very low, it can lead to intense envy, often unconscious and disguised. 'One of the most deceptive masks of unconscious envy is contempt'[2]

Envy is double-edged. At times, as suggested in this advertisement, it is satisfying to become aware that one can arouse envy in others. At other times, especially in our cultures where the gaze can harm, we can also be somewhat paranoid about having attracted attention and therefore the envy of others. Envy coming towards you as waves of negative energy is seen as destructive and sapping of health and goodness. Not standing out, and blending in with the background is therefore also considered protective.

What arouses envy? Many things actually—'Men and women envy others if they feel the other is superior in strength, beauty, intelligence, potency, power, prestige and above all, in our society, in wealth'[3]. This is certainly applicable in today's modern world. But an emotional lexicon is not built in a day or even a decade. In our cultures, which have prized asceticism, dharma, renunciation of the material world for centuries, what desire could be so deeply embedded that it leads to the creation of terminology to refer to itself—a desire of acquisitiveness but where this desire cannot be fulfilled? A desire to possess alongside an anger and hatred that the other has something you do not? What do we all desire so deeply, wish to possess and fear the loss of?

Love. Of course.

When we look at who is most susceptible to *nazar*, where is the greatest amount of care taken to protect someone vulnerable, we notice that nowhere is this stronger than when it comes to childbirth, newborn babies and young children. Mothers and babies are protected from strangers, from unnecessary visits by neighbours and others in various ways. The 40-day ritual of confinement, the feeding that takes place out of sight, the *kala tikas* of various sizes on babies—are all suggestions of how a culture protects the newborn child and mother from infection, unnecessary demands from the social hierarchy, judgement and the gaze of others. The *kala tika* absorbs and/or deflects the effect of others looking upon the baby.

What feelings are stirred in us as observers of a mother and new baby pair that are so powerful as to leak out from us, unknown to us, and cause harm to this new vulnerable couple? *Nazar* assumes that seeing a baby and mother together will make the viewer yearn for that once-exclusive relationship which can never be recreated. This is jealousy but there is something more at play here, something that makes it worse, that being outside of this new mother-baby couple, the viewer will want to ruin it for them by putting something bad into it.[4] *Nazar* is our culture's way of acknowledging that the exclusive relationship with our mothers is the stuff of paradise; that once lost, nothing can bring it back; that the effects of it and the desire for it linger in every one of us and it is reactivated when we gaze upon such a scene. Parts of us are sad, longing and dewy-eyed. Other parts are green with envy.

This 'bad feeling' that is put into the mother, baby or the mother's capacity to mother, can manifest in many different ways. Milk flow stops, babies fall ill, become cranky, refuse the breast, get unsettled or stop thriving. *Nazar* is commonly blamed for many ailments in young children, from common childhood infections, to loss of appetite, poor sleep; the list is long.[5] In fact, any positive attention to a young child, especially praise delivered verbally[6] is considered suspect. I am not quoting decades-old studies but interviews from the twenty-first century, educated, well-travelled, urban parents, including myself.

My 20-month-old daughter was eating spaghetti in tomato sauce at great speed. Suspiciously great speed! Watching me feed her was my neighbour, whose child's poor appetite was a frequent cause of distress for her. She commented on how well my daughter was eating her meal (perhaps too well, as I was to later find out). Meal over, we moved over to the sofa to chat and minutes later, this entire aforementioned meal had come out on my hands and lap. Pieces of spaghetti, whole and red, almost unchanged from how they had appeared on the plate, were out. And all I could think of was '*ise nazar lag gayi*'. What's more, my neighbour agreed with me. Perhaps in order to preserve our relationship we didn't specify whose *nazar* it had been. Perhaps we needn't have bothered. That was four years ago and she has not visited me at home since.

My daughter has never eaten pasta with tomato sauce again. Four years later, she continues to refuse tomatoes in any form.

I consider myself well-travelled, well-read and liberal. But I have noticed that the power of what some may call 'irrational' when it comes to the protection of loved ones, knows no barriers of class, education and breadth of mind. This phenomenon can be found in all families with young children irrespective of socio-economic class, western-style education and career orientation. One woman I know stopped putting photographs of her child on Facebook because she noticed each time she did, the child fell ill. I have always avoided baby showers that take place prior to a birth because in my mind the attention on the unborn baby left too much room for *nazar* to operate. How could one celebrate when there is always so much uncertainty about the postnatal mother and child?

From a group of women working as aanganwadi workers in the Jama Masjid area of the walled city of Delhi to liberal arts professors with doctoral degrees and some years of psychotherapy behind them—when it comes to babies and *nazar*, there is little dispute. '*Bachhon ko to nazar lagti hai*'—it sticks and therefore periodically, almost as hygiene, it must be removed. And it is always women. It is only the women who speak of *nazar* this way, as if they are closely acquainted with its ins and outs and its workings; a nexus of women, children, love and envy.

Women will tell you who is susceptible to *nazar*; who is more prone to having '*buri nazar*' leaking out of them and how to remove it—referring to it as a concrete agent that causes an affliction, like a virus or bacteria. You can use whole dried red chillies, mustard seeds and salt; or you can use fresh green chillies and lemons. How much you use depends on the potency of what you are dealing with. How often you use it to cleanse the aura of the mother and child depends on how well they are doing and how paranoid you are that this health and prosperity may wane.

Some will go further and tell you about a mother's envy of her child: a mother's *nazar* on her own child; *bachche ko maa ki hee nazar lagti hai*. When I first heard this after my first child was born, it made no sense to me. *Nazar* was what others did. Now it was being suggested that there were parts of me, outside of my conscious awareness, that were being seen as subtly damaging to my own child? What is more, it was being said as a matter of fact. That it was an accepted reality, with no need to contest it, fight it or deny it. These are culturally very widespread ideas and they may be repudiated by the rational logical world but they are held onto by all mothers of small babies.

Many years later and after closely watching several mother-baby pairs together[7] and after two children of my own, I understand this more. I can clearly state 'yes there is such a thing. Us mothers can be envious of our children.' In most of us this is one of the many other emotions we also feel towards our children but it is often a real, yet denied part of the mix. Also, wanting our babies to stay little, to not grow up or move away, to not get a life separate from ours, to remain dependent—are also forms of envy. Not letting go is also about envy, not wanting the other to have something different from what we had or what we have together.

Some say *Maa ki hee nazar lagti hai*. Others say *Maa ki nazar nahin lagti*. But truly, a mother can be envious of her child. It is so excruciatingly difficult to give of yourself to another if you have not had enough of it yourself. We all envy our children the attention they receive from us. Especially for a woman who has survived being a girl child in India (with all the odds stacked against her) but perhaps bears the emotional scars of that battle. Especially the mother of a girl.[8] The child in her, in us, rebels, is jealous, is angry: 'how can you have so much of what I yearned for and did not receive enough of?' At times in return this little child in the mother wants gratitude but in a culture where dharma is so binding, and the mother's dharma is to love and care, while a baby's is to receive and devour, do such feelings have a space? When, as a culture, we acknowledge *maa ki nazar*, we are giving permission for this process to exist, only out of consciousness.

If we are honest, we all recognise when we have reacted with envy—to people's photographs on Facebook, which suggest that they have lives different from ours; to someone's beauty, grace, qualities, skill or worse, to a relationship we don't have and someone else does. A child, a marriage, a lover.

Usually we 'other' envy. Remove it from ourselves and place it in others. By acknowledging that '*maa ki nazar lagti hai*' we may be willing to consider ambivalence. We may be willing to look within and acknowledge that we both love and hate the same person. Love and anger together, nowhere does this become more relevant than in the experience of mothering. Interestingly, since in a patriarchal arrangement, women are othered and women other women, it is the gaze of the mother and the gaze of the other woman that is problematic. *Nazar* is the bastion of women. Patriarchal society makes it such that women understand envy and the cultural structures exist for it to be disavowed and projected onto another.

And what about the men? How have they absolved themselves of their ambivalence and envy? Or have they? What do men envy? Or more pointedly, what does our society permit men to be openly envious of? After all, some envy is more tolerated than others. 'I believe the most widespread example of this is the male's contempt for the female. Despite all of the male's advantages in our society, men envy women's certainty about being feminine. Girls just have to get older to become feminine, while men have to continue to prove their masculinity…. I also believe men envy women's capacity to bear children.'[9]

One quality inherent in envy is that it includes admiration for whomever one envies. Happy and contented people, especially a happy couple, are among the most envied and unconsciously hated people in modern societies, especially by the unhappy and discontented majority.[10] North India also specialises in othering this envy and placing it upon widowed and unmarried women, using it as an excuse to 'other' widows and unmarried women, thereby making it safe. As if 'Envy is something widows, unmarried women feel, for the wonderful things I have—my married status, my fertility. Not I; I want for nothing.'

Envy is a miserable state of mind especially when it is intense. It can lead to self-hatred, depression, compulsive acquisitiveness and addictive urges. Envious people have to possess the best or be the first. It is not sufficient to be successful and there is no internal yardstick. It is all about the comparison. This comparison is also deflected onto children, whose parents demand they be the best, the most attractive, the smartest, etc.; such children have to make up for their parent's deficiencies. Other examples are of middle-aged people who become envious when they see the greater beauty, intelligence or success of younger people, including their own children. Instead of enjoying the achievements, they grudge them their development and become belittling, cold, dismissive and depressed.

Perhaps the most piercing and perplexing question of all is whether it is possible to make envious attacks on yourself. We have all heard the phrase '*Mujhe apni hee nazar lag gayi*', suggesting that there are conflicts within us, that parts of us do not want other parts to succeed. That working toward success in something—a career, a skill, a relationship is not a straightforward enterprise. Perhaps because winning is also losing:[11] a previous status quo, someone's affection or the way things were.

Most of us are aware of being intimidated by other people's envy of our talents or our loves, knowing somehow, that envy seeks to spoil. So if we do not want our relationship or our skill to be damaged, it is best to lie low, not get too much attention to it, to not do too well, to succeed less. Sometimes to fail. To protect ourselves, or the ones we love, we sabotage our own success, perhaps because sometimes, to live as an accepted part of a family or a community, to belong to a larger whole, to preserve love is more important than individual success.

At times, no one is more envious of one's gifts, that oneself.[12]

The fairy tale of Cinderella may be useful as a story that illustrates this complexity. It is a psychological tale about how women don't want other women to have pleasure. And given that women, like their mothers, are women themselves, it is therefore a story about how women, or parts of themselves, can be the enemies of their own desire; a story about how women, out of fear of other women's envy, want to frustrate themselves. If Cinderella's stepmother and stepsisters represent parts of herself, then they are saboteurs of her pleasure, recruited to stop her getting to the ball.[13]

Cinderella who, by all accounts, was beautiful and resourceful, had imposed upon herself (by recruiting these other parts of herself) a wretched home life. This way she would be safe from the envy of others, or other parts of herself. 'As though women will do anything to avoid other women's envy. If we read the story as an internal drama—in which everyone in Cinderella's story is a part of herself—it is as though what Cinderella does, all that endless housework, is an attempt to keep at bay those female parts of herself that hate her pleasure and her pleasure-seeking because it incites envy.'[14]

Not just Cinderella, but for millions of women in the world, it may hold true, as Adam Phillips writes, that it is not satisfaction the woman fears, but the envy of her satisfaction.

NOTES

1. Melanie Klein. 1980. *Envy and Gratitude and other Works 1946-1963*. London: Hogarth Press, p. 181.

2. R. Greenson. 2016. *On Loving Hating and Living Well: The Public Psychoanalytic Lectures of Ralph Greenson*. London: Karnac, p. 286.

3. Ibid., p. 287.

4. Melanie Klein. 1980. *Envy and Gratitude*, p. 193.

5. H. Keller, M. Abels, B. Lamm, R. D. Yovsi, S. Voelker & A. Lakhani. 2005. 'Ecocultural Effects on Early Infant Care: A Study in Cameroon, India, and Germany. *Ethos*, 33, pp. 512–41. doi:10.1525/eth.2005.33.4.512

6. Nupur Dhingra Paiva. 2008. 'South Asian Parents' Constructions of Praising their Children'. *Clinical Child Psychology and Psychiatry,* 13(2), pp. 191–207.
    N.D. Paiva. 2014. 'Who Observes Whom? Infant Observation Observed: An Experience of Setting up an Infant Observation Skills Training in India'. *Infant Observation,* 17(1), p. 519.

7. I teach psychoanalytic infant observation on the MPhil psychoanalytic psychotherapy course at Ambedkar University, Delhi through the weekly seminar group with MPhil students and have the opportunity to be witness to the close observations students make of mother-baby interactions.

8. Urvashi Agarwal & Nupur Dhingra Paiva. 2014. 'The Uncomfortable Subject: Observing the Indian Girl Child'. *Infant Observation,* 17(2), pp. 151–66.

9. R.R. Greenson. 2016. 'Jealousy, Envy and Possessiveness'. In R.A. Nemiroff, A. Sugarman & A. Robbins (eds), *On Loving Hating and Living Well: The Public Psychoanalytic Lectures of Ralph R. Greenson.* London: Karnac, p. 286.

10. Ibid, p. 289.

11. Stephen Grosz. 2013. *The Examined Life.* New York: Norton, p. 133.

12. Adam Phillips. 2000. *Promises Promises.* London: Faber & Faber, p. 63.

13 Adam Phillips. 2010. *On Balance.* New York: Farrar, Straus and Giroux, p. 300.

14. Ibid., p. 305.

Fathers
Their Presence and Absence

This is the thread running through the lives of many of the young people I work with—the absence of a supportive father. From the eight-year-old boy anxious about death and bullies to the 26-year-old woman struggling with her relationship to food and all the self-harming adolescents in between, the thread of their father's absence accompanies them right through their emotional lives, affecting their relationship with their bodies, their inner worlds and their own feelings. Each responds differently to this absence but mostly they seem lost and overwhelmed. Life, death, desire; strong emotions of love, anger, guilt; being connected to oneself and to others— the stuff that makes life worth living also provokes too much anxiety and seems to be too much of a risk.

It has different effects at different life-stages and it appears that the inevitable loss hidden in every life-transition hits hardest when there is a parent missing. The six-year-old whose father is aloof, busy or otherwise unavailable can make do with his mother for all his needs, or so it seems. She can cook, feed, get him dressed, drop and pick him up from school, help with homework, perhaps take him out to play in the evening if she has the energy, tell him a story and put him to bed at night. What does he need his father for then? The socially created and accepted roles for man, woman and boy child in India leave out so much yet it is the ideal that many families work toward—the gender roles and work divisions between care and work. Care Vs Work. As if care is not also work. In this ideal, women get to be little else than mothers and men get to be many things other than fathers. This is a problem, since it certainly creates one for their children.

Around age three, the father begins to become important in an obvious way, even to the more inattentive among us. It begins in small ways, mostly to do with play, trips outdoors and sports activities. The mother remains important for care and it is rare for fathers to be involved in the daily care routine of their young child even at this age. When hungry, tired, ill or scared, mother or her surrogate is still the one who is trusted. Fathers often have little idea about what to do: often because no one lets them early enough and often enough. Simply put, they lack practice so it is unfair to blame them for not being good at 'care'. Between society, gender roles and lack of exposure they don't stand a chance. Which does not mean they cannot be good at it or don't want to. They often just don't know who or what all they can be to their children. The loss is huge for the two involved, for the mother and for our society in India today.

This is changing in many families now and about time too. As families become more nuclear and hired help replaces the extra support of grandmothers and aunts, fathers often have to come in to the picture and do more with their young children. Whether it is taking them to the toilet, the school run in the morning, time spent on the weekend or stories at bedtime, fewer adults around means all existing hands need to be on deck for childcare.

It is not enough though. A closer look shows that six- to eight-year-olds are straining to get their fathers to play a leading role in their lives. Involvement in schooling, physical activity or in the politics of the playground are more common but they also ask for their fathers; they badger them for time, they ask to play word-games or help with math problems. Sometimes more subtly, they are more amenable to getting dressed in the morning or to doing homework if their father helps instead of their mother. Often these demands or subtleties are overlooked by the father or fulfilled by a mother, grandmother or hired help—maid, tutor, teacher, driver. 'Your father is a busy man, he has important meetings to attend, people to meet, money to make and after he has done all that, he is tired and needs to relax' is the message the child receives. The message the child imbibes, unfortunately, is far less benign, more along the lines of 'So he does not really have time for me and perhaps it's because I am just not good enough and he does not love me; or there is something wrong with me, it's my fault that my father, of whom there is only one in the world, does not have time for me.'

An eight-year-old I met was very clear about wanting more time with his father. He said 'Mumma can go to work and Papa can stay at home', clear about who was rejected and who was desired, for now (our emotional states are dynamic and do not stay the same). He was angry with his father, pummelling him with toys during their game of throw and catch, saying he was either at work or resting on a couch or bed. Unfortunately for him, he was rejecting the parent he had around and did not have the parent he wanted around.

One seven-year-old I met resolved this problem for his family by refusing to go to school. On the surface, Madhur struggled with the classroom and it was a challenge for his school because he did not want to sit in one at all. By all reports, he was fine until he was in Class I. Now he avoided going to school, by bus or with his mother, refusing to separate from her at the school gate. He would cry, scream, become angry and to buy peace, his mother would stay. Madhur's parents said that he threw wild, violent tantrums if he did not get his way. His father said that Madhur was unlike any child he had ever encountered; that he was embarrassed to take his seven-year-old son to a social gathering because he was out of control.

The family lived as part of a joint family in south Delhi with the father's younger brother, his wife and their three-year-old son as well as the paternal grandparents. Madhur's father worked long hours, six days a week and was only available on Sundays to spend time with his family when he admitted to being uncommunicative and wanting to rest. He said it would not be possible for him to attend sessions with his wife or son; that he was very busy and yet he needed help because he felt desperate.

The parents blamed each other—mother blamed father for being absent and too aggressive with Madhur; father blamed mother for her lack of discipline with their son. Madhur's mother talked incessantly about her difficult relationships and her isolation in the family as his parent because everyone disliked him. I felt she was terribly needy and lonely, something her son confirmed when he said he did not want to go to school because he was worried what would happen to his mother. Father wanted Madhur to grow up; feed and dress himself, polish his shoes—memories of his own childhood of valuing things that his father had given to him—but wanting this from afar, without involving himself in the daily routine was not working. Madhur's mother overcompensated for his father's absence and firmness by giving in or being un-boundaried and confusing. Both parents were physically aggressive with Madhur. His father was also occasionally violent with his wife.

Both parents admitted to difficult dynamics in the family. They described the grandfather as depressed and silent after retiring and moving to Delhi to live with the sons. The drastic change in lifestyle, the restrictions and loss of freedom had been extremely difficult for him. The relationship between father and sons was described as one of low communication. Madhur's father admitted that he did not communicate much with his parents or his wife and child because he did not see the point.

When a new baby was born to Madhur's uncle and aunt, the other women in the home pitched in to help. In the process Madhur, who was used to having his mother and grandmother exclusively to himself, suddenly lost them both. His mother noticed that it had been a very difficult time for Madhur and she now made a conscious effort to give him more time. This helped to explain why she was overcompensating for her own and his father's absence; the pattern had continued from the time Madhur turned three, which is when he started nursery school.

When the family arrived for a session one morning, Madhur was being dragged into the gate, screaming and hitting his mother. I was told that Madhur was very angry because his parents had refused to let him sit on the front seat of the electric rickshaw. By the time he arrived at my consulting room, his outburst had reached a level where it could not be intervened with verbally. Madhur was alternating between wanting to approach his mother for comfort and hitting her. After watching this for a while, his father intervened very calmly by picking Madhur up, physically removing him from the mother and slowly walking away toward the consulting room. He held Madhur in his arms, the child's head rested on his father's shoulder as if he was a much younger child and this helped to calm him down. Madhur stayed in his father's lap for the first part of the session in the room while we requested his mother to sit elsewhere.

When asked how he felt about this very public display of the family's difficulties, Madhur's father reported that he felt angry toward his son. Yet, I pointed out, that he had been able to control his anger, hold Madhur and calm him instead, something that the child needed at that moment. We agreed that Madhur's anger was bigger than him at such times and that perhaps Madhur needed to feel that his parents, particularly his father, was stronger than him in a safe and caring way. It was helpful to have father stand up and ask Madhur who was bigger. He said he knew his father was bigger and he knew that he needed to listen to his parents but that it was difficult to obey them if they did not speak to him calmly. Madhur seemed to be informing his parents that he would be more tractable if he was negotiated with rather than controlled or infantilised. While at times it seemed to Madhur that there was more to be gained by being a baby, there were clearly parts of him that wanted to be helped to grow up. He was struggling between wanting to be the favoured little child, with multiple mothers, especially the grandmother he had lost, and be treated as the older child in the house. This was extremely difficult to do without the support of his father. Madhur's actions of hitting his mother, moving away and then coming back to her, painfully illustrated his difficulty, and his father's entry as the third who could break the cycle was quite poignant. I wondered if an alliance with his father would help him.

This session proved to be a turning point in our work together. Madhur's father became more communicative and made an effort to attend late evening sessions after work. He spoke of the father of his own childhood, the distant, uncommunicative father who he was scared of; from whom he received little affection but new shoes and books annually, which he valued immensely, making them symbols of his father's affection (hence the reference to him wanting Madhur to polish his own shoes, value his father). He spoke of his mother who he felt was clearly partial to his younger brother; of having spent many years, as a child, living with his uncle, away from his parents. He spoke of how he was aware of his father's sadness and sense of loss about having to leave their hometown and was honest about his desire to have his son be more like the child he had been.

This last theme—of differences between him and his son— was central in helping me understand the distance between them and I saw it as the father's struggle with envy. There was so much that his son currently had that he had not received as a child, especially the attentions of a dedicated mother.[2] For Madhur's father that old wound had been reopened when he saw his son not only with a loving mother but also having taken away his wife. He had not wanted a child to start with and was only reluctantly a father to Madhur. He seemed to be out in the cold as the third and feeling the isolation, which he had partly created. He was ambivalent toward his son, at best.

'Expecting to be looked after but fearful of dependency, men who become fathers must struggle with the gap between their own fathers' emotional absence and their own needy response. …What is hardest of all to do is to find a way of meeting the child's actual demand for presence, calm, and thoughtful love.'[3] I would add, especially when you have not had your fill of it.

His fantasies were of sending his wife away to her parents so that their child would not be so mollycoddled. He would dismiss his wife saying that being with his mother will only teach Madhur to be a housemaid. It was much easier for the father to acknowledge anger than envy; to dismiss the mother-son relationship completely instead of imagining sharing, even though this option deprived everyone of a relationship.

Madhur's solution of refusing to go to school actually achieved the opposite; it got his parents together.

Alongside feeling envious, Madhur's father was not sure he had anything useful to offer his son. He could fantasise about getting Madhur away from his mother but had no clue about what to do with the empty space. It was as if he was afraid to offer whatever he had. In order to reach out to his son in a loving way, he required 'a shift of masculine consciousness, involving not just some more gentleness but a whole gamut of alterations in relations of dependency, intimacy, vulnerability and trust'.[4] Even in the current family arrangement where everyone lived within six feet of each other (but were emotionally miles away), he could not see what fathers were for. He certainly could not see how he could be useful to his son. Having had so little of his own father, he was poverty-stricken.

After 14 sessions with the family, Madhur's father was much more involved with him. He had made a visit to the school, something he had not done since the child had gained admission two years previously. He had started taking Madhur to school and Madhur had started staying in school without his mother. The tantrums had reduced. Madhur's father took him roller-skating in the evening, which he enjoyed. The child was very clear that he liked to spend time with his father, which was helpful for his father to hear and in their last session together, it was his father who brought him in. The family left town for the summer break and did not return to therapy. Six months later, the school reported that Madhur was stable, yet when the time came for another transition—the move to the next class a year later, the upcoming loss of another maternal figure, he was back at refusing to go to school. We met for two sessions during which I experienced Madhur to be more confident in his play and communication with me. A year later he was doing well at school, and his relationship with his father continued to improve, slowly. At the time of writing this, Madhur, is almost

10, a fantastic drummer, diagnosed as mildly dyslexic, going to school regularly and getting into fights with other boys. His father brings him for a review every few months and they are working on building a stronger father-son alliance.

I wondered how things would have worked out had I been a man.

Vidur would not eat if his mother did not cook for him. He needed her to tell him when he should use the toilet and also to wash him after he had. They shared a room and a bed, because he could not sleep alone.

Ajay would spend a lot of his time playing video games and his grandmother would feed him his meals while he played, fearing that he would not eat if she did not. His mother would read his textbooks out to him so that he would at least hear something of the study material the night before his exam. Vidur and Ajay were angry and violent, mainly toward their mothers, hitting them till they bruised. Both mothers said it had started when they were around eight-years-old and they had not been able to stop it. Vidur would hit his mother, sit on her to smother her and threaten to kill her if she refused his demands. Ajay would hit and threaten to break his mother's arm if she dared to touch his things or did not buy him expensive things.

Vivek and Krishna were gentle and bullied, angry but afraid of their own aggression and unable to assert themselves. They would both substitute emotional pain with physical pain through direct deliberate self-harm like cutting wrists or in more insidious ways such as eating excessive sugar and becoming obese, regularly breaking bones, unable to attend school and ignoring bodily signals like hunger, thirst, pain and sleep.

They are all 16 years old.

Vidur was a big boy but easily scared. The prospect of taking the Metro by himself was too overwhelming and the same bullying, brutish boy turned into a blubbering child, whining to his bruised mother, asking her to accompany him for his sessions with me.

Ajay avoided all responsibility in academics, his mother would do his homework and in the words of the school principal, 'bail him out'. There were never any consequences. Ajay's father has a job that keeps him away from home a lot and he likes to attend parties when he is in town. He does not believe his wife when she complains that their son hits her. Hard. He says 'you have spoilt him', conveniently abdicating responsibility for his role in this production. I found the parallel between father and son hard to ignore.

Deep down, a place they allow themselves to reach with immense difficulty after weeks of 'emotional gym' with a psychotherapist, these boys acknowledge the grief they feel about not having a father around. They experience the distance as a rejection and are extremely angry as well. The absence of a relationship with a father for a boy on the verge of manhood is experienced as a huge gap; a loneliness; an emptiness—one that is all too easily experienced as a deprivation; of love, care, attention, guidance, safety. This deprivation, perhaps a hole, is so painful to experience that they would rather not, and instead seek to fill it with material goods. They make incessant, desperate demands (on who else but their mothers) for 'things'—a scooter, an expensive watch, new clothes and electronic gadgets. Demands that have no end; demands demanding an end.

By the time they were 16, these boys with busy absent fathers, who have 'made do' with their mothers were often a deprived lot. (The eight-year-old I mentioned earlier certainly felt deprived.) Not learning to read your own needs and be able to ask for help equals being unable to attend to yourself. Being unable to do so means being deprived of a life-skill. Many families don't know it because they can't see it; because in our society raising boys, for a long time, has been the mother's work, and not allowing him to want for anything is the measure of her success. The hints appear often in underachievement at school; taking drugs, struggling with bullying or low self-esteem; difficulty handling frustration and aggressive relationships at home; and a subtle devaluing or active violence against women.

By the time they are 16, the mother for whom this child meant the entire world and who believed that her love and attention was the most crucial ingredient, begins to feel powerless, devalued and resentful. This becomes a self-fulfilling prophecy—our society is raising boys who devalue the very women who love them.

Ironically, love is not enough.

In 10 or 20 years' time, one way or another, each of these young men will probably father a child. And what kind of fathers will they make?

Legend has it that King Janaka, while ploughing a furrow in the earth, found hidden within it a healthy radiant baby girl and she smiled at him, as if she was waiting to be found. He wondered how she could have been waiting for him; after all this was not the fruit of his seed. 'But then', Janaka said, 'Fatherhood springs in the heart, not from a seed.'[5]

What quality of fatherhood will spring in the hearts of these young men when they are so poverty-stricken themselves?

The word parent, in our country, still manages to effectively mean 'mother'. Parent is used as a politically correct term perhaps to sound inclusive but in reality it rarely is. This may be because the word is too vague and permits enough space for the absent parent to remain, well…absent. In any 'group' or 'talk' at school the overwhelming majority of the persons attending are mothers. In a casual outside-the school-gate-in-Delhi conversation, one mother commented that she had noticed how our four-year-old daughter was very attached to her father. 'It is very rare', she said. 'I have seen how they play together when he comes to pick her up. I watched him re-do her hair the other day. Usually fathers leave everything to the mother. They don't really want to be bothered.' We laughed wryly, I agreed and we parted ways, but her comments stayed with me.

My class of 1996 was planning a 20-year reunion and a two-day itinerary was proposed. A classmate wondered out loud if anyone else was bringing children and husbands because her husband would 'faint having to look after my son for three days'.

It is his son too, I thought to myself.

This is not by accident. It is a constructed reality. Our society has helped this reality to come into being whereby the busy parent who has the responsibility of providing for the family monetarily, can be absent from or relinquish all (or most) of the 'bother' of the upbringing of the children to the other, the mother. Apart from the burden that this creates for the mother, whether it is experienced as such or not, it seems to be ignored that there could be some significant impact on the child of having a powerful but largely inactive male member in the family. In fact, to have a father who is alive but absent seems to have a far worse impact on children than his being dead and therefore unavailable.

There is a crisis of fatherhood today in urban India and it manifests itself across class. From the richest families with extreme amounts of disposable wealth to the poor in unauthorised housing and the wide middle class in between, men are not becoming fathers, in the true sense of the word. They are fertilising eggs with their sperm but seem to have little clue about what their role is to be after that stage has been completed. (These are not just my words, they are also Barack Obama's in a 2010 speech on Father's Day: 'We need fathers to realise that responsibility does not end at conception. We need them to realise that what makes you a man is not the ability to have a child—it's the courage to raise one.'). This theme is taken up with sarcasm, satire and gloom across many forms of writing. *The Economist* has had a front cover story on the uselessness of the male more than once in the last three years. Feminists have argued for years over whether it is even necessary to have men in families.

I am arguing that it is. It is important because the growing child needs his father to step up and be one.

Ideally I would have liked to assert that it is as important, for different reasons, for both boys and girls to have their fathers present but for now I am going to have to stick to the needs of the young boy because 'in childhood boys are more vulnerable to parental failures'.[6] This was an extremely difficult choice to make since there are few relationships more ignored in India than the one between father and daughter. Even in my consulting room, the relationship between father and daughter is only subtly in the air. Alluded to but then quickly overshadowed by the mother's presence or the internal conflicts involving generations of women. It is ephemeral, difficult to grasp and hang on to. On the other hand, the relationship between fathers and sons is right there; palpable, obvious and yet tiptoed around. To not address it would be to ignore the elephant right at the centre of the room. The sheer pressure created by the confluence of this theme rising to the top in my consulting room, boys' emotional needs demanding attention above all others,[7] and the current (hopefully) collective introspection on what we are doing to young boys as a society that makes them so violent toward women, made the choice for me.

From birth onward, there is often little space for separation between mothers and their sons in our communities in India and the mother is often blamed and caricatured for this:the overprotective mother—chasing her son with the glass of milk or plate of food; the anxious mother of the young man, keeping an eye on his friendships with girls; or the overbearing and possessive mother-in-law, making life difficult for the son's new wife. Yet this space between mother and son can only emerge if the father enters the picture early enough and is valued by his son. For there to be greater distance between mother and son, the distance between father and son needs to reduce.

Is it that the gap left by the father's absence is filled by the mother or is there no space between mother and child for father to fit in? Which came first? It is a chicken and egg situation. Trying to answer this in an all-or-none way will lead us into the familiar terrain of blame and shame, neither of which are helpful. The truth perhaps varies across families, communities, social class, and life-stage but most importantly, what matters is how the father is kept in mind by the mother and child. Who do they turn him into? What of him do they remember? What is he considered useful for and does he have any say in the matter? It is well-acknowledged though, and not only by the lady at the school gate, that fathers are often reluctant to enter into child care and may have to be dragged in, initially kicking and screaming till they can see what is rewarding in it. In the myth of Shiva and the Devi, Parvati draws Shiva in from being the detached hermit to being the involved householder.[8] He is happy to be far away, uninvolved and deep in meditation but she is not okay with that. What is significant is that she does not disrupt his meditative state (loosely translated as his job or work) by seduction, which had been the modus operandi of many *apsaras* including Vishnu transformed into Mohini, but through determination and devotion to the aim—i.e., by consistently keeping him in mind. Thus, Shiva becomes Shankar and together they become Gauri-Shankar—the parental couple that is capable of nurturing the world. Without the Devi/Goddess, Shiva is distant and disconnected from the world. Only when the Devi keeps him in mind is he capable of being paternal.

The distance between father and child is created very early, from birth, and we all collude to make this so. Some say[9] that the pattern for whether and how the father is a part of a child's life is determined by the manner in which the new triangular relationship between mother, new baby and father is negotiated in the first month of the baby's life itself. For this to happen, for father to be involved, not only the mother, but the family, workplaces and society[10] have to all be able to imagine (and tolerate) the father's inclusion in looking after a new baby. What can he do to get to know his baby and this new mother (he knew her all this while, but she was not a mother then, so things have changed) in the early days? I say 'do' because when we are very little, vulnerable or ill, physical care is love. Love is best expressed through a physical presence—feeding, holding, carrying, changing and bathing. It creates a reservoir of intimacy[11] between father and child like little else can. And it is this reservoir that is tapped into in difficult times later.

Can father help to burp the baby or change nappies? Is he patient with a tiny person's incessant crying in the middle of the night when all else has been tried and mother is fatigued? Most families may never know simply because the father is kept out of this early messiness of anxiety (though he feels it too, silently), feeding, dirty nappies and disturbed nights, saying that it saves him the trouble. Yes it is true. Being kept away from all this does save him the trouble but then it also keeps him from two new relationships. Caring for a baby is a huge amount of trouble, let that be stated up front. Whether the trouble is worth it in order to develop a new relationship, is a question every new mother-baby-father triangle needs to consider. In the majority of, even middle-class India, there is no triangle. Father starts off being and continues to remain on the outside of the mother-baby couple, whether the tradition of mother and baby remaining in a confinement of sorts for 40 days after the birth is followed, or not. While many more children in urban India are now brought up in nuclear families, it does not necessarily translate into fathers taking on more early caring roles. A grandmother, aunt or nanny continues to feature more regularly in a child's life than a father. Helpful and reassuring as it is for a mother to have an older female family member for support, it can be dismissive and undermining of the care that a father can provide his wife and child at this time.

Mother-son closeness is built into the Indian social fabric; after all, having borne a son changes a woman's place in the pecking order like few other things can. A son gives a woman an important place in the family hierarchy, her one stab at some power in the system. Giving up her son to the father or deliberately creating space between her and her son in order to permit closeness with the father is not the easiest thing to do. It is potentially an exercise in ambivalence.

A friend called me one morning, telling me that her three-month-old baby, who had had a vaccination the day before, had been unsettled all night, refusing the breast and squirming out of her arms. After struggling with this for hours, she handed the baby over to his father and he immediately relaxed. He looked calm with his father, yet began fighting her again when he was returned and still refused to feed. Even on the telephone I could tell she was finding this hard, despite the fact that she is a very aware new mother and is doing a very good job at avoiding 'maternal gatekeeping'. 'Are you feeling rejected?' I asked. 'Yes. That is. Exactly. It.' she said. Her words were deliberate and her tone subdued. Because I know her well, I felt she could bear it, I said, 'I know, this will happen a lot.' I was honest with her: that her distress at the baby's distress was perhaps not helping him. That perhaps he wanted a firmer hold from someone less upset, which his father's arms provided and that he will ask for her and for a feed when he is ready; that he won't starve himself; that she had to trust him.

The next day he only wanted to be with his mother and he refused to go to his father. I was later told that mother asked father, 'Do you feel rejected?' and he said 'Yes!'.

A few weeks later this baby and mother travelled to another city to visit relatives, leaving father behind to attend to his work. The journey was not long, an hour by air, and while his mother was anxious about this trip, she had used it to be extra prepared for many eventualities. The baby, his mother said, did not sleep at all for the first night in the new environment. He sleeps between his parents, his arms stretched out wide so he can touch them both. She said 'He is okay but his smile is not as bright…. I think he is missing his father. He recognised his voice on the phone especially when he sang the song about the t-shirt' (part of a daily ritual between father and son).At four months of age, this mother noticed, perhaps also mirroring her own feelings, that their baby could keep his father in mind.

It does a child no end of good to have two involved parents. It works best for the child's overall emotional economy to have two trustworthy parents because there is a good chance that at any given point, one parent is going to be experienced as overwhelmed, anxious, tired, angry, too strict, unavailable, otherwise distracted or liable to be murdered in a fit of rage. At such a time to have an alternative beloved parent available to take over, or at least make this bearable, is a relief.[12]

Even this tiny baby was able to communicate that he preferred his father for that particular job and his mother for another that day. Even this very well-meaning mother-father pair felt rejected in turn by that choice. This, in an egalitarian relationship. What happens when the child's attentions are part of a larger picture of marital hierarchy or active discord when it is important for one or the other to feel important or for the child to pick a side?

The father's involvement will change things all around though because he will do things differently. Are we ready for that, as a society? Is the father a potential intruder in the new mother-baby bliss, as experienced by the new mother? In the story about Ganesh's birth, Parvati created a child by herself to keep her company while Shiva was away for long periods of time (er…at work. Again). When Shiva returned and wanted to approach Parvati, interrupting her bath, the boy followed his mother's instructions and treated him as an intruder, preventing Shiva from entering.[13] What was Parvati's experience of the event, I wonder? Shiva's entry did immense violence to the peaceful mother-child relationship that had been going on for years in his absence. (From a young child's point of view, time with mother is experienced as an endless ocean, peaceful and uninterrupted. All the more reason to be resentful of breaks in this continuity.) Shiva realised that this child was important to Parvati when she insisted that Shiva repair the damage he had caused by chopping off the boy's head. His locating an alternative head and bringing the new form to life is what creates Ganesh and makes Shiva a father to Ganesh. It is no longer the same child Parvati had created by herself. When the father appears, everything changes and yet without Shiva's intervention, Ganesh would not be in his current form. It is a risk to let the father in and to bear the changes that will follow when the two-person dynamic changes to three. It is so much simpler to retreat into the warm familiarity of mummy's world that promises sameness and safety.

So while it is potentially inflammatory to say so (I struggle with mixed feelings as I write this) to some extent, 'It depends on what mother does about it whether father does or does not get to know his baby.'[14] Inflammatory, because there are few situations in the world more powerless than that of a postnatal first-time mother in India. (Ironically, for a baby, there is no relationship more powerful than the one with his mother.[15]) This paradox, of a powerless woman being extremely powerful in her relationship with her son, is potentially the source of many emotional conflicts for the son right now and in his future relationships. Between the vulnerability built into the postnatal situation, and the power exerted by older women who are also her caretakers and the medical establishment, the new mother has little space to express her personal views. And this is when things go well. If the birth is difficult or she or the baby is ill, this vulnerability rises exponentially. Still, at the risk of further provocation, I will say that if there is any chance for the father to enter the early scene, it is if the mother urges him to. This is because it's the mother who mediates all of a child's relationships, including the one with his father. She is the beginning.

Unfortunately, this portends further complexities since the mother's capacity to make space for the father in her mind and therefore in the life of the child depends on her relationship with the child's father but also comes from her experience of having had a father in her life or at least in the mind of her own mother.[16] We are all a part of a skein of thread linking generations; many of our relational and emotional capacities come from what was passed on to us, not genetically but by words, gestures, hugs, family stories, caresses, tone of voice and physical presence; in other words, through the air in the home. This endowment is both our wealth and our poverty.

Manav came to me because he was struggling in his relationship with his wife and his five-year-old daughter. His wife accused him of being too aggressive and short-tempered with their daughter and he, with a combination of anger and defensiveness, said he could not see what he had done wrong. However, as he described his interaction with his daughter, expecting her to move more quickly in the morning so that they did not miss the school bus, I noticed that he had forgotten that she was just five years old. He was expecting a sense of responsibility to task (brushing her teeth) as well as an awareness of consequences of actions (i.e., 'if you dilly-dally you will miss the bus') that his daughter did not have the cognitive capacity for. (He had also not noticed that by 'dilly-dallying' she got more exclusive father-daughter time, even if it was only him shouting at her. That is how children's logic works. They will make do with negative attention. It is far better than being ignored). As we talked, it emerged that his first memory of being slapped by his father was at age three-and-half-years for not understanding some math concept. He remembers the shock and fear he felt and that he did not in fact learn what he was being taught. This was the beginning of many years of experiencing his father as short-tempered, violent and unpredictable. Manav could never tell what would annoy his father. He tried his best to be 'good' and he was. He internalised a sense of responsibility such that by the time he was 10 he was a very upright young man, adult beyond his age, often angry but very quiet, not sharing his feelings with anyone and definitely not sharing a relationship with his father that could entail talking about emotions. But that was by the time he was 10. Not five.

From early on, Manav was expected to have a cognitive capacity that was beyond him. Thirty years later, unwittingly, he was doing the same to his child.

Most, if not all, of the young men I work with experience either a distanced or actively damaged relationship with their fathers. These are not stories from slums or from poor families which make it easier for us to explain away violence as something belonging to 'the other'. These are middle and upper middle class families who also use a 'this can't happen to us' version of denial as a force-field. Poverty and deprivation add layers of complexity that are way beyond the scope of what I am presenting here. These boys, along with their mothers, often turn the father into an actively rejecting figure who is good for monetary support but not much else and sometimes not even that. On the face of it, mother and son have convinced themselves that they are better off without him.

If only it were that simple.

It is not enough to say that a father's involvement does good things to the young person, which it undoubtedly does. Research after research finds that a father's involvement in his children's lives has a positive impact on their development, school achievement, social skills and future relationships. It also makes fathers happier and healthier suggesting that what is good for a developing child is good for their adult carers too. What that means is that mothers and fathers discover those parts of themselves only in interaction with, in relationship with, their children and in the process of caring for them.[17] They don't exist separate from or outside of the relationship. A report on the State of the World's Fathers[18] finds that 'fathers matter' and that involving fathers early in their children's lives has many advantages for families and communities. Children could have told you that, if anyone had cared to ask or listen to their response. Children not asking for their fathers is not because they don't want them but because they have rarely, or never, had them.[19] They don't know it is an option. They know their mothers very well and they grow up learning that care=female. As a result their relationships with their fathers is not on the dimension of care at all; food, washing, clothing, school, friendships and homework all become mother's work. So what dimension does father bring in?

The sad fact is that mostly neither father nor child has the answer to that.

It is important to underline the damage that the father's absence creates for the boy, his view of himself and his capacity to love and to work and therefore to his community. Whether through distraction, divorce, disinterest, drink, disease or death—each form of absence has a profound impact on the child in the world. Most significantly, urban India today needs to recognise the link between a father's absence from the life of his son and the child's capacity to regulate his aggression;[20] whether this aggression is turned out toward other relationships (usually female, starting with his mother and moving on to other women) or toward himself in the form of self-doubt, self-neglect, apathy or depression.

We need to pay attention to this, individually, as families, and as a society. What are the ideas of masculinity that young boys are growing up with today? What does it mean to be a man in a particular time, in a particular apartment, *mohalla* or *basti*? The 16-year-olds described earlier are a decade or so away from becoming fathers. What emotional endowment will they manage to bring to their families? To their girlfriends, wives and children? What blueprint of parenting do they turn to consciously or unconsciously? How can they trust themselves as parents when they could barely trust their own?

In every generation, but perhaps more so now, there are boys who don't see men or know men. Surrounded by females as mothers, carers, teachers, disciplinarians, this is what boys see and imbibe, that men do not nurture, do not teach, do not learn and are not usefully around. For a young boy growing up without his father's presence, the chances are that his view of 'man' as powerful but unavailable, destructive, disappointing and distant is filtered through the eyes and lived experience of his mother. What chance does he then have of developing a range of emotions of which affection and caring for friends and family is a part? He gets stuck in an either-or-place where he can either be 'a man' and fulfil his socially reinforced gender stereotype or be considerate, caring and affectionate. A 17-year-old explained this to me, saying, 'I used to want to be only male, testosterone-fuelled and remove everything and anything that could be remotely female.' When asked to elaborate he included even his not bathing, slouched posture, swearing when speaking, not ever talking about feelings and a distaste for expressing positive feelings toward his closest relationships in the list of 'man' attributes. He realises that it is not working for him anymore because he finds it restrictive and that it makes him lonely.

'I don't know how to speak to girls my age', he added.

'Anyway, which girl would want to speak to a smelly, slouchy, swearing and unaffectionate young man?' I asked, driving home the point not too subtly.

This split, furthered by society (neighbours, school and friends) and media (films, songs and advertisements), does not help him deconstruct the matter either. Care and affection have been co-opted and constructed as belonging to one gender and by not protesting, we all permit this to happen. Caring is not just feminine. It is a life-skill and it keeps us human.

Most mothers I meet in my consulting room come across as strong, capable women who are not timid pushovers, yet they are physically bullied by their teenage sons and feel powerless to place a boundary. On further exploration it emerges that the sons feel powerless too, especially in the outside world, with their peers, in school but mostly when faced with the intensity of their mother's emotions. These teenage boys feel overwhelmed by the power that their mothers have over them, emotionally. There is therefore a desire to push her away, physically and psychically. To find space for themselves where they can find themselves. Therefore, the oft-heard 'leave me alone!'. A young man explained to me that he felt his mother treated him as an equal at times. He did not want that. 'Just because I am good at listening does not mean I am her companion. There is a line, one that she has overstepped too often. I do not need to know the details of her life.' He did not add '… with my father or any other man' but that is what he meant since that was the context of our conversation. Having such direct access to detail about his mother's intimate life and implied sexuality was traumatic for him. It took over his mind with images and feelings that he was not prepared for. He wished she would protect him from that by 'drawing a line' and when she could not, he did. He is aware that his father's absence leaves his mother alone, lonely and therefore indirectly places pressure on him. This young man, in psychotherapy for four years, is able to verbalise his 'I love my mother but there is a line' conflict and does not need to act it out. Otherwise, physically hitting and pushing their mothers away is often how boys express their demand and desperate need for a boundary.

There is one other option for where this desperate need and anger could flow—back in toward themselves, creating a terrified, helpless, shrinking monster. In the larger scheme of society, both are damaging. Attacking another or self-sabotage —a pattern of punitive self-attack or a harsh conscience are both destructive. A conscience that exacts too much, without any associated reward or recognition of effort is a punishment. A rulebook composed of 'shoulds' ultimately becomes self-defeating since the rules come in the way of the young man's spontaneity and his experience of himself in the world. Hemmed in by these voices which are not his own, it also keeps others from really knowing him. Usually these voices have the theme of 'I will not/must not, turn into my father because then even my mother will reject me'. A fatherless child creates a father in fantasy, a personal myth, full of distortions and harsh rejections (i.e., the version he has experienced and through the versions his mother holds in mind). In this process, rejecting themselves and their own potential, they turn into nothing at all. They fear all intense feelings and clamp them up instantly, deflating themselves, draining their own source of fuel and power. They are so afraid that any intensity may mean aggression that they don't explore it enough to find out who they may really grow into. Angry toward, yet scared of hurting the only one parent they have, they prefer to remain small and helpless.

A young man gave me a detailed version of how this works.

He is angry with his father, very angry toward him for all the random beatings meted out to his mother, brother and himself. Very angry for scaring him: 'if you go out cycling some stranger will rape you.' Even though at the age of seven he had no idea what that meant, he knew it meant that people outside the home were dangerous. But so were the ones inside the home because he had a father who would come into the bathroom and take pictures of him naked, then threaten to send them to his school.

Real men don't cry; real men don't have feelings; real men are rocks. That is the rulebook. Something he has heard over and over again and something we discovered is his hidden ambition—to be rock-like. It explains why he needs nothing. No food, water, affection, company, stimulation of mind or body, use of mind or body. Why he smokes marijuana to dull the internal parts of him that he cannot control, usually the anxiety. Each time he does something different, which is the attempt through psychotherapy, a critical punitive mechanism in his mind (like an aggressive policeman) comes in and zaps him with bolts of electricity so he freezes into inaction. He literally turns to stone. Is petrified. The way he was in front of his father when he was seven.

He has tears in his eyes. Almost. But not quite. I can see he is struggling to feel his own feelings and not bow down to a rulebook that is not his own but one that he has owned and lived by for the last so many years. He smiles a small smile. I point it out; that it is very difficult for him to fight off the policeman and be himself. It was the only way. The only way to get his father's love was to become more like him.

But this is not logical, you say. He hates him, so why would he want to be like him? He keeps saying he does not want to turn into his father. So why want his father's love?

Yes, that is also true. Yet, there lies the honest truth about us all—that our feelings don't come in one at a time.

He hates him too. Not, he hates him only. There is love as well. There is always love as well. More than anything else, there is a desire to be loved by his father. An unfulfilled one. 'I never got anything back from him. 'All these years he was a dead weight. I would try to talk to him but he would not respond'. And, with his childlike logic, this young man's mind had turned that into 'I am not worth loving', a belief he had lived with for at least a decade.

However, when I asked 'So whose problem is that?' he replied, 'His, not mine.'

'Yes, just because he could not reciprocate your love, does not mean that you are not worthy of love,' I said, relieved.

The look in his eyes changed. I could see my statement had gone in somewhere deep.

'I just had an epiphany,' he said.

Fathers are just as important to their children as mothers are.

NOTES

1. W.S. Merwin. 1993. 'Separation' from *The Second Four Books of Poems*. Port Townsend, Washington: Copper Canyon Press.
2. S. Kakar. 1997. *Culture and Psyche: Selected Essays*. New Delhi: Oxford University Press, p. 82.
3. Stephen Frosh. 2001. 'Fathers ambivalence (too)'. In *Mothering and Ambivalence*. Wendy Hollway & Brid Featherstone (eds). London: Routledge, p. 51
4. Ibid., p. 50.
5. D. Pattnaik. 2013. *Sita*. Penguin, p. 9.
6. S. Kraemer. 2005. 'Narratives of Fathers and Sons: "There is no such thing as a Father"'. In A. Vetere and E. Dowling (eds), *Narrative Therapies with Children and their Families: A Practitioners Guide to Concepts and Approaches*. London: Routledge.
7. In the Child and Adolescent Mental Health Services in the UK National Health Services as well, boys take up the majority of time and effort in children's services and girls, in adolescent services. See S. Kraemer. 2005. 'Narratives of Fathers and Sons'.
8. D. Pattanaik. 2006. *Myth = Mithya: A Handbook of Hindu Mythology*. London: Penguin. p. 178.
9. M. Marks. 2002. 'Letting Fathers in'. In J. Trowell and A. Etchegoyen (eds), *The Importance of Fathers: A Psychoanalytic Re-Evaluation*. Hove: Brunner-Routledge.
10. anne marie slaughter. TED Talk. https://www.youtube.com/watch?v=tH5iEf9oxaI
11. Neil Altman. 2008. 'From Fathering Daughters to Doddering Father'. *Psychoanalytic Inquiry: A Topical Journal for Mental Health Professionals*, 28:1, 92–105, DOI: 10.1080/07351690701787135
12. It is important to add that the mother and father as two parents usually get subsumed in the male and female genders in a heteronormative arrangement. However, in psychodynamic thought, it is not the gender that matters but the attitude. The maternal attitude of playing safe and the paternal attitude of getting ready for the outside world. This attitude could be displayed by women or men.

For a single parent, this becomes a huge challenge since the same individual has to often display/own both the maternal/paternal attitude. Which is to both be available and be no-nonsense when the moment demands. The paternal function interrupts a boy's exclusive bond with his mother. The task may be performed by anyone, even by mother herself. However, it is exhausting to say the least. Breaks can be/are had in other ways—whether a grandparent or hired help or daycare to mitigate the aggression and exhaustion. A loved other is always beneficial.

13   Here I won't go into the obvious territorial 'she is mine and who the hell are you?' attitude in the story, from the boy's perspective, since the focus is on the mother's experience.

14.   D.W. Winnicott. 1964. 'What about Father?' In *The Child, the Family and the Outside World*. London: Penguin, p. 113

15.   Wendy Hollway. 2006. *The Capacity to Care*. Routledge: London. Here, the 'omnipotent mother' has huge influence, a figure given little attention within dominant feminist literatures because of their emphasis on women's objective lack of power. Many currents of psychoanalysis have concurred in the idea that, because of the infant's total psychological dependence, the mother that predominates in its internal world is omnipotent; that is, has complete power:'I believe that the premature condition in which the young of the human species are born and the fact the infant continues for a considerable period of time after birth to be totally dependent for survival on the mother or her substitutes is one of the principal explanations for the creation of an all-powerful and invading maternal imago'.

16.   M. Target and P. Fonagy. 2002. 'Fathers in Modern Psychoanalysis and in Society: The Role of the Father and Child Development'. In Trowell and Etchegoyen (eds), *The Importance of Fathers*.

17.   Wendy Hollway. 2006. *The Capacity to Care*.

18.   http://www.menscare.org

19.   Atkins gives an interesting example of this, of a five-year-old patient who sighed and said 'I don't know daddy so good.

Children spend a long time with their mommies, I think. I used to, too. Mommy and I were home all day together. And then, after such a lon-n-ng day…daddy came home from work. So you see, you don't know daddy so good. Not like mommy.' R. Atkins. 1982. 'Discovering Daddy: The Mother's Role'. In S.H. Cath, A. Gurwitt & J.M. Ross (eds), *Father and Child*, Boston: Little Brown, pp. 139–49.

20. S.H. Cath, A. Gurwitt & J.M. Ross (eds). 1982. *Father and Child*.

On Why We Need Two Parents

G. was large and lumbering as he walked into my consulting room but I saw him as a snotty-nosed spoilt child who I struggled to find warmth for at first. He did not admit to it but his mother said he needed her to wash his bottom, give him his food and tie his shoelaces—to look after him the way one would an invalid or a small child. He is 16 now, not six, which is what he was when he and his mother moved back to India to his maternal grandparents' home without his father, whom he has not seen since. This being another thing he does not like to admit, that he has many hidden feelings about not having his father around. How can he explain it to his friends, of whom there are few anyway? He feels bullied, excluded and lonely. Not that anyone would guess. He was sitting in my consulting room on charges of being aggressive, demanding and bullying, not small and scared. Initially I found myself wanting to protect his mother from him, from his demands, his aggression and what I experienced as his constant whining.

Yet, the other side began to show up after a while and I wondered about the circularity in the mother-son relationship, something that they were both so stuck in. Perhaps he was unwittingly being infantilised by a collusion. Perhaps, as her only child, a part of his mother needed him to be a little boy for longer, to not grow up and move away from her because then she would be completely alone. He was complying. She was being a good mother, fulfilling his every need. In turn, he was being a good baby and practising being demanding. Dependency was being encouraged and yet she despaired at how he was not taking responsibility. Perhaps propelled by an unconscious, irrational but real and powerful force, her own fear of loss and loneliness, this woman who was otherwise very successful at dealing with teenagers in her profession as a schoolteacher, found herself powerless and unable to put her foot down in the face of her son's demands. As a north Indian Punjabi woman, somehow she did not seem to have cultural permission to be anything other than a caring, though nagging and smothering, mother.

He could not bear her nagging, he said. That is what drove him to hit her; he felt desperate because she controlled him and he wanted out. His response was to try to control her in return, trap her into fulfilling his demands, the way he did one evening when he locked the bedroom and forced her to watch a film, not letting her out for water or to use the toilet.

His compliance was double-edged; desperate to move away from her and scared to as well, and this conflict left him petrified in one place, unable to grow. G. was very much like a toddler who was squirming out of his mother's lap only to walk away and panicking when he turned around to find himself without her and then becoming angry at her for abandoning him.

Their private solution was for him to stay in the lap, kicking and screaming, occasionally pause for rest and then resume the struggle.

There comes a time when a child needs something more than mother. Not because she is no longer good for the child, but because mother is not enough.[1] Just like after a point breastmilk is not enough and every baby has to be weaned, both away from and onto something else. New resources *have to* be found, new relationships are *needed*.[2] In order to understand what this means one needs to look closely at the relationships as they unfold from the start, from birth.

Babies, we will agree, have limited cognitive capacities to make sense of the world. They desire and need comfort and attention and they complain, often loudly, about any frustration, be it cold, hunger, dampness or delay. Often the care and the delay come from the same source: the mother. After all, she is still learning and is certainly not perfect. Sometimes she gets it right, sometimes she does not. Either way her baby has an opinion about it and usually lets her know, often loudly, though this varies. (Some babies are more forgiving than others. Psychically, a baby who can complain loudly is a more hopeful baby because some previous experience has given him the idea that he can trust the world to respond to him.) For a long time, in their minds, babies have to keep these good and unsatisfying aspects of their mother separate from each other because it is impossible to imagine that the satisfying, responsive mother is the same one as the disappointing or frustrating one. The simplest way out of this is to split the two. It is an unforgiving, somewhat ruthless strategy but it preserves the fantasy of the perfect and loving mother in the baby's mind. Perfect is always a fantasy. The disappointing parts of mother are rejected as a bad mother. Therefore, when the baby experiences his mother as frustrating and infuriating, it is *she* who is rejected, by his turning away from her.[3] It makes the relationship between her and her baby a far more complex one.

Every mother will be able to identify times when her baby has not accepted comfort or food from her and somehow, inexplicably to the untrained eye, some less emotionally involved person (such as an aunt) has been able to rescue the situation. In the baby's mind, there is a good mother and there is a bad mother and they are not the same person. Anger and love cannot live together. This is what psychotherapists mean when they say that a child with two parents has the advantage of always having a parent to love when the other is hated. [4]

The situation is more complex because the 'bad' mother is also the scary one. She is the one the baby is afraid of which is why he cannot accept comfort from her, which is why he is inconsolable, and someone else, perhaps the nanny or the father or a grandmother comes in to take him away and he calms down (much to the mother's dismay, irritation or perplexity).[5]

The point of this close look at a mother-baby relationship is to elaborate on how they often need a third to get them out of a stuck place. It begins, and perhaps for a long time, regularly returns to our need to develop a capacity to bear hatred and anger in the face of frustration, the capacity to think in the face of intense emotion, 'to keep your head when others around you are losing theirs'.[6] It is the principle of the third and this becomes the central metaphor for newness and loss, and the capacity to rise above it.

There needs to be more to help the child build these capacities—the capacity to deal with school, take responsibility, the discipline it requires to do stuff you don't like or that makes you feel inadequate, and the capacity to deal with failure, hurt and try again. *It is absolutely possible for the mother to help her child develop these capacities* as well but in our culture, where gender roles are often so rigid, the role of the mother is often fixed and immutable. Mother is care and nurturance and the anticipation and fulfilment of needs even before they are expressed.[7] This is all wonderful, up to a point. A child also needs discipline and boundaries, and she needs to be told 'no' because paradoxically, a child's tendency to be demanding is simultaneously asking for an end and for a boundary. Asking to run up against something. Just like the shoplifting child who is almost relieved to have been caught.[8] Relieved that there is a power greater than him; that in reality someone else is in charge.

In order to acknowledge that there is truth beyond what one can conjure in one's mind and that which the mother-child couple believed as the truth; in order to acknowledge that there are some truths that belong to the world outside the mother's embrace, one needs a third perspective. Having only the mother do the two jobs for a child is extremely difficult for both because she is resented for having introduced the frustration. Before the inevitability of loss-and-change-as-necessary-for-growth is accepted (plenty of adults struggle with this), there is anger at the mother, as if somehow she made it happen. She is responsible for the loss. This can deteriorate into a language of control. 'She controls me. I control her. I imagine that I can get what I want from her by controlling her. I cannot see her as independent of mind, as an autonomous agent who can exercise choice. I find the frustration unbearable.' But at the same time 'If I control her and get what I want, it does not taste as sweet because it is tainted by the violence of my demands. And if I let it go I run the risk of losing her because she will be outside of my control.' This can then be extended to other relationships with women.

The triangular relationship, or the three-person relationship is the crucible for the growth of these new capacities. These are both cognitive and emotional capacities. Not either-or but both, making real learning both a cognitive and emotional experience. Before the age of 10 or 11, it is difficult for a child to sustain this way of thinking, that there is another perspective other than his own.

There is always a larger perspective from which a situation might look different from what we currently see or imagine it to be—(this) helps us to enquire into the darkness of what is not yet known.[9] Till then we think others laugh at us. Once we see this, we can laugh at ourselves.

But being able to see and truly accept how it changes the certainty with which we had lived previously, are two different things. Because the entry of a third person or this third view pushes the child to painfully acknowledge that he does not have exclusive claim or control over his mother, it sets up jealousy and competition and an immense feeling of loss. The child realises that the 'timeless bliss' of early babyhood satisfaction is over and that the same mother whom he adores is also the one who he is angry with for having others on her mind or other points of view, other *ways of viewing him*. A different attitude, other people, other activities—his siblings, her work, a partner or his father. Someone or something else that is not-me. That he is in fact, part of a triangle and at any point, may be the one on the outside as the observer of a relationship between two significant others and not a participant.

'The triangle is only closed if there is a recognition of a link joining the parents'[10]; only when the child accepts that the parents have a relationship independent of him does he truly see reality. This suggests that the parents' relationship with each other is very important to the child but for our purposes here, it suggests particularly that in the case of an unlovable parent or a barely-there parent, closing the triangle would be difficult for the child. The child has to accept the reality of difference and accept difference as the seat for creativity and new possibilities. He is different from his mother (in gender). He is different from his father (generationally) and his parents were in fact an item before he came on the scene. This simple fact of life and how it is taken in is one of the most powerful forces propelling learning, curiosity and the acceptance of difference.

Unfortunately, this truth is also one of the hardest to swallow.

Envy is hard to bear.

Realising that the two parents share (or shared) a relationship (a sexual one) that the child cannot rival (because of the generational difference) is difficult enough. Alongside this is the painful realisation that he can never be like his mother (because of a gender difference) and have babies. Patriarchy, of which we have copious amounts in north India, provides ample opportunity and strategies of how he can get over this disappointment and pain by rejecting his mother (which is related to but not restricted to his real mother, therefore extended to all women) and denigrating her (simply put: reject the grapes for being sour when, like the fox, in fact he cannot reach them). Dismissing women/his mother as a separate entity who has the capacity for creativity may seem like a good way to feel good about himself but it places this boy in a difficult emotional position: of loneliness, since he has just rejected his primary love and core validating audience. Now all he can hope for is closeness to and recognition from his father, who he is at least similar to (in gender).

These losses can be made palatable by a growing closeness between father and child, if he is lucky, because the child gets to be recognised by another. He gets to have his capacities and potential acknowledged by a significant other. His father or father equivalent, provides him recognition and validation.[11] If a boy has an established relationship with his father, that is based in recognition, then the boy may not need to ground his separation from his mother entirely in denigration and rejection of what he does not have, especially since he can see that his parents have a relationship with each other. By giving up his ideal relationship with his mother he is not left unloved. Part of the motivation to be like his father also comes from his mother's love and respect for this father.[12] So the quality of the relationship with the real father can make the crucial difference. Provided he is around.

Enter: father, if he is around. Hopefully. He can be very useful. If anyone would let him. Between gender roles and the pressure on the father to be the provider, the complexity of 'family math' (the phenomenon through which each person has less and less time to spend with individual others as the family size increases) and sheer lack of opportunity for practising their parenting skills, the most well-intentioned fathers remain the 'other' parent.[13] Because he does not get to flex his 'care skill' muscles very much, he and the child don't know whether he is any good at it. He is good at giving instructions, often at telling off and drawing boundaries but that right has to be earned and it can only happen if there is a reservoir of intimacy between father and child built up in the early years; only if the father allows his son emotional access to him from an early age. What begins with physical care then moves on to conversations about feelings and conflicts around growing up.

Krishna's father had a series of serious health problems from the time Krishna was 13 which ended up isolating them from each other. As a result, Krishna lost his father's support during a significant life transition, puberty. In the struggles with his peer group—bullying from the boys and mockery from the girls—that followed, he felt unable to approach his father and felt his absence very deeply, which created a desperate loneliness in him. He eventually resorted to cutting himself as a way of dealing with emotional turmoil. In a conversation that I was privileged to witness, Krishna explained to his father that since the latter's illness, he had not been able to speak to his father, feeling he would damage the other, give him a heart attack with the burden of the child's troubles. That what he wanted was a relationship with him that was 'without female intervention'. How much more plain could he make it?

Krishna's father's gentle and thoughtful response displayed that he had heard both his son's desire for closeness with him and the fear that this demand would be a burden.

On the other hand, it was painful for his mother and older sister to hear, that their fulfilling Krishna's needs before he expressed them was not only unappreciated but actively pushed away. It was difficult for them to see that 16-year-old Krishna was in a space between being boy and man. He did not want to be infantilised. He needed to and wanted to learn when to ask for help. He did not want the food put in his mouth before realising he was hungry.

Once Krishna could verbalise his emotional pain, he stopped causing himself physical pain by making cuts on his body. A year later, when convalescing after a minor surgery, he was able to notice how much his father had looked after him through it when he felt powerless and in pain. Having been bathed and fed by his father for two weeks, Krishna could now acknowledge that this too was love.

Mothers need fathers as a support and they do often use them that way, even if invisible, with the 'wait till I tell your father/wait till your father gets home' line.[14] So fathers exist in mothers' minds anyway. I wonder what fathers feel about being used as the gremlin with which to scare the child? It may be painting father in a shade that he does not feel like living up to or perhaps he would have another version he would like to try out. 'Go to sleep or the gremlin (Bhoot/ghost or its equivalent—generic-evil-child-snatcher) will come and get you' is another way in which the 'third' is used by mothers to instil fear, maintain compliance yet deflect the child's anger away from themselves. In this process, the third has to be a demon who wants to get the child away from mother.

It is not surprising that the father function has such bad press.

A father missing from the life of his young child is very common, not just in my consulting room but also in the world outside my translucent glass doors. When I ask fathers to come to the session, they do but they are never the one taking the initiative. They leave that to the mother. I have learnt over the years that persistently asking fathers to join us early on pays off; otherwise it is only too easy to be seduced into a collusion, to believe that he is disinterested (whereas in fact we have lost interest in him) and uninvolved (while we continue to not involve him). I find it saves us a lot of time and agonising over a problem to have both parents in the room from the beginning, though it can cause other kinds of anguish when carefully glossed-over marital conflicts emerge in front of their child and a total stranger.

However, no father has ever refused to come: even the supposedly peripheral ones, the busy, divorced or reluctant ones show up. Then it is up to me to get him involved in the conversation with and about his child. Some take time to warm up but mostly they behave as though they have been gagged for years and are desperate to be let loose and speak up; or shout out.

Rahul's very thoughtful and concerned parents came in saying that he was unduly concerned with death, his own and that of his loved ones. He was afraid of going to bed and of being alone in his room at night. He often complained of being bullied at school but was a terrible bully to his younger brother and, according to his mother, had extreme emotional reactions to disappointments. These were beyond tantrums, she called them 'meltdowns' because he seemed distraught and inconsolable and nothing seemed like it would ever be fixed.

After about 15 sessions, for which I had insisted Rahul come with his father, during which we explored Rahul's anger toward various family members and his other difficulties at school, the family went on a holiday and I did not see Rahul for several weeks. Upon their return the parents described a very different child—better adjusted at school, going to bed with ease, no longer scared and no longer bullied. When I asked what they thought had changed, the father, who had always liked to see himself as the 'bystander' parent, took over the conversation. He had clearly reflected upon this substantially because he was able to point out the links between his making changes in his lifestyle and time-structure and the impact this had had on his son, through their relationship. We noticed together that nine-year-old Rahul, who had been struggling with his angry feelings toward his mother and sibling for years, had been encouraged to look at what potentially wonderful things lay in store for him if he was to move closer to his father and give up his devoted yearnings to be a little child again, that too his mother's exclusive child.

In our sessions, Rahul had liked to sit on his father's lap, fitting his body into the curve of his father's torso, uninterrupted except by his own anxiety. In this posture father and son had talked about similarities and differences in their childhoods; their feelings towards their respective siblings; the link between grandfather, father and Rahul; bullies at all ages, in school and at workplaces and perhaps most significantly, Rahul had noticed that his mother perhaps did not have all the answers because 'she is not a boy'. On this family holiday, father had encouraged Rahul to join him in his favourite hobby, buying him his own kit. Similar to Madhur (in the previous chapter) being a small child in his father's arms, Rahul too had time in his father's lap. However, he moved through the lap to spending time observing older boys and perhaps saw something of value in that. Being taken seriously by his father, having his potential validated, seemed to have helped Rahul want to grow up.

This boy had been struggling with his anger toward his mother for having given birth to his younger brother. He was stuck with being in competition with his brother, the baby in the house. He is not alone. He represents all of us when we get angry with the person we love so much because it is hard to share them. It is hardest to share our mother's love with another child or another 'project' that needs care as well. Irrational as it may sound, we want to be the only loved one. Accepting reality is hard and it makes us feel rejected or left out and the mother bears the brunt of the anger of the child. The child in all of us. The father helps because he can be the relief feature who can provide both mother and child with an antidote to the adverse effects of too much mothering[15] which we all desperately want should last forever. The father is responsible for otherness, newness and the boundary that stands for the 'no'; the 'no you cannot have mother all to yourself; no, I sleep beside her and not you; no, you cannot be the baby at the breast forever; you will grow up and go to school and leave her behind. And it is all made more palatable because I also love you, I show you how you are my child too; that we have things in common and I show my love for you.'

If the father is not around for whatever reason, we can't help it and I do notice how that makes things harder all around. For the child, because he or she has to accept the reality of the father's absence and the feelings toward him for not being around, plus the feelings toward himself for being fatherless. For the mother, because she is alone in this enormous task of parenting and has to be both maternal and paternal, which may not be easy for her or she feels stuck in one place. And for me, because at times I have to play the role of the father, symbolically. I take on the role of the 'bad guy' who has to be clear about the fact that reality exists and cannot be wished away by magic, fantasy, aggression or sadness. Mostly this is in the form of the boundary of the session, the timing and its simple but consistently applied rules: 1. we tidy up any mess we create; 2. we don't hurt anyone or anything in the room; and 3. we stop one hour into our scheduled time, regardless of when we started. It is surprising how children can find ways to try to bend even these scanty, scaffolding boundaries, simply because they are there.

The child's experience of two parents is about the experience of the coming together of differences and seeing differences as life enhancing.[16] In Indian myths[17] there are symbols that connect that father with the bones in the child's body and that see the flesh and blood as the mother's contribution. So a relationship with the father is what gives the child the capacity to stand, walk, move forward, move away, have a spine, explore the world, consider alternatives beyond mother's milk and blood. Ideally, the father helps develop the capacity to think in the face of intense emotion. Fathers can often come in with fresh energy and perspective when mother's love and care inevitably runs into fatigued and persecutory heavy weather.

Fathers' actions seem to suggest that they want to be providers and bystanders. They leave the list of care-giving tasks to a combination of mother, grandmother and hired help (usually female) to handle. When my intervention is asked for (another female) as a professional, I find it is the mothers who make the first call. In all these years of practice, I have had one father who made the call. Over the years I have learnt that it is invaluable to ask for fathers to attend the first appointment. If I hear the mother's version only, it becomes too easy to believe that the father is too busy, disinterested or generally the villain of the piece. If I persist and ask for the father to attend the sessions anyway, they always do. They seem to be torn between the desire to be in the wings and dying to be called onto centre-stage. They want to be involved but they don't seem to know how. Their reluctance often hides a lack of confidence in their own capacities as a father. They simply are not sure they are valued. And they really do want to be.

NOTES

1. In the book/film *About a Boy*, Nick Hornby's character, age 10, reaches the same conclusion, that just his mother is not enough. He needed to have other people around him and he searches out and creates a relationship with a man (played by Hugh Grant) who reluctantly becomes his father-figure. Or in the film *The Kids Are Alright*, which has a same-sex parent-pair, Nic and Jules (played superbly by Annette Benning and Julianne Moore respectively), both offer the 'other-parent' perspective alternatively for each of their two children.

2. Even in a single parent arrangement, whether through choice, divorce or death, other relationships can exist for the child—either through the relationships in mother's mind/past or through day care, school and extended family. It is important for the mother to notice how a child uses these other relationships.

3. Splitting is a very common though not very sophisticated defence mechanism. Not only infants but adults, communities and an entire country's foreign policies can be seen doing this too.

4. D.W. Winnicott. 1964. 'What about Father?' In *The Child, the Family and the Outside World*. London: Penguin, p. 115.
    Single parents need to be made aware that parental roles can be played by many people who are reliably and consistently nurturing and present. The word parent does not need to be taken literally and neither does the word 'father'. It is about the presence of a 'third' to provide an alternate vantage point. Therefore it is about the attitude and mindset, not the physical embodiment.

5. I watched a mother-baby-father trio enact this. We were at a Sunday gathering of families. The mother was tired and handed the baby (about 14 months old) over to the father but the baby started to lean out of his arms crying 'mama…mama'. Father moved away from the mother, jigging the baby up and down, taking him to the window to distract him perhaps. It could have worked but we will never know how it may have turned out because the mother, though tired, followed them and took

the baby back into her arms and sat on a nearby couch. The father walked off.

6. Rudyard Kipling. 1910. 'If'. In *Rewards and Stories*. New York: Doubleday, Page & Co.

7. Which brings to mind how the best hotels and hospitality services market themselves also as the most attentive services—that they have the attention to detail and speed of responsiveness that will make us feel no frustration whatsoever. That our needs will be anticipated, we won't even need to ask. Thus the emphasis on the personal butler, the exclusive attendant, the well-trained staff. All attempts to re-create (in exchange for large sums of money) the once-upon-a-time feel of what it was like to have our mothers attend to us as infants in a seamless way.

8. Stephen Fry talks of his relief at having been caught shoplifting in his autobiography which covers the first 20 years of his life. Stephen Fry. 1997. *Moab Is My Washpot*. New York: Random House.

9. Marylin Charles. 2009. 'When Cultures Collide: Myth, Meaning, and Configural Space'. *Modern Psychoanalysis*, 34 (1) 2009.

10. Hollway 1997/2001, p. 69 quoting Ronald Britton 1993, p. 84 'The Missing Link: Parental Sexuality in the Oedipus Complex', in D. Breen (ed.), *The Gender Conundrum*, London: Routledge, chapter 3: 82–84.

11. Jessica Benjamin. 1988. *The Bonds of Love: Psychoanalysis, Feminism and the Problem of Domination*, London: Virago Press.

12. Anna Freud quoted in Ralph Greenson 2016 *On Loving, Hating and Living Well*. Edited by Robert A. Nemiroff, Alan Sugarman and Alvin Robbins. London: Karnac.

13. Workplaces and the culture of capitalist work has to answer for this as well, taking workers, both men and women, away from families for long hours.

14 D.W. Winnicott. 1964. *The Child, the Family and the Outside World*, p. 10.

15. Joan Raphael-Leff. 1991. *Psychological Processes of Childbearing*. London: Chapman and Hall.

16. Which more than before, north Indian society needs to consider seriously at many different levels —gender, family, community and religions.

17. Devdutt Pattnaik. 2006. *Myth = Mithya: A Handbook of Hindu Mythology*. London: Penguin.

Mindblowing

I am watching eight-year-old Pia play with the doll's house. In the story, she is putting a male and female figure together in a double bed, saying that the parents are going to bed. Then there are suddenly a lot of babies emerging all over the house—two were found by the help in the kitchen, one by grandma in the bathroom and another by grandfather outside the front door (these are the people who look after Pia when her parents are away at work).

Mother and father woke up to all this and wanted to know where all these babies were coming from. They were told 'that is what we don't know and that is what we have to find out.'

That evening, Pia went home and asked her mother about the story of how she was born. She has heard this story before. Her mom has told her that she 'came out of Mummy's tummy'. That was good enough at age four but at age eight, Pia wants more detail. She wants to know 'Where was I *before* I was in your tummy?' Whatever answer she had been given till now was not satisfactory because now she specifically wanted to know 'What does Papa have to do with it?'

How much more specific does a child have to get to convey the message that she is desperately curious about the only question worth being curious about? The question of her origins; the 'Where did I come from? How was I born? How was I made?' And because the answer involves referring to the coming together of male and female genitalia, parents are squeamish about giving them the honest truth and sure, young children do not need the elaborate details, but they need to know. Give them the amount of information they can understand but stories about storks or Gods or other magical events need to be avoided. 'It ruins the trust if you make up a story that you later have to correct'.[1] An explanation about 'mummy's egg and papa's egg' coming together is usually enough to help sort out the basics—that it takes two to make a baby that each one has a contribution, that there was perhaps even a relationship here before you were born.

This last part, even in theory, is difficult enough for young children to conceptualise—that they are not the centre of the world; that there were relationships that preceded their existence; that there is a lot in the world that they are not a part of. This experience of being the observer to a relationship that you are not exactly a part of—the beginning of the acknowledgement of our insignificance—what 12-year-old Aira called her 'existential crisis'—is not an easy one to stomach. Beginning with 'I am not the centre of the world', through 'the world existed before me and will continue to exist after I am gone' and 'one day I will be gone' to 'I am a tiny dot in this universe'—is such a huge shock that most of us try hard to not think about it at all. If one were to pay heed to the fact that our existence itself is a matter of sheer chance, the narcissistic injury would almost be too much to bear. Certainly enough to blow the mind.[2] Resolving the complex and painful feelings that this raises (usually outside of our conscious awareness) is a fundamental part of our capacity to learn, to be curious and dare to want to find out about that which we do not already know.[3] It is the work of a lifetime.

Aira seemed to have taken this shock in her stride though.

A fortnight after speaking to me about her existential crisis, she returned saying that she had discovered newfound interest in her schoolwork. She had surprised herself by opening her textbook and making notes on a chapter on respiration in humans.

I wondered out loud 'How come? What happened to YouTube?' which had previously been her way to escape into fantasy and avoid the reality of needing to apply herself to schoolwork.

She smiled and said 'After a while I realised that there was nothing on it that was interesting to me.'

I must have raised an eyebrow and she did not look pleased.

I explained 'I am wondering, how come this desire to plug yourself into reality?'

She laughed and replied 'After my existential crisis, I realised that if I wanted to be seen and recognised, I would have to work for it; that day-dreaming would not get me there.'

'So how does it feel to realise that?' I asked.

'Awesome!' But also familiar'

And how did it feel inside your body? How did you experience this inside you?'

'Something exploded in my chest, and in my mind'.

She looked very pleased with herself. I realised that we were both smiling.

There is a gap between the outer that is trying to teach the child about the world, life and people, and the child herself, who is concerned with her own world, where the issues are of far greater import. Our childhood is fraught with deep mortal fears, intense rivalries, loneliness and isolation, and because imagination and reality are not really differentiated in childhood experience, such emotions hold a lot of energy. Perhaps it is for these reasons that there is also an anxiety around learning. Around *having* to learn. When learning is seen as new knowledge, something one was hitherto ignorant of, if the child is not ready to take it in, it is an imposition of the outer world; a narcissistic injury; a nuisance created by meaningless material.

Alongside the curriculum in a classroom there is always a personal experience of that material, one that is concerned with making sense of it.[4] Some of this personal meaning, for a primary school child, revolves around sorting out the complex wishes regarding sexuality, jealousy and parents. It is the reworking of such issues throughout childhood, which lead to a capacity for engagement in learning in the classroom. To understand the child's version, to understand his/her spontaneity or its lack, these factors would have to be taken into account.

In other words, our curiosity (initially about our origins and perhaps eventually about our future) fires the imagination and drives the intellectual mind. Education becomes valuable when it satisfies our curiosity about our internal realities. This begins with the child's experience that someone in her life (parent, teacher, grandparent, aunt, uncle, therapist) is curious about her internal reality. The child who can bear the emotional upheaval of not being the centre of the world, can be freed up to learn about other such truths. Let's face it, every new learning, whether in scholastic, spiritual or relationship terms, points to how we are an infinitesimal part of this universe—of knowledge, of the cosmos, and perhaps even our family tree. We are but a part of something much, much more unimaginably immense. You can imagine then that it takes a certain courage to want to step out into the vast unknown.

It is enough to blow your mind.

Many children struggle with learning; very often, despite being surrounded by good teachers and resources, they do not, cannot learn. It is as if there is a conflict in them over being able but disinterested, and becoming un-able because of it.

We will succeed in teaching our children only if our children have a capacity to believe *in* anything. The development of this capacity is not a matter of education. It is a matter of the experience of the person; of whether, from birth onward, the environment has been good enough, facilitative enough to inculcate trust and create a trusting, believing child. 'What you teach can only be implanted on what capacity is already present in the individual child based on the early experiences and on the continuation of reliable holding in terms of the ever-widening circle of family and school and social life.'[5]

Toddlers/pre-schoolers are the most curious people on the planet with their incessant 'why?', poking their fingers into everything including their bottoms and attempting physical feats with fearless abandon. After that, depending on how this urge to gain knowledge and experience is treated, they may continue to be interfering, bright pesky ones who are full of questions or turn into convenient, compliant humans with nary a thought of their own in their heads. How does the world treat their curiosity?

Of course, it is true that 'They need to trust us to know better than they do in many matters, and often, for convenience' sake, they have to do as they are told without going into the whys and wherefores….But from a very early age, that varies from one child to another, *children's interest in the connections between things leads them to want to know* why we tell them to do this, forbid them to do that'(italics mine).[6]

The vital part here is the 'connection between things'.

Children hate to be ignorant, especially of some great mystery that their parents are privy to, something that seems to happen in their bedroom, in the dark, that their child is kept out of. It is no wonder children fight to stay in their parents' bed or fight sleep. They are convinced something interesting is happening when they are asleep. They aren't wrong about it either! They feel terribly deprived if they are kept out. Feeling left out is an extremely difficult experience to bear.

For all of our lives, taking in new information, adapting our minds to any new reality, learning new things is a struggle and it begins with this original struggle of accommodating to the reality that we are but part of a triangle where sometimes we are the observer and not the participant.

'As we know, the effect of new knowledge in the scientific world which transcends our pre-existing view of things is at first disrupting: it needs investigation, abandonment of some existing order, and its integration demands modification of our world view. It arouses hostility, threatens our security, challenges our claims to omniscience, reveals our ignorance and sense of helplessness and releases our latent hatred of all things new or foreign: all things, that is, that we do not regard as some extension of ourselves, or as encompassed by the familiar boundaries of our mental landscape.'[7]

Many vague or difficult to specify learning difficulties in children are in fact emotional blocks to the unbearable anxiety created by the awareness of this reality. Some of us would rather be blind than to face the truth that is so painful.

Six-year-old Akshay was brought to a clinical psychologist for not being attentive in class and seven-year-old Mayank, because he was refusing to go to school. Their respective schools had asked the parents for cognitive assessments; in other words, 'is there something wrong with their capability to learn?' Both boys, both only children, were eventually diagnosed with specific learning difficulties. Their cognitive assessments interestingly indicated high intelligence but a struggle to put things together: literally, in spatial terms and also in language. Both were struggling to make the move to school as the new addition in their lives, a parallel to the struggle of accommodating to the original triangle. This new life stage needed them to separate from their mothers and engage with school and both these boys were, in some ways, struggling against their developmental capacities 'to perceive, to recognize, to remember, to locate and to anticipate experience'.[8] In other words, they would rather not know, even though their bodies and minds could take in more. They were intelligent, they just did not want to use their intelligence to make connections between things in the world because too much would change in the process.[9]

A child's capacity to bear the emotional disruption that new knowledge (originally, of his parents' intimate relationship and his, the child's, exclusion from it) creates and the distressing loss (of his exclusive relationship with his mother) that follows has a direct bearing upon his capacity for curiosity, symbolisation and rational thought. It is a simple question: has my curiosity paid off or led to a traumatic discovery?

Why is the parental relationship so important, one might wonder? The parental couple is the symbol of 'it takes two'. The coming together of the parents as a couple in the child's mind, is the coming together of differences, the realisation that diversity is reality, that the individual is a tiny event in the scheme of things yet carries the potential to become a potent force, is a fundamental symbol of our capacity to learn. Not learning by rote, which is what our national education systems encourage but learning that matters, that can be believed in, that may actually be included in the personality—learning that can blow your mind.

❧

For the middle-class urban Indian child, especially the boy child, learning is considered central to success but it is learning a prescribed text. Not learning as an attitude, not an opening of the personality or the mind. Learning is fact-oriented not subjective and not emotional, very much adhering to the binaries of rational and irrational where the emotions are irrational. Music, literature, reading, poetry, all fall under 'cultural but useless' skills that have little commercial value, often leading to a poverty within because there is little attention to the link between learning and the growth of the personality or on the emotional aspects of learning. As a result, there is a lot of innovative work in schools focusing on children's learning, but on little else. With a premium on science and commerce coupled with the low status of the liberal arts, learning becomes a lonely, painful, individualised and alienating task, which is separated from life outside the classroom and especially from one's inner life, with the family only permitted to view the end product in the form of a 'grade' or 'result'.

This is a conveniently compliant human in the making.

Regulations insist that schools employ a school counsellor but most schools do not know how to use one other than to increase compliance in the heretofore non-compliant: compliant to the curriculum or to a person or to the norms of behaviour in the classroom. Counsellors teach 'life-skills' or 'moral science' or they act as substitute teachers. If they do not provide learning support, they are seen as useless. Seeing the school counsellor is usually a matter of shame for a student and a wastebasket-space for other teachers to send difficult children off to. A school counsellor is usually a management tool to control an unruly group and to make them comply. Toeing the line is crucial. Children's creativity or emotional reality is not.[10] With this view of learning, we neglect the essential link between children's lived experience of the world and what they can take in.

On the other hand, perhaps as parents we can try to focus on the view that creativity and personal meaning are what may be considered the very basis for learning.

Strictly realistic stories run counter to the child's inner experience; he will listen to them and maybe get something out of them, but he cannot extract much personal meaning from them that transcends obvious content. These stories inform without enriching, as is unfortunately also true of much learning in school. Factual knowledge profits the total personality only when it is turned into personal knowledge.[11]

The way it had done for Aira.

NOTES

1. Gail Saltz, 2005. *Amazing You: Getting Smart about your Private Parts.* Puffin.

2. Bill Bryson does an excellent job of trying to convert this narcissistic injury into awe and amazement. B. Bryson. 2004. *A Short History of Nearly Everything.* London: Black Swan.

3. 'Some day children will find out that we are not so important in the world as they had supposed and the disillusionment is for them less of a blow, or less of a triumph, if we have not been fostering the illusion.' M. Harris. 2011. *Thinking about Infants and Young Children.* London: Karnac, p. 80.

4. B.J. Cohler & R.M. Galatzer-Levy. 1992. 'Psychoanalysis and the Classroom'. In N.M. Szajnberg (ed.), *Educating the Emotions: Bruno Bettelheim and Psychoanalytic Development.* New York: Plenum Press.

5. D.W. Winnicott. 1986. 'Children Learning'. In *Home is Where we Start From.* New York: W. W. Norton, p. 149.

6. M. Harris. 2011. *Thinking about Infants and Young Children,* p. 80.

7. Ronald Britton. 1992. 'The Oedipus Situation and the Depressive Position'. In R. Anderson (ed.), *Clinical Lectures on Klein and Bion.* London: Routledge, p. 38.

8. Ibid., p. 37.

9. N.D. Paiva. 2016. 'Keeping Father in Mind'. *Journal of Child Psychotherapy,* 42(2), p. 122.

10. A mental health professional in an educational institutional

space arouses suspicion (females outnumber men in this field so it is safe to say 'she'). If she does her job well, for which, please note, she was employed in the first place, she becomes a thorn in the side. An irritant who is either ignored or actively fought off. Management regularly asks themselves whether having a counsellor *creates* more emotional problems: 'Are we being indulgent by encouraging people to talk about their difficulties?'

11. B. Bettelheim. 1976. *Uses of Enchantment: The Importance of Fairy Tales in Children's Lives*. New York: Knopf, p. 54.

First Day at School

For months, I had my editor's voice in my head, usually emerging at three am when something had woken me and the streetlight danced eerily on my bedroom floor; her voice would invariably be saying 'School anxiety. School anxiety, you have to put in something about school anxiety'.

Clearly this was giving both of us anxiety. And we were not alone, I thought.

School was ghastly; most of the time for the most of us, I thought to myself. Large classrooms, lots of white noise so that the teacher could not be heard, often not worth hearing, if you did manage to, because the curriculum was tedious and dull, the environment competitive and isolating. Yet we all went and now have an obligation to send our children.

At the same time, I am also so glad to have my children out of my hair for some hours of the day, so I thank God for school. I am not sure about the value of the scholastic content of what they are taught but I am sure that they will learn something. If school was not entirely ghastly for us, all of the time, it was because of the relationships we made, the friendships and how we learned to bear the drama of failure and success as it unfolded over the 12 years. Or it was the relief provided by art, music, drama, debate, sports or something non-academic. It was character building. Sometimes.

Pan the camera away from schools of the 1980s and the scene cuts to now, where I am the parent with this suffering behind me, not the child anymore. Schools have changed in the last 30-odd years and there is an effort to make them cheerful-looking and the content more interesting. How cheerful the children may be feeling, however, is a mixed bag on any given day.

It is present-day Delhi in the month of April; the days are hot, the large red flowers of the silk-cotton tree lie strewn on many streets and the wailing of three-year-olds going to school for the first time fills the air. The emotional event of the month is the new school year for nursery, that is if you are lucky to have gained admission in the first place.

Nursery admissions in Delhi have been so fraught over the last some years that as parents we have been forced, not by the system but by the sheer absence of one, to focus on getting a place and not on what happens once our child is 'in' except to heave a sigh of relief. As parents and educators, we are in grave danger of missing the wood for the trees. Getting a nursery place is so anxiety-provoking for us as parents that we may easily forget how worrying it is for the child to be going anywhere at all by themselves. Our children do not care what nursery it is, which school it is or where it is located. The large majority of children are just scared at the prospect of leaving home, being with strangers in an unfamiliar environment, and having to communicate with adults who may not understand what they are trying to say.

More anxiety. The inevitable, unavoidable anxieties of a small person.

A three-year-old is not always functioning at the peak of their capacities. Like all of us, they are sometimes (most times) younger than their chronological age and when tired, hungry, ill or scared, regress to being the babies they were. Besides, let's be honest, a three-year-old is still incredibly small. Going to nursery then is less about learning content and more about negotiating the separation from parents and home. Nursery is only the beginning of this enormous task since it can go on for years. Separating from the people we love is our hardest task. It starts at weaning and it never ends.

We all have fears, real or imagined, about what will happen to us and to the loved other if we were to leave their side and these are not easy for us to verbalise. Children understand a lot more than they can explain though, so I was relieved that when I finally asked her what she was afraid of, my three-year-old daughter said she was scared that I would get lost and never return to pick her up, implying a connected fear that she would get lost in this new place and not be going home again. Her being reassured then depended on my reliability over a period of time, of showing up when I said I would.

Each child's struggle is different and it is not possible to generalise but we can find familiar shades in the stories of other lives. My younger daughter's classmate cried for months at the school gate while mine had luckily (whew) decided she loved her teacher and was happy to go after a first week of reluctance. However, that first week was torturous for us both. Having spent most of the first day (to be read as one hour) crying under the tree outside her playschool, I realised exactly how hard this separation was going to be for us, though I could not quite figure out whether I was crying for her struggle or my own. Our feelings were very intertwined. *We* were very intertwined. That was the crux of it.

In that first week, we would return home and play-act our separation with her stuffed toys. One pink coloured bear was designated as her teacher and another bear was her 'mumma'. A tiny bear represented her. Tiny-bear and mumma-bear went to school together and then kissed each other goodbye at the gate. Mumma-bear said 'I will be right here waiting for you under the tree'. Tiny-bear would go into the school gate with teacher-bear. She wanted this enacted on three consecutive days and then, to my enormous relief, declared that she now felt better about leaving me at the gate because she knew I would be there when she came out.

So many of our fears arise out of not knowing. It helps to talk to our children as honestly as possible about what to expect. This talking gives children permission to bring up their worries, howsoever small or fantastical. They may worry about how to use an unfamiliar toilet or who will help them with their trousers or whether they will be sleeping in the school or that mumma/papa will leave them there. Be clear about what you will say to her when she asks 'Why do I have to go to school?' (because one cannot expect a three-year-old to not ask 'why'; it is part of their job-description). On the other hand, there are some children who are not talkers, they find it difficult to express themselves in words and show them in other ways, by changes in their everyday behaviour—waking up at night; wetting the bed; throwing tantrums; not eating. The list is as long as children's temperaments since each child is unique. The point is to notice that something is the matter. The parent is best placed to decipher hidden communication if they are able to see the link between the behaviour and the intended emotional communication.

Stories of 'when papa and mumma first went to school' have always been irresistible to children I have worked with and have helped to address the 'not knowing'. It becomes more interesting when you throw in stories involving *masi, mamu, chaacha,* even grandparents and their early days in school. It makes going to school commonplace. It was hard enough for my daughter to imagine that her parents ever went to school, let alone her grandparents as little school-going, four-year-olds. She was very entertained by the different names of schools and laughed hysterically at the photographs we showed her. She was intrigued at how schools were different through the ages and in different towns; that her father used to go to school by a horse-pulled 'tonga', her mother by cycle-rickshaw, her aunt by a shared taxi and that her grandmother along with her siblings were driven to school by their father.

Start early with picture story-books or perhaps even a visit to the school for her to see what it looks like a month or so before the emotional temperature rises in April. Be prepared for repetition for as every parent of a young child knows, once is never enough. Stories that matter the most must be repeated endlessly, without variation so that they can sink in.

The story of how everyone leaves home and goes to school is of central emotional import. It is not meant to be easy. In fact, it is a rite of passage.

A majority of children settle down with this level of intervention, preparation and repetition. Some struggle more. There is always a percentage that is still crying at the gate six months later. Their individual struggles need closer attention: why going to school creates such distress or anxiety, once every other child has accustomed to it or at the very least decided to make the most of a bad job, needs to be wondered about.

Some children are unhappy about going to school because they worry about their mother's feelings—'What will mumma do at home without me?' Leaving the mother may feel like a betrayal, especially if she is lonely, sad or there is a tension in the home, usually in the parents' relationship. All children have an unspoken awareness of difficulties in the family and they often feel responsible for them, especially if they experience their mother as fragile. It is extremely difficult for a child to begin to enjoy a different space if they feel they are betraying a loved one in the process.

A seven-year-old I am acquainted with started refusing to go to school after having apparently settled down in nursery.

It turned out that there were regular fights between his parents and he felt he needed to take care of his mother. Once this was unearthed, it became easier to know how to intervene. He was back at school within a few weeks.

Conveying a sense of firm yet gentle clarity can go a long way in helping the child not feel guilty about going to school. Parents can help by putting feelings into words—that it is sad one cannot be a baby forever but it is also fun to grow up; that they can go to school and enjoy it without worrying about what has been left behind at home; that their work is to grow and learn and that adults can take care of themselves. They may be angry with you for this, for some time, but that is part of another story.

Fathers are particularly useful in this process of helping their children separate from their mothers[1]—not by dragging them away kicking and screaming of course but by helping them to see that there is a lot to be gained from an interest in the outside world. There is a significant amount of research that suggests that a father's involvement in their children's lives has a positive impact on their adaptation to school as well as their interest in learning new things.[2] When my husband became involved in the school-going process and started getting our first-born dressed and dropping her to school, his presence itself became an incentive for our daughter to stop whining about waking up early. His style was more playful than mine (which tends to be more fraught, finger-waggling and you-will-be-late-for-school-oriented), yet firm and it worked. When he praised her for being responsible for small things like washing her hands, finishing her glass of milk, dressing herself, tidying up or remembering her manners, I noticed that it had a greater reinforcing effect than when it came from me. It became more fun to grow up a bit.

Many first-time school-goers might also simultaneously be in the process of gaining a sibling, which may make it doubly difficult to leave home and mother. It is bad enough to go to school without the added envy that mother is being monopolised by a new, potentially 'replacement' baby. Sharing parents with a new sibling is difficult at any age; even seven-year-olds who are school-going veterans may struggle when there is a new baby who gets to be at home, cosy and safe while they face the outside world of rules, homework, heat and dust. Activities shared exclusively with father, like going to the park, activities that exclude mother and the new baby (and include an ice-cream), are often a favourite and can help to initiate the process of moving away from the mother when a sibling is born.

It is rare for us as adults to recall our own early schoolgoing experiences with fondness. Most of us focus on the good parts, on the one teacher we liked and the friends we eventually made. We gritted our teeth and got through it, one might say. Does school have to be this way? Is it not possible to actually enjoy the many years we spend in educational spaces? I am suggesting that the early experience of separation from parents, the first day, the first weeks and months in nursery may form a blueprint for what the future may *feel* like—an internal wrench that has to be borne by supressing anxieties, i.e., not thinking about it.

Could we not co-create a version that has space for good experiences to come in too? If we understand the fears, there may be freedom to look forward to learning new things without being too scared about losing something in the process. After all, learning is an emotional task and the patterns are set very early in our lives.

Let us not forget that in any separation there are at least two people involved. If going to nursery is hard on the child, what is the other person feeling? How do the parents feel, leaving their baby at the gate, in the care of someone they have no choice but to build trust in? For the mother who has kept an eye on every little detail for this little person, is it easy to let go? No, it isn't. You may be relieved that you have a few hours of peace but watching them cry is also gut-wrenching for us. I can distinctly recall my daughter's first day at nursery and me standing and weeping (yes, that tree again). The school principal felt the need to come out and reassure me that my child appeared to be doing okay. Luckily, my daughter did not see me cry; she had enough worries of her own without having to think about my feelings too. We parents have mixed feelings toward our own schoolgoing histories, whether consciously remembered or not. We also have mixed feelings toward the idea of our babies growing up. It becomes manifest in our hanging on to them in the last lingering hug at the school gate or the standing and watching till they go into the gate.

NOTES

1. Martha Harris. 2011. *Thinking about Infants and Young Children*. London: Karnac, p. 84.
2. See Nupur Dhingra Paiva. 2016. 'Keeping Fathers in Mind', *Journal of Child Psychotherapy*, DOI: 10.1080/0075417X.2016.1191199 http://dx.doi.org/10.1080/0075417X.2016.1191199

Siblings

A sibling is a disaster.
A blessing.
A friend.
A reality check.

This is a subject that is not given enough airtime in psychological thinking yet like many neglected parts of our inner worlds, it is crucial. The arrival of a sibling changes everything and adapting to it creates an upheaval for us all. Yet it is central to the growth of the personality adding valuable richness and depth.

If we can acknowledge that a significant part of being a mature adult is to learn to share— this planet and its resources, our living spaces, our loved ones, the attentions we receive, our opinions—then we need to acknowledge the enormous debt we owe to our siblings, for it is in our relationships with our sisters and brothers that we first learn how to share.

The arrival of a sibling is (sometimes outside of our immediate awareness, sometimes within) a seismic internal event. With it the world of exclusive attention of our parents and grandparents comes to an end. The world of being the only baby is over and nothing can ever bring it back. In short, it is a disaster. Pocket-sized older ones are known to have said things like 'take this baby back' or 'put it in the bin' and other less-than complimentary remarks. Of course, older ones always know way before the actual arrival of the baby that something is changing. They can see the change in their mother's body and the change in her mind, her preoccupations and the quality of her presence. Older ones know about new pregnancies even when mothers are not showing a bump or when they have not been explicitly told. This is because when things are going well between any mother-baby pair, they are communicating with each other perfectly well without words; pre-verbal; before words; perhaps even beyond words, and so they know when there is something else on mummy's mind.

'Your toe is crossing the line onto my side of the bed!' Or

'don't breathe over my book' Or

'Mom! She is standing on my side of the room!' Or

'What the hell is your problem? I am not touching you. I am just keeping my finger here near your face!'

It may all sound familiar, it may sound ridiculous, but we know siblings can fight about anything and violence is commonplace where overt hitting, scratching, biting and teasing is easier to deal with than sly hurting, pinching and tipping over. It is also important to point out that later rivalries over money, property, possessions, really all begin from the original difficulty in sharing attention.

Indeed, the most crucial experience that the arrival of a sibling brings on is that of hate.

Older one's hate their younger siblings. Yet, like all statements of truth in psychodynamic thinking, the opposite is also always true and given the opportunity, chinks begin to show up in the wall of hate separating the two. Gradually love enters and this experience is at the basis of our humanity. Love turns up, for the same person who was also hated and that is where the transformation begins. The acknowledgement that we have actually begun to care for and have tender feelings towards the one who displaced us, whom we hated, whom we wanted to be rid of because his/her arrival ruined the world as we knew it, as the younger baby becomes a person and can be played with and enjoyed as an ally—this experience enriches our personalities and makes us human.[1]

This cannot happen if our basic aggression is denied, which is common enough for the following to have been written in 1955 and still be relevant

> Take the example of the child who beats the little baby sister and the mother with this phony smile says 'I know you did not mean to hit her.' Sure he meant to hit her; he probably would have liked to kill her. But the mother prevents the child from recognising that people have such impulses. What happens as a consequence of this? First of all, there is complete confusion about what is real. If you hit out of jealousy and rage and mother who is the authority says, 'you didn't mean it', then your own emotions cannot be real; they are strange and unique. What can you trust, what mother says? Or what you feel?[2]

The older sibling will often be very upfront that they hate their newly born brother/sister. They will want to return them to the hospital; put it back in mummy's tummy; poke them, hit them, make fun of them or even be able to say, 'I hate her!' They struggle with the intense jealously they experience when they see their mother feeding, holding, caressing a baby that is not them. Sometimes young children will have to destroy something else in the house, or hurt a pet or even their mother in order to protect their new sibling from being damaged by their aggression. I went out into the garden one afternoon to discover that my three-year-old daughter had systematically destroyed all the small *nasturtium* plants I had grown from seed. It took me some time to connect the dots and acknowledge to her that she was in fact furious with me for growing a new baby (from seed) and at the baby for existing. This experience of being able to first put up with, and later perhaps enjoy, a scenario where you are not the only recipient of good things is what builds character. Being happy for someone else. It is a long, painful road and it begins by learning to share your mother and acknowledging hate or envy.

This is very hard for the mother to bear; yet from here on, both parents have a huge part to play in how the relationship between the siblings will pan out. Parents who wish to deny that their older one has negative feelings are deluding themselves and also pushing this falsehood onto their child. Denying a child the satisfaction of having their feelings validated, not being given permission to own up to difficult, messy negative feelings, means a child has to pretend to be all nice and pristine. So where does all the crap go? It does not. It is repressed out of immediate awareness and finds ways to express itself in other surreptitious ways— cruelty to animals, bullying other children, a weary depression, clinginess and regressing, bedwetting, hitting and hurting oneself for having had bad feelings that the family won't see. The list is endless and is only restricted by the enormous creativity of the human mind to deal with emotional pain.

Six-year-old Nidhi was an energetic, enthusiastic child who loved to run, more helter-skelter than with purpose, and had become used to being able to overwhelm her mother's resources. Exhausted by this, Nidhi's mother often pressed the older sister, eight years older than Nidhi, into being a secondary parent, telling her to be patient to Nidhi's demands, indulging one of her children at the expense of the other. The mother did not realise that she was killing the relationship between the siblings but also damaging her older child's relationship with her. Nidhi knows that she and her sister do not like each other and is able to state it in these words. We have not got the older sister's version but can imagine that it is not pleasant either.

To be seen for our internal truth is what we all desperately seek. We all want to be seen and heard for what we truly are within, even if it is not that pleasant. We want our complexities to be seen and known, our ambivalence to be noticed, not denied. Even little children do not enjoy palliatives of 'everything will be fine' or 'no, no that is not true, you do love your sister' because they experience them to be untrue. Children thoroughly enjoy stories about evil monsters, naughty children, wickedness of all kinds because it is reassuring to know that it exists in the outside world as well, that the rage and hatred inside is not an aberration, that 'I am not an aberration for feeling this way. Perhaps there are others too'.

Parents who are aware, somewhere at the back of their minds, that the sibling relationship between their children will usually outlast them and their presence, would do well to encourage the bond between them from early on.

> He needs to be prepared for the fact that the baby is produced by his mummy and daddy and that he is going to be its elder sibling. He needs to be prepared for the fact that when it's born it will sleep most of the time, and maybe cry some of the time, that it will take up a great deal of his mummy's attention, that she'll be feeding it as she fed him when he was so little. It's a help to be prepared for the fact that it's not going to be much company for him to start with, and that there won't be a great deal he'll be able to do for it in the very beginning, but that there are many little ways in which he can help mummy when she is getting things ready for bathing and feeding and so on.[3]

Protecting one child from the aggression of the other, stepping in to resolve arguments or fights too often is a sure way to do the opposite, since the battle is for the parent's attention. Remove that reward and the relationship between siblings actually strengthens. A friend often tells the story of how, as eight and 10-year-olds, he and his brother would fight long and loud, hoping for their mother to come and take sides. She did not; instead he clearly remembers the day she walked into the room, refused to hear the pleas of either party, slapped them both and walked out. The boys looked at each other and said words to the effect of 'What a bitch! Can you believe she did that?' and in their shock, ganged up against a common adversary. They never called her again to be the referee.

For Hera the situation was markedly different. His parents could not see or imagine the distress that had been caused to him by the birth of his younger sister and the subtle ways in which he expressed his jealousy, his anger towards his mother and his subsequent guilt for that. Hera's parents only noticed when he began to get extremely aggressive in school and at the age of six began hurting himself by deliberately squashing his fingers between doors and strangling himself with rope. In Hera's mind he deserved this punishment because he had extremely violent feelings toward his family and he had no permission to own them (in the form of stories or aggressive play or even a 'we know you are angry' from his parents) since his parents found it extremely hard to link the two facts of Hera's behaviour and the huge change in his life of having to share them.

In groups of children, whether in a classroom or on a sports field, the rivalry among younger children is usually for the attention of the teacher. The child who feels she cannot receive positive attention by being good at the task, will often settle for negative attention by being the pest. Our education systems, classrooms and individual sports encourage this individual-based competition, and a direct one-to-one relationship to the teacher or the coach, which encourages rivalry and mirrors the sibling relationship in the home. Team sports on the other hand, encourage 'the siblings' to work together and band together in order to gain advantage over another team. You lose individual attention from an admired adult but you gain feelings of belongingness and appreciation by a peer-group. This is reality.

Through some of my work[4] it became evident that girls who were the older siblings had an easier time adapting to teamwork, team dynamics and giving of themselves to a group. The younger siblings really struggled in this process. If they attended the programme with their older sibling, the struggle was mitigated somewhat. If they were there by themselves they alternately behaved as if persecuted by the group, superior to the group, unattended to by the coaches or too self-important to need coaching, all this between the ages of 6 and 8 years. They kept themselves out of team huddles and discussions and attributed it either to their self-sufficiency (a false narcissism, I don't need anyone) or the insufficiencies of the team (I don't need them, they are no good; grapes are sour, perhaps). Yet, they seemed to respond very well when the team encouraged them to join in.

The team, not the coach.

Their siblings, not the parent.

Seven-year-old Anita was a case in point. She was the youngest in her family with a many-year gap between her and her older sibling. She found it extremely difficult to share her mother and wanted to be her only child. In the sports group Anita really struggled because she was not the special one to the coaches and resented the hard work she had to put in to gain respect from the team or praise from the coach. Most of all she could not bear being one of a group. To her it was the equivalent of being ignored, even invisible. That which she feared the most had in fact already happened, since her older sibling had in fact sucked up all the attention and energy in the home. Now she perpetuated it by denying the reality that she was in fact, part of a group. Her family.

One afternoon she refused to join in the sports practice drills, hanging around at the periphery of the field saying she was tired. When it was time for the group discussion at the end and she watched her teammates sitting in a circle on the grass, it seemed she was in a state of internal conflict. She came near, hovered behind me as I led the group but did not join in. It was as if she wanted her conflict to be noticed: 'Please see that I am struggling. That I want to be here but I will not ask because then I may be seen as small and needy; which I am but I will deny it.' I asked the siblings(i.e., other children in the team) whether they had noticed Anita hovering and wondered out loud 'what do you think she would like?' Without any further assistance some children in the group shouted 'Come and join us! We miss you!'

Anita came and sat by me with her head down and proceeded to spend the next few minutes avoiding eye contact with her peers and instead poking my bare thigh with a bit of grass. Her anger toward me and toward the team was all there in its flagrant glory for me to feel and everyone to note.

She had a long, lonely road ahead of her if she were to choose to continue to deny the reality of being part of a group and focus only on her desire to be her mother's only child or the only student to the coach.

How else are we to learn to live together?

Notes

1. D.W. Winnicott. 1964. 'The Only Child'. In *The Child, the Family and the Outside World*. London: Penguin, p. 133.
2. *On Loving, Hating and Living Well, the Public Psychoanalytic Lectures of Ralph Greenson*, 2016, p. 7.
3. Martha Harris. 2011. *Thinking about Infants and Young Children*. London: Karnac, p. 64.
4. The Art of Sport programme for the overall development of young girls through football and group therapy. www.theartofsport.in

Anger: Beloved Demon

Anger: The demon in each one of us. We despise it, apparently. Yet we are drawn to its power.

Aggression is a necessary part of living. It is 'the innate urge of the child to use force in order to control, to dominate, to overcome, to master, to influence something in the outside world. Aggressiveness is necessary in order for man to establish contact with an external object, to maintain this contact and to control objects in his environment.'[1] The roots of our aggression are the roots of our life force. The pleasure we experience in movement, even if it hurts at times, the rage we experience at frustration, have the same roots.

The demon of anger is in us all. It is us. It makes us; it makes us different, it makes us stand out, stand up and move ahead. For it is the same energy that powers a tantrum or a rage that also powers our capacity to assert ourselves, have an opinion, to be heard, to place a boundary or go beyond one. Our aggression is what helps us differentiate self from other.

This demon is constantly repelled in order to prove our piety, goodness and uni-dimensional nature, usually the feeling of love. But it is a precarious state, often a front, or a false self, like the little girl who keeps a smile on her face even when she is nervous. Yet, like the inevitable age-old relationship between the *devas* and the *asuras* in Hindu creation myths, this demon is near. Always near. And like the *asuras* who are honest about their quest for *amrit*, anger is honest. About want, greed, desire, about being self-serving, perhaps to the point of destruction of what we also hold as good and valuable. Acknowledged openly.

Repelled but present, whether as envy, greed or jealousy, whether unconscious, repressed or displaced, controlled or sublimated, this demon is always present. And when we deny its existence, we miss the point it is trying to make and perhaps miss out on an important part of the truth; our truth.

My five-year-old daughter, when really annoyed with me would say 'Mumma, you are such a zebra!' One time, when I was urging/forcing/cajoling her to take some medicine (for her own good) she frowned, screwed up her eyes, curled her little hand into a fist and air-punched me, one inch away from my face. I was taken aback but returned the air-punch to her fist and it turned into a game. She had rebelled, got her point across, no one got hurt, there was no retaliation and I did manage to get the medicine in as well. As a six-year-old, my daughter could verbalise 'Sometimes I think you are a monster'; she said it with some trepidation, lest the monster-mumma emerged at that moment. A year later she would wonder out loud 'DO you still love me? Then why do you shout at me?' And she could ask 'How can it be that you still love me when you are shouting at me?'

At other times it did not go so well. She would walk into our bedroom in the middle of the night plagued by 'bad thoughts' or nightmares in which she was being attacked or I was being killed. I found myself trying various things as panacea—'it's nothing, go back to sleep' or 'it's only a dream, it's not real, go back to sleep' or just 'It is the middle of the night, GO

BACK TO SLEEP!' Eventually I decided I may try some of my psychoanalytically informed theories, that in fact her 'bad thoughts' were fuelled by her unacknowledged anger that she was projecting outward. In other words, 'she was angry with me, in real life and instead of being able to talk about that, she was covering it up but the cover was flimsy and was not working; that it would just be simpler if she would be mad at me when she was mad at me', or words to that effect.

It worked.

By the time she was eight years old I began to get written notes telling me off for some omission or oversight, telling me I had lost points and was now scraping the bottom of the barrel and needed to pull up my socks if I wanted my status to improve. She could say 'I hate you right now' and more complex ideas such as 'I love you but I don't like you'.

The 'bad thoughts' stopped. By nine, I was 'the best mumma in the world'.

Let's see how long this lasts before rage returns.

❧

I love you.

I hate you.

Cinderella and Snow White solved this problem by splitting their hatred and anger, into the step-mother they were persecuted by. That way the love for their adored but dead mother could be preserved. And this is true, that is how it happens, a love that is preserved is in fact dead because it is unreal. Our real selves are far more complex and that complexity is painful but it is not uni-dimensional. Because we are dynamic, and we have our opposites right there next to us, like our shadows, which can only be seen by us depending on how the light falls.[2]

All of our emotions are painful when experienced intensely

but none so painful as anger toward someone we love. For it is only those whom we love and depend on who cause us frustration and pain. Because 'Anger is the loudest of all the emotions'[3]; it can effectively work to cover many of the other feelings that may live alongside it—sadness, disappointment, guilt or the search for parental love. Anger can be used as a defence to hide our other feelings behind, or it can be honest. Either way it predisposes us to violence, in action and inaction, in words, in fantasy, both conscious and unconscious, and also through neglect and abandonment. We neglect our own feelings and those of our children when we judge and condemn angry outbursts; we fail to let them experience their angry parts and eventually deprive them of a nuanced, unbiased view of their inner lives. This is an uncomfortable, daily, ordinary occurrence in every family, between every parent-child pair.

Myra was asked to look for her slippers and went to rummage in the shoe cupboard. Watching her, her father was getting really irritated; he knew the slippers were not in there. As she continued without success, he found his irritation rising. And in a voice which he later admitted was too loud, asked her what she was doing and why. She was scared and he could see it. And she went silent, looking at him with what I imagine were large scared eyes. He said 'I am asking you a question and you are not responding and it is getting me more irritated, why are you looking in this cupboard?' A few more repetitions and she finally gathered her mind to overcome her fear and responded with 'I thought they may be in here'.

Once she left to look elsewhere, her father calmed down, and the voice in his head told him that perhaps he had used too large a hammer for a tiny nail, that he had overreacted.

Once the slippers had been found (next to her bed) he went

to her and said 'I was very proud of you that despite being so scared you answered my question.' The voice in his head said 'Yeah right, that was a poor attempt at back-pedalling'. Still, it did the job because the breach between them was repaired somewhat and the look in her eyes told him that Myra had forgiven him.

Myra's father told me this story with some amount of guilt at having overreacted and hurt his daughter. True, she had been scared and he could have done it differently but he did all right actually. What I could see was that for Myra, faced with a shouting parent, this had also been a good lesson on how to strengthen relationships. After all,

1. We are never in 100% attunement with our loved ones.
2. An absence of conflict is not what we need.
3. What we need is repeated experiences that misalignments will be repaired, that conflicts will be resolved, that love will be greater than anger. That is what builds a stronger relationship, not the avoidance of conflict.

Her father had given her one very important lesson— by praising Myra for standing up for herself, he had done something that is crucial for us to handle the outside world, i.e., to think in the face of intense emotion.

Myra's father is only human. What propelled him to shout this way? He admitted that he could feel the irritation rise up in him as he watched his six-year-old daughter mess about. What he was less aware of was that he could not bear the discomfort it caused within him and so it flew out. He discharged it risking the love his daughter has for him in the process. At that moment he had split off his love for her, yet it returned soon enough and he could feel guilt, and repair the damage.

We are taught from early childhood that our anger, our aggression, is 'bad'; a value judgement is placed upon a feeling and this is when the trouble begins; the surreptitious hatred, the shouting and sulking, the rage and tantrum or the self-punishment, depression and apathy and the fascination with violence. In this drama of extremes, so easy to dismiss as unhelpful, we forget to see anger for its honesty and its presence. When our innate aggression is not openly acknowledged as real and existing, if it is either denied and controlled, smothered and squashed, worse stuff may happen.[4]

We do much more violence to babies and young people by neglecting their emotional realities and moving them further away from an honest relationship with their internal worlds. Living with a theory of *'bacche to aise hi pal jaate hain'*, we abandon children and let emotional poverty and hunger continue, and it returns to us all. One of the jobs of a parent is to be a kind of emotion coach, and certainly to help children regulate their emotional states. Children cannot do this for themselves. *Bacche apne aap nahin palte.*

Look into the personal history 'of the criminal, the assassin, the delinquent or the fanatic, we find that all these people have suffered from excessive frustration and deprivation or they have been neglected, humiliated or starved in early childhood and usually also in adolescence. The lack of any enduring loving human relationship, the absence of a reliable caring person in terms of love, concern, food, compassion and understanding makes for free-floating aggression, hostility and violence.'[5]

In other words, it pisses us off and we propel that forward, exponentially into external violence or internally into self-destruction.

The ordinary human baby is born with a drive that propels us toward people as well as an aggressive urge, which drives us to overcome obstacles, to get rid of things or people that hurt and give pain. Our aggression is propelling, compelling and protective. As this baby grows, if he is fortunate, he is able to move through rage, through destructiveness on to anger and hate; and further to modulate hate into dislike and competition and to master problems. If the world around us reacts to our anger by producing a stronger, larger, more frightening anger, it squashes us, only teaching us that we have to wait till we get to be bigger and more frightening. It does not teach us to regulate, understand or communicate what is beneath our anger or to make changes in the world.

Let us take the example of hunger since it is easy to recognise. We acknowledge that a baby's hunger creates an impelling need and if the food arrives at the right time the baby can devour it with an energetic interaction, take it in with greed, which is very satisfying and gratifying. This is a picture of aggression meeting something on the outside.[6] At the same time, babies also go through periods of great frustration when their needs are not fulfilled and these frustrations, in health, lead to anger, even rage.[7] We may not be used to seeing a screaming hungry baby as enraged but mothers know that they are often at the receiving end of such a feeling. *This anger is a sign of health because it means the baby has got someone to believe in and someone to be angry with.*

As this baby grows, he/she needs to test the environment, to see if the parents really truly mean the love and holding. When all goes well this innate destructiveness gets channelled into other actions that need force—eating, kicking, playing sports, competition, etc., and the destructiveness becomes an idea rather than an actual acting out.[8]

We take a huge risk whenever we experience strong emotions fully because these experiences of excitement and rage are often painful. So even our normal healthy selves, from childhood, will try to discover ways of avoiding the most intense feelings[9]. Even before we are taught anything, we experience our intense emotions as painful, as overwhelming. Whether it is anger or even an excess of desire—to take in, greed, to grab, to HAVE. So intense love and intense anger are both denied or dampened. But there is a price to pay for this: a dampening of life itself, because it is the intensity in us that is at the base of our life force; that intensity, which can also be destructive, is the basis of aggression, of strength, of force. And we need that.

This chapter has been by far the most difficult one for me to write. I, as do most of us, have a checkered history with anger, having been described as a 'thoughtful and considerate' child for most of my growing years but never really basked in this praise. To me it was a burden since I was aware of a secret wish to be a shark who could bite people's heads off without remorse. It took many years to accept that in fact, I am everything: thoughtful and considerate but also angry, dull, asocial, envious, arrogant, hysterical, contained, loving, warm, cold, wise, childish and the opposite of all of this as well. This permission to be many things and not just a few frees me up to be in the moment, whatever it is. This is why a split that keeps reality (thoughtful and considerate) and fantasy (remorseless shark) is a dangerous, self-defeating one that many of us live with. I meet young people regularly who are struggling with this split; they are either explosive and impulsive, spreading their anger about and getting labelled as having 'anger management problems', or silent, afraid of confrontation but destructive in their silence buying peace at the price of abandoning their own corner, losing their voice or throttling their desire. Unsurprisingly, this latter lot feels helpless and powerless in their relationships, using silence and sulking as their weapons. It does not endear them to others even though this silence is both their gift of love and their defence armament. Neither lot feels effective or understood in their relationships. Both lots of young people confuse the experience of anger with the expression of it. They remain focused on how it comes out. Not on how it feels within. Living in the mode of action or reaction means they miss out on the internal experience. They don't get to understand themselves or the nuances of the life force in them.

Angry silence needs special mention here. Also called sulking it is excruciating if you are at the receiving end of it and you are a pain in the ass to anyone else if you sulk. Sulking is a silent anger clearly directed at one (usually hapless) recipient. They are the only person who can fix it while also being attacked by it.

At the heart of a sulk lies a desire to be understood, wordlessly. Only wordless and accurate mind-reading can feel like a true sign of love and trust. 'Only when we don't have to explain can we feel certain that we are genuinely understood.'

> Sulking pays homage to a beautiful, dangerous ideal that can be traced back to our earliest childhoods: the promise of wordless understanding. In the womb, we never had to explain. Our every requirement was catered for. The right sort of comfort simply happened. Some of this idyll continued in our first years. We didn't have to make our needs known: large, kind people guessed for us. They saw past our tears, our inarticulacy, our confusions; they found the explanations for discomforts which we lacked the ability to verbalize.[10]

It is the child in us who does the sulking. The sulkee (i.e., the recipient of the sulk) usually has little to do with it. The child in us feels helpless and powerless, angry and insulted that there is a need for dialogue at all because the ideal is wordless understanding.

As adults when we choose to sulk we prevent ourselves from enjoying that which we would ordinarily enjoy and we give away the responsibility of our joy to the beleaguered sulkee, who is simultaneously responsible for and prevented from rescuing us from our sulk. We *want* them to suffer as we suffer. We *want* to create an impossible situation for them but it is one we are mired in as well.[11] As a child we were powerless in the face of a relationship with an adult—parent, teacher, sibling —who had hurt or disappointed us in some way. We often call this 'upset'. 'I am upset' is two feelings, a combination of hurt and anger, with arrows in opposite directions. The hurt feeling is toward ourselves, the anger is toward the disappointing/hurting other. A sulk is both.

Not a terribly adult way of handling anything.

In our closest relationships, we are often not adult at all. We may look it, we may be chronologically older but our emotional patterns, especially of intense feelings, and how we treat them (and therefore how we treat ourselves) always reverberate with something in childhood and we find it impossible to actually see the present for what it is. Usually, we find it impossible to see that we are no longer small and helpless and that we do have agency. Anger may give agency but do we want to take it?

NOTES

1. D.W. Winnicott. 1964. 'Roots of Aggression'. In *The Child, the Family and the Outside World*. London: Penguin, p. 232.

2. In literature this has been alluded to in countless writings. Phillip Pullman's *Northern Lights* has this theme where humans' souls naturally exist outside of their bodies in the form of sentient 'dæmons': talking animal spirits that constantly accompany, aid, and comfort their humans. Children's dæmons can freely and instantaneously change their appearance into that of any real or mythical creature; once people reach puberty, however, their dæmons settle into one permanent form. This sentiment daemon is what psychotherapists call the inner world and the permanent form, character.

3. Varun Narain. Personal communication.

4. See www.psychcentral.com And how we convert emotional pain into physical pain https://blogs.psychcentral.com/

liberation/2017/09/7-types-of-pain-directly-linked-to-your-emotions/?li_source=LI&li_medium=popular17

5. Ralph Greenson. 2016. 'The Fascination of Violence'. In *On Loving, Hating and Living Well*. Edited by Robert A. Nemiroff, Alan Sugarman and Alvin Robbins. London: Karnac, p. 195. 'A history of chronic malnutrition, degradation, brutality, humiliation, frustration and emasculation may lead to acts of violence. If this occurs in a person who sense he is being pushed to the brink of feeling helpless, an act of violence is apt to occur. Violence is not only an act of hatred and revenge against one's oppressors, but it is also a defense against falling into despair, resignation or deadly apathy. An act of violence may give one a temporary sense of power, in fact, it may create a feeling of omnipotence, the exact opposite of helplessness. Violence is quick and therefore enticing for those who have been forced to endure indignities for years. Violence is magical. It transforms one by suddenly changing one's identity from a feeble, dependent nobody into a sense of some-bodiness, a sense of manhood' (p. 196).

6. D. W. Winnicott. 1964. 'Roots of Aggression', p. 94.

7. Ibid.

8. D.W. Winnicott. 1986. *Home is Where we Start from: Essays by a Psychoanalyst*. Penguin Books.

9. D.W. Winnicott. 1941. 'Observation of Infants in a Set Situation'. In *Through Paediatrics to Psychoanalysis: Collected Papers*. London: Karnac, p. 52.

10. Alain de Botton. 2016. *The Course of Love*. London: Penguin. pp. 61–63.

11. I am grateful to Dr. Rachana Patni for sharing her thoughts on sulking. Jasper Juul, Aggression and Empathy. https://vimeo.com/55093210

Childhood Desires

Four-year-old Freya has a story where she is the queen, her father is the king and Freya's older sister is the princess. Mother is the servant.

Three-year-old Isha and her mother are walking down a long carpeted corridor back to their hotel room when she turns to her mother and says 'Mumma, let's race. The winner gets papa!'

At age 5, Iman tells her mother 'Why did you have to marry Papa? He was my last chance.'

A few weeks later, she adds, 'Actually, it is okay that you married Papa. He makes a very good Papa.'

Nine-year-old Tania tells her father she likes his face and wants to kiss him on his mouth.

Her father is stunned at this directness of her attraction towards him.

Eight-year-old Urvashi play acts with her father where he is Barack Obama and she is his wife Michelle.

Six-year-old Arjun loves his father but when it comes to bedtime, he tells his father, 'You go and sleep on the floor because the bed is not large enough for four' (Arjun's sister and mom as well) and he wants his mom.

Four-year-old Samir is asked what he wants to be when he grows up and says he wants to marry his mom.

The child's attraction to the parent of the opposite sex is well-established in psychoanalytic literature and even Wikipedia will inform you that this is unexceptional. The examples above will not shock most people who listen to their children's fantasies, imagination and comments. Yet, when most of us think about children and desire or childhood sexuality the concept seems to be an oxymoron, because children and sexuality are considered to be on opposite poles. Perhaps the difficulty here is with our limited understanding of the term sexuality as much as it is about our blinkered awareness of children's inner worlds.

Sexuality is more than sex and genitals.

It includes gender

It includes emotion

It includes all our communication—verbal and non-verbal.

It is our desire to join up with people and be close to them and to have them be close to us.

It is our creativity and our beauty.

It is what makes us attractive to another, the inner beauty. Sexuality has very little to do with the outfit we pick. It is more about how we use the outfit we are in, whatever it may be. It is everything in us that draws people to us and us to others: our spoken and body language and how we treat others and ourselves.

It is pleasure in the physical sensations of our body, not just sexual organs, which incidentally are never just sexual organs anyway. The penis has a more everyday function of passing urine than sexual pleasure and the vagina is also designed for another purpose. Also, the adult sexual act is more than penetrative sex and sexual arousal continues to be more in the mind than in the genitals.

Those of us who refuse to imagine children as being sexual have a limited understanding of sexuality and are confusing mature adult sexuality with children.

Of course it cannot be similar. Children's bodies are not developed and their minds are not comparable to an adult but children have desire too. And children also love.

Children too seek to complete that love by being physically close to the one they love. Just the way adults do. In fact, it is more truthful to state it the other way around. Adults seek to be close to the people they love, the way they did as children. The holding, the caressing, the kissing—all of which has nothing to do with sexual organs or with reproduction—began in infancy.

In fact, I may go so far as to say that when we go out seeking love as adults, it is often the child in us who goes out seeking. The vulnerability, insecurity and anxiety, the desire to be looked after and adored, to have exclusive attention, to be kept in mind, to be held gently, to have your needs understood and met wordlessly, are some of our earliest desires, ones we experienced first in our relationship with our mothers. That is what forms the template for love.

Early attachments, including the satisfaction, gratification, touch, physical proximity, safety and warmth, the stuff that came before words, continues to propel us in all our future relationships. Love is physical and no one knows that better than babies. It begins from the first day we come out in the open air. From when we are tiny, love is in the holding, caressing and feeding. And forevermore love is in all of this, especially when we are ill, upset or naked and vulnerable. Love is in *how* we are touched. The quality yardstick is set very early in life.

So why are we surprised when slightly older children want to be physically close? And why are we surprised when all our lives we crave touch?

It would be odd not to.

This desire is not one-sided—parents desire their children too. Both mothers and fathers derive an intense pleasure from holding their children, hugging and kissing them, from watching them use their bodies, grow and become competent. There is a mutuality of pleasure in the cuddles and the bedtime routine of sleeping with limbs entwined. There is satisfaction and pride for the parents as they watch their tiny infant become a capable, responsive child. Because early attachments in childhood are the template for later adult relationships, parents need to be real about the desire they feel for their children, not chastise themselves for the attraction they feel towards their child and not enact it as they would with an adult. That is the key. Physical warmth is the building block for the future and this applies equally to boys and girls. Caring, emotionally responsive boys and confident, expressive girls emerge from families where their physical presence has been acknowledged as existing and as one that has an impact on their parents. Not subdued, hidden, cloaked, dissociated from, ignored, shamed or exploited.

The parent's attraction for their child is not incestuous in itself—it becomes incestuous when the parent reacts to their desire/acts on it as they would with another adult. When they treat the child's attractiveness the way they would an adult's. Then force, exploitation or power enter the picture and change/destroy the child's safety in the world, the safety to be a source of light. And they have to fear their internal glow that draws people to them. They have to learn to hide it or hate it.

Children also having desire does not mean that children who are sexually abused were asking for it. When a grandfather physically molests his 4-year-old grandchild, it is the grandfather's responsibility, not the child's. Children's desire to be physically close to the adults they love and trust is purely just that. Similar to the way adults define their own idealised, mature, sexual relationships, mutually consenting, with vulnerability and intimacy, and shared pleasure. We can see where the ideal comes from. Children do not confuse it with power, exploitation and hurt. It is the abusive adult who betrays trust, uses their power unfairly and exploits the weaker person.

It is not by chance that children end up being abused within family relationships or by a person whom the child knows and trusts. It is for the adult to know the difference between a consenting adult who is seducing them and a child who wants to be loved. The child only ever wants the latter but is fully involved in the desire, with their bodies as well, the way as children we all felt everything intensely with our entire beings.

A parent always has a reaction to their child's body, whether it is the mother as she breastfeeds her infant, parents as they watch their children sleep, watch their son grow into a strong, sinewy teenager, or not, their daughter develop curves, or not. It is never a neutral occurrence. It usually involves pleasure, but could also arouse envy in the parent and in most cases the pleasure and pride, unless it is denied and defended against, outshines the envy and anger. Anxiety is common because the parent is only too aware that their child's body is precious, beautiful and attractive to them (or not as complete as they would have wished, when children have developmental delays, chromosomal irregularities or physical ailments/ disfigurements). How we as parents respond to this anxiety has a *huge* impact on how the child experiences their body and the effect it has on their world.

These reactions, this attraction is the stuff from which the child's sense of being desirable is made. It is what they carry around with themselves for the rest of their lives. Their sense of being lovable and desirable. Attractive. Beautiful.

The Air in the Home

It all began when a dear friend and fellow psychotherapist pointed out to me that adults had little or no idea that their children were tuned into the state of their relationship/ marriage.

That whether it was going well or there were cracks in it, their children knew about it. When he said this, I found it reverberated through so many parts in me: personal, clinical and theoretical. He was right. Not always a conscious awareness but an under-the-skin kind of knowledge, the kind you have by virtue of having breathed it in every day till it becomes part of you. Knowing but not knowing about knowing.

It is true. 'I know this', I thought to myself, beyond my awareness of this as a professional who is trained to understand children's emotional worlds, I knew this in my bones as a child. At the age of twelve, I knew before I was told, that my parents would be getting a divorce. They did not know that I knew. I did not know that I knew. I also did not know that I was carrying this burden around with me every single day and that it was taking a toll on me.

There is another kind of not-knowing as well, which is more about un-knowing; the breathing it in, taking it in but working-to-deny-it kind. A bit like living with the air in Delhi that is killing us, poisoning us all slowly, imperceptibly and us knowing it but not reacting or perhaps denying it. Living as if normally. Families do that all the time about the state of their relationships.

Either way, it is safer to not know about knowing. Perhaps we are doing something like this when we as adults un-see that the parental relationship affects the emotional atmosphere of the home and that this may be having an effect on our children.

It matters to children whether their parents are happy together or not, whether there is affection between them or a silent freeze, friendship or active aggression. I think about my childhood and I know that I could sense whenever there was tension between my parents but I now ask myself, *how* did I know? I know I felt happy when I heard my mother's two gold bangles clink or when I heard her heels click-clack down the corridor as she came back home from work. There was very little overt shouting and there was no physical violence or verbal abuse between my parents, that I can remember, so what was I picking out of the air? Most of us can easily imagine that a child reacts to, is scared of and scarred by enraged adults, by violence witnessed or borne, but what of the subtleties? What do we pick up in the silence or in the spaces between them? As I look back at my childhood, at the scenes of my parents' interaction stored in my mind, I know these are visuals created by emotion and I know that I must have watched them carefully. Unknowingly I followed their eyes, their tone of voice, their ease in each other's presence, physical distance between them, laughter, smiles, touch and reactions to phone calls. This is the stuff that fills the air, like microbes or particles—perfumes it or poisons it, makes it rejuvenating or dangerous. Compound this over years and it seeps into our pores.

This is not about obvious trauma, abuse or violence that crushes the senses, things which we can identify without dispute, which is not just air, it is noxious. This is much more about the ordinary stuff that slips and slides under the door and escapes and that we don't really see. It is the sulks, the silences, the meals not eaten, the excessive smoking, the absence of touch. It is about the parent who is there all day long but where the child's experience is one of neglect in their presence; it is about repeated experiences of mis-attunement, of having a person physically present but with no connection. And we can tell when that is happening; most of us are good at knowing the difference between genuine emotional involvement and a false front.

A young woman of 21 is propelled to come and see me because her parents are considering a divorce. She tells me that she noticed years ago, before she was 12, that her father would not chat affectionately or share jokes with her mother. She had wished he would. It mattered to her that her parents were not that close to each other, she said.

It reassures children to see their parents' affection for each other.

Strange, right?

Who knew?

An eight-year-old watched her parents give each other a sideways hug at the station platform as they parted for a few months and thought 'oh good. They do love each other'. Thirty years later, she recalled that sideways hug on the station platform and imagining parting from her own husband for a few months, noted that it was a telling death knell for a marriage, given how the intervening years had unfolded, such forms of embrace being reserved for those one has conflicted feeling towards. Sideways hugs were for the slightly creepy colleague at work or the person you did not know too well, not someone you love and were going to desperately miss. Unless of course your love is conflicted by other feelings; things that eight-year-olds do not consciously know about but can feel in the air; in the space surrounding that non-hug.

Eight-year-old Kanika tells her mother 'I know that you and papa don't like each other' and seeing her mother's shocked expression, she tries to make the truth more palatable, adding 'but you don't fight *too* much' but it was too late. It was out. She had let her mother know that she, the oldest of the three children of her parents, could sense and verbalise that her parents who had been living in separate cities for three years, apparently for business and financial reasons, were in fact, not very happy together. It was a truth her mother had been avoiding, denying her feelings of anger toward her husband for his decisions which had left her alone to look after three children in a foreign country, in a city where she had no family, and where she lived in a one-bedroom flat, taking tuitions to make ends meet.

Kanika's mother is very restrained, biting her tongue, holding back her anger, ensuring she never let her husband know the truth of her feelings. In fact, she went a step further and denied that she had any feelings at all. So how did Kanika know? She could tell from the quality of the air; because our feelings leak out of us in more than just words, because absences are not empty.

One answer to the question of 'how did I/she know?' comes from the fact that children are very closely tuned into their mothers and into their mother's state of mind. This is one relationship, the first one, perhaps the only one, where wordless communication is the norm rather than the exception. Babies and mothers spend a large amount of time together and when things between them work well enough, they understand each other without words. Our earliest communication is wordless. It is in the body—in muscle tension, in facial expressions, eye contact or the lack of it and inflections in the tone of voice. As we get older, we lose the awareness of how important these subtleties are for us. We are so focused on learning to get the right vocabulary and the correct verbal communication that we vastly underestimate the power of the unspoken.[1]

Four-year-old Nayantara was sitting in the back seat of the car one afternoon when her mother was driving. It was just the two of them and while mother was physically present in the car, she was mentally preoccupied with thoughts and feelings about the state of her marriage with Nayantara's father. Specifically, she recalls, she was thinking about 'How would things work if I was to move out? What would happen to the children? How would things turn out?' All of this silently to herself, up until she heard Nayantara say, as if in response to her questions 'I will stay with you and bhai can go stay with papa.' Seemingly out of context, out of the silence of the car but fitting the noise in her head, Nayantara was connected to her mother's state of mind and responding to it.

It is September 2016. Manav walks into the 32nd session. Our work had begun a year ago with his then five-year-old daughter was having nightmares and feeling afraid of ghosts and terrorist attacks. In the first session itself, it had turned out that she was bringing her parents in for therapy, for the state of their relationship.

Today, it is just him. While describing a fight between him and his wife, he said that when his wife starts to shout, 'the windows shake and here is our six-year-old cowering under this deluge' and the cab driver valiantly pretending this is not happening in the back seat in his full view.

As he spoke, Manav became aware of so many complex, painful feelings but mainly a deep sadness in him at the sight that he and his wife were as a couple to this stranger. 'And what of their daughter?' I thought to myself. In just an hour I had come away from this session with a rawness within me. I was carrying a pain inside. An awareness that Manav's pain had been in the room, palpably present. I had not hidden the few tears that had rolled down my face as he had openly wept; at his many losses and the painful realisation that there was very little trust in his marriage. 'We trust strangers' he had said 'We get into a cab and say 'yehan le jaana', trusting that the cab driver will not drive us over a cliff, and here, she does not trust my intentions. How can we be on this journey together without trust?'

And more and more, I wondered about their daughter. She was breathing this conflict in through the air every day. I had this pain inside me after an hour of being in the room with these complex, painful feelings. She had had it around her all her life. The air was painful to breathe. These were the ghosts she had drawn, saying there were 42 of them in the room in the dark. This was why she could not sleep. She knew there were attacks, not veiled and underhand but direct, overt, violent, humiliating, degrading. These were the terrorists she was afraid of. They were in her home.

'There is no one more likely to destroy us than the person we marry.'[2] And as I was reminded, parents are often unaware of the collateral damage to the silent cowering witness who holds both these adults dear, each one alternately damaging the other.

There is also no one more likely to damage us than the persons who gave birth to us, linking us across generations with more than just our genetic matter. Sometimes unwittingly they put into the air the stuff they do not acknowledge to themselves or say in words. Sometimes directly, in a much more lethal approach, parents find that it is easier to deflect the conflict between them through and into their child. In order to keep an artificial peace between them, they say 'See? Because you wanted to buy that toy, now papa is angry with mumma', giving their child both the power and responsibility for a dynamic that, in all honesty, belongs between the adults; power and responsibility that is fake, an illusion. So now this child is not only sensitive to the dynamic between her parents but also sucked in and dumped upon by the leakage from this. When conflict becomes routed through the child, she becomes the barometer for the state of her parent's marriage and is no longer free to just be herself. She is forced to take sides, have allies and is deprived of an honest relationship with her TWO parents, with TWO opportunities for love and growth.

Twelve-year-old Yogesh wanted to remain his mother's baby, wanting to get into her lap and speak in a babble. His mother could not bear this, wanting to get away from this version of him, because it physically repulsed her. Their timing together had just not worked for her. She had not wanted him even as an embryo, let alone as a baby. Giving up her dreams and ambitions in order to look after him for a decade had been a penance. She was a good-enough mother but a depressed one and her denial of her feelings only ensured that it amplified and leaked out of her. His growing up (in size, and age at any rate) was a huge relief to her but it was as if he knew something about her truth because he refused to. This cost him his spontaneity but he had (so far) figured it was worth it. If he grew up and started doing the things she wanted him to be independent in—choose his own clothes, eat his food, make small decisions for himself, sit and read by himself or play, display his own mind—he would lose her completely.

He said he felt he was a disappointment to her. He was more right than he knew. It was his very existence that had disappointed her. It was not his fault, any more than it was hers.

He did not ask to be born. But he seemed to take responsibility for it and for her anyway. He was so keenly attuned to his mother's mood that her low mood did not just upset him, it sucked the oxygen out of his world. He did everything to make her feel better and never really succeeded. At 12, he had not even begun to know himself or live a life because he kept his eyes only on her and he existed only if he was on her mind.[3] The alternative world, one where he could have had the love and potential from two parents, something a relationship with his father could have provided him, was nowhere on his radar. His father's presence was almost irrelevant to him. He was entirely preoccupied by the air that surrounded his mother.

Nobody is to blame here. No one is judging the adults here, who were once children and who are also responding to the air/what they have in them/had around them. But the child, for whom these parents are everything, all of what the adult is saying or not saying, is worth keeping an eye on. It will inevitably sink in and become part of them. We need to know this.

Indeed, just like we don't think about the air we breathe or the very act of breathing and yet it is the very basis of life, there is so much we take in by breathing in the air in the home, which, unknown to us, forms the very core of who we turn into. We call them choices, when they may just be extensions of something we inherited or a reaction to that inheritance. We react one way or another to the air around us, whether it is to follow what our parents did or want or to do the opposite. Either way we are tied down to our origins. We are far less original than we may like to believe.

A friend recounts that as a teenager his mother had moved to Calcutta from Dhaka (during Partition) leaving her parents and her history behind. Growing up he did not really know how this affected her. As an adult, he found himself choosing to move out of mainstream corporate careers to film-making, social activism, teaching in night schools, working with streetchildren, and linking art with people's remembered histories. He now helps communities come together by linking their personal histories, collecting the stories of ordinary people living in the area.[4] which is ironic given how his own story unfolded and he discovered a part of his own unknown yet personal history.

Having already made these life choices, years after his mother's death, he discovered a collection of photographs of his mother, informing him of a part of her life that he (thought) had known nothing about (consciously). She had been a social activist and reformer working alongside people like Jai Prakash Narayan, with deep political interests in a newly independent India. When he confronted his father with a 'How come no one ever told us all this?' he received a grunt by way of a response. 'It was never ever talked about' he said, his eyes wide for emphasis. As he found out more about his mother, he was overwhelmed by how much he seemed to have unknowingly known, so much so that he had followed in his mother's footsteps.

After all, he had been breathing it in. For years.

In failing to notice the air around us, or rather, to notice that we do not notice the air that surrounds us in our growing years, we fail to see much of what connects us to others—to our parents, to the spaces we call home, the city, our neighbourhood—and how we continue to carry along and respond to the feeling-world we were born into. In other words, we fail to notice our emotional origins, instead pretending to ourselves that emotionally, we almost gave birth to ourselves. That we are 'original'.

NOTES

1. A. Mehrabian & S.R. Ferris. 1967. 'Inference of Attitudes from Nonverbal Communication in Two Channels'. *Journal of Consulting Psychology*, 31(3), pp. 248–52.
    The study described the relative importance of words, tone of voice and body language in understanding an underlying emotional message. Non-verbal communication accounts for eye contact, gestures, inflection, dress and proximity; all of these play important but subtle roles in determining our understanding of a person's meaning. Without these indicators, the totality of a person's statement is impossible to interpret. They concluded that the interpretation of a message is 7 per cent verbal, 38 per cent vocal and 55 per cent visual. The conclusion was that 93 per cent of communication is 'non-verbal' in nature.
    Adam Phillips. 2010. *The Beast in the Nursery: On Curiosity and Other Appetites*. New York: Knopf Doubleday.
2. Alain de Botton. 2017. *The Course of Love*, London: Penguin, p. 34.
3. D.W. Winnicott. 1984. 'Reparation in Respect of Mother's Organized Defence Against Depression'. In *Through Paediatrics to Psychoanalysis: Collected Papers*. London: Karnac.
4. http://www.cckonline.in/   www.jatantrust.org   http://www.fondation-langlois.org/html/e/page.php?NumPage=2070

A Good Divorce

There is no such thing, unless you are talking about the amount of money that changed hands, I thought to myself as I wrote the title of this chapter.

The divorces I have seen, and there have been a substantial number of them, have all been exercises in negative feelings—anger, bitterness, betrayal. Ex-couples who cannot bear to speak to each other, let alone see each other or be civil, are the norm. In this well-trodden, predictable though never-dull path, since there is no shortage of drama, there is rarely anything to be cheerful about.

Close friends got in touch with me the other day, quite out of the blue, saying that their marriage was over. No one on the outside really knows the truth of what is happening to a couple in a relationship, so it often feels out of the blue. Speaking to one and then the other, it struck me that a divorce is a split on many levels. There are intense feelings to choose from, judgements to make, sides to take. All readily available, lying there for the taking. And we are trained to choose between one or the other. Whose fault is it? Who is being wronged? Who deserved it? Who had it coming? Who wanted out? Then there is stuff to divide or destroy and the question of who gets what. Land, money and buildings are the ones that make the headlines but what about the stuff of everyday life? The kitchen, the books, DVDs, and the ones never mentioned: the feelings, the relationships, the people. The family, friends and children. I found myself thinking that I did not want this to become a '*batvara*' of friendship and yet, how could I know? How could I know what feelings of hurt and anger would come up and shove me around? Would I be able to keep them both in mind and not give in to a split?

So who is a divorce good for, other than the lawyers?

More than 20 years ago my parents got divorced, ending a 15-year-long marriage. My sister and I were in boarding school, at a developmental stage where blending in with peers was supremely important and neither one of us wanted to wave the 'my parents are divorced' flag. Whatever our individual emotional responses were on the subject then and have been since, we agree that our parents were paragons of restraint and cooperation when it came to their joint custody of the two of us. School events, annual days, birthdays and vacations were negotiated, attended to and attended in such a way that unless we explicitly came out and said so, our classmates could not tell that there was anything amiss with our family. It was not perfect for us of course and we have our personal traumas, but really, it could have been a lot worse, both in the way our parents behaved and in our internal worlds. But since children's (our) inner turmoil remains unseen by people around them, the impact is never evident in its complete floridity. So, to meet a child, like the one below, and gingerly be allowed into his inner world is a rare privilege and an act of courage and faith on his part, which is ironic, given his experience of adult behaviour.

Rishi was about nine years old when his class teacher referred him to the school counsellor for his inexplicable behaviour. She said that he was very reluctant to take his notebooks and work home and that he was fabricating some far-fetched excuses about his incomplete class work. A meeting was arranged with Rishi and his parents.

Rishi's father seemed to be uncomfortable speaking in front of his son or listening to him. He kept suggesting that one or the other leave the room for some time. His mother continuously gave Rishi instructions: sit up, don't put your fingers in your mouth, don't fidget. His father said he thought Rishi was low on self-esteem and did not understand why his son didn't want to share his talents and achievements with the rest of his class. He was sure Rishi had a lot going on within but that he did not want to openly share his thoughts and feelings with his parents. Although he pressed Rishi to speak in the session, giving him permission to share his thoughts with the counsellor, there was no real space for him to verbalise anything since the adults spoke continuously. The father suggested that he would feel helped if the therapist could somehow draw things out of his son and convey them to the parents.

While the father seemed to be feeling disconnected from his son, the mother communicated that she experienced a very clingy and needy version of him; that he was like a much younger child with her; she couldn't go to the bathroom without having him knocking and standing by the door; she couldn't leave him and go to the gym, for example, because he would insist on her time, attention and physical proximity. She too had noticed an increasing gap between home and school, since Rishi was not carrying books and information between the two.

The only recent significant change mentioned was that Rishi's grandmother had fallen ill and moved into their home. Rishi's mother wondered whether her divided attention was difficult for him to deal with since he was an only child. Rishi chose to remain silent throughout the session.

The very next day Rishi found the counsellor in her office and blurted out very quickly that his parents were getting a divorce and that neither of them had wanted to say anything about it in the meeting. However, when they had returned home, Rishi's father had told him that it was okay for him to speak to the counsellor. As a result he may have felt that it was up to him to tell the counsellor the truth. That if he didn't, no one else would. At least now he had permission.

The counsellor agreed to meet his parents once more to discuss how they could help him. Almost a month passed in trying to do so. Eventually, the parents acknowledged the truth of their son's account and over email gave their consent for him to see the therapist once a week.

In his first session Rishi was overwhelmed and uncontainable. Unlike other nine-year-olds, he was not interested in exploring the room and its contents at all. He launched into his narrative, which was distressing to hear, speaking of how lonesome and torn he felt in the middle of this separation. He described himself as an 'overflowing bowl of milk' where his parents kept pouring their own worries into him without noticing that it was spilling all over and how he could not hold it in any longer.

Rishi used his weekly session to unburden himself and to have his complex, painful feelings acknowledged. He wanted to know if his therapist could sense the awkwardness between his parents. He said he felt saddled with the 'unnecessary' details of his parents' dispute. He spoke of the agonising choice of having to pick between his parents and, worst of all, failing to find any reliable adult in his family who could help him in this situation.

It become clear that Rishi's parents had not told their respective families about the decision to separate and were therefore not ready for anyone else to know either. As a result, the child felt a strong sense of guilt in divulging the details of his family life to his therapist, yet expressed great relief from time to time to have a listening ear and to be able to share what was really on his mind. While his parents were preoccupied with their own lives and their parents' health, Rishi was left feeling like there is no space for his very fragile and vulnerable parts. With two ill grandparents there was no space for yet another one who needed mind space. He was trying to take responsibility for his own schoolwork but often struggled with it. 'How can I manage all of this?' he often asked. One morning, he described how his father slapped him for not completing his work. Angry at his father and sad for himself, Rishi earnestly wondered out loud how his father expected him to concentrate on his school work at a time like this.

Although this child was given some explanations from time to time for the upheaval in the home, there was no real space for him to communicate and work through his own inner turmoil. What Rishi experienced in his daily life at home was an uncontainable weepy mother, a practical and strict father and extremely anxious or ill grandparents. Through this the adults expected him to somehow continue as 'normal', as if *his* inner turmoil had no consequence in the outside world.

This is the average divorce story, from the child's perspective I suspect. Give or take a bit. Rishi's counsellor and I were just extremely privileged to hear it first-hand. I did not think it could ever be substantially different for a child, till I met G and M.

G and M came to see me for the first time about a year ago. Although they had been friends for a long time before getting married, they felt the marriage was no longer working. They had been seeing a psychotherapist to help them with their difficulties as a couple but for various reasons had decided that they could no longer remain married to each other. However, they had a six-year-old child and they were aware that just as they had been helped to be thoughtful about splitting up, they needed to help him.

In my first meeting with them, I found the couple, or not, as the case now was, to be struggling less with what they were going to say to their son and more with how they were going to break this news to their parents. Theirs had been a marriage across states, languages and cultures and I got the sense that their respective parents had been somewhat tight-lipped and sombre-faced about it to begin with. I got the impression that both G and M felt more ill at ease and squirmy facing their own parents than anything else. The mother had tears in her eyes as I pointed this out and the father, who clearly used humour as a way of covering up his pain, laughed as if laughing at himself, his parents and their predicament. I referred them to a colleague who was nearer where they lived so that in case their child really hit it off with the concept and person of the psychotherapist, it would be easier for them to make multiple trips.

I heard from them a year later. G and M had definitely split but the father was staying in the same apartment complex in the building opposite so that their son had time to adapt, if there is any such thing from the child's perspective, to the new arrangement. This time they came to see me as parents, not as a couple going their separate ways. They were clear that they both wanted to remain parents to their son and they wanted to work hard to keep that bond. Today was about 'How do we divide time?' and 'How do we react when he sees us together and looks hopeful that we are going to get back together as a family?' Father went over for bedtimes on occasion, to read his son a bedtime story and had his son over for the weekend regularly. We spoke about how a seven-year-old boy really needs his father, what his father can mean for him and areas that mother does not manage to get to. Mother agreed when I wondered out loud whether their son was protective of her and holding back expressing his own feelings. Father had noticed that like him, his son had begun to brush away painful subjects by laughing over them. The boy, it seemed, was getting a lot of practice at covering up his hurt feelings.

G and M are remarkably attentive and perceptive parents. So far, they have achieved something extraordinary, deconstructing their roles as spouse and parent. They were disregarding the convention of 'thou shalt hate thy ex-spouse' and attempting to remain cordial, even friendly, enough to keep communication lines open. Their parents, I was told, were not able to make this jump and could not understand it. According to them, you were either together as a couple, or not. There was no in between. This is the typical social reaction to a divorce but what then of the one person who does not see it that way? The one person who feels torn within: rejected, forgotten and most often, irrational as it may seem to us adults, responsible?

Most divorcing parents do not manage to notice, let alone spare, their children the anguish of being split in two. I recall a 13-year-old saying 'I feel like I am Kashmir'. I filled in the rest of his thought, about how India and Pakistan were trying to pull him in different directions. Another child, a 12-year-old, could speak to his mother in terms of politics and ask her 'why do countries have to split up?' referring to his family but could not bring himself to directly talk about his feelings. Children, of all ages, feel like they are being forced to make a choice in such a situation. My work is often as simple, and as complex, as helping parents acknowledge that the child is not the one being divorced, that the child wants a relationship with both parents for as long as they are alive. That they will remain parents forever. You can un-marry but not un-born your child.

The task for these parents is to find a way to remain father and mother and not get it entangled with the anger, envy and active hatred for their ex-partners. That their disappointment, betrayal and hurt are separate from the relationship that the daughter or son has with them. This is extremely difficult because often the presence of the child is a direct and potent reminder of the presence of the ex-partner in the world since the child was a joint creation. The hated, disappointing, betraying ex-spouse is not part of a history that can be erased. As a result, the child often becomes a pawn for one parent to prove that the other is unreliable, disinterested, amoral or otherwise useless.

Children can also blame themselves for a divorce, especially if they are under the age of 10. It is an unavoidable consequence of their stage of mental development, that they can only see the world from their own perspective and therefore see themselves as the centre of the universe. Add to this an often punitive conscience and the result is a personal theory that mummy and papa would still be together if the child had been 'good', though what exactly that means is a mystery. On the whole it boils down to 'It is my fault' and 'I should have done something'. The post-divorce child who is going off the rails and getting aggressive with mother, father or peers or the one who is retreating into a shell or crying themselves to sleep, are often struggling with the ordinary messy feelings of hurt, anger and guilt, one acting out 'badness' and the other suffering from guilt. Since our feelings are never neatly arranged and certainly do not come in one at a time, messiness is a guarantee and children may also feel forgotten and not kept in mind by parents who are preoccupied by this huge change in their lives.

The task for the child of divorcing parents is to acknowledge, often prematurely for their cognitive and emotional stage, that their parents are not perfect, which they aren't of course, and in fact, that they may have serious flaws but that they are still loved and it is worth preserving a relationship with them both. Most of us are lucky if we can become conscious of this by the time we are 30 years old. Young girls, especially, can sound terrifically sensible, even wise for their age, fooling everyone with their outward composure. Sure, intellectually they get it but often there is an emotional cost of being cut off from their own pain and from themselves so that they are shells of their former selves, stunted and afraid to really love again.

Most divorcing couples, and other adults in the family, have a way of displaying their vulnerabilities and incapacity to tolerate anger, their lack of boundaries about what is adult conversation and lack of awareness about what a child needs to be exposed to, in a way that is overwhelming to their children. A 17-year-old was very angry that his mother told him details about the unfulfilled sexual life she shared with his father. He was very clear that he did not want 'to have these images' in his head. 'I am her son, not her partner' he shouted. A 12-year-old told me repeatedly that he was very upset that his father spent hours on the phone with his relatives, complaining loudly about his ex-wife. His son did not want to be witness to that; he did not want to be part of his father's anger toward his mother. He wished he could be spared at least that.

A 13-year-old was furious with her grandmother who had been grieving out loud and crying for months about her son and daughter-in-law getting a divorce after almost 15 years of marriage. For the young girl, her grandmother's reaction was salt on her wounds. She could have used her grandmother's affection and understanding and perhaps an expression of their shared grief could have followed. Instead, the grandmother's reaction was experienced as so 'over the top' that the girl felt she had no space to air her own. She felt dropped from the minds of the adults in the family who were absorbed in themselves. Who would listen to her if they were so busy falling apart? So busy with their own feelings? So she just kept quiet about both, her loss and her anger till she found a psychotherapist more than 10 years later.

G and M are working on something I have rarely come across, to live apart but to actively keep their minds together for their son. So far, they were getting themselves a good divorce.

Opinion

I believe, or perhaps I like to believe, that people have asked me my opinion on this question; perhaps no one has actually asked me and it is all in my head; perhaps I am talking to myself but the question that comes up is – "Should we stay together for the children?"

Children have very sensitive radar and they always know when there is trouble between their parents. They pick up the nuances of tone of voice and choice of words, as well as silences and eye contact and avoided gaze. They add two and two and often make six. When there is tension between parents, the strain becomes part of the air the children breathe. The strain or tension becomes the environment the children's emotional, relational and physical systems adapt to or respond to. Unfortunately, it is an environment where they have to be on alert (in case there are raised voices, verbal abuse, sarcasm, physical violence, humiliation or silence and avoidance), their baseline response becomes what for a human body is actually a hyper-vigilant state. These changes take place at the level of the quantities of hormones in the body and neuro-transmitters released in the child's brain. Depending on how early the home environment was stressful and for how long, this hyper-vigilant state becomes part of the wiring in the child's brain. Changing these at a later age therefore becomes exceedingly difficult.

When a couple persists in a marriage 'for the children' while everyone knows they are unhappy, the children have a unique problem. Their radar works accurately, but the message they get from the family in words, contradicts their internal-radar. Because we humans are wired to want to believe our parents, we learn to deny our internal truth and just go with 'everything is fine'. What then becomes warped is our idea of what 'fine' feels like.

Unwittingly, we humans tend to move toward recreating what we were familiar with in childhood, – what we call comfort food, are usually the foods from our childhood, what we associate with affection and safety; we do the same with relationships. It is for this reason that children who are bullied turn into bullies, children from abusive families will either turn into abusers or get themselves into other abusive relationships. Unknowingly, unwittingly we end up recreating the familiar patterns of our childhood with some minor variation in the power dynamics of the cast.

Even if it turns out that this is a conversation in my head and even if no one really takes advice, here is my opinion: It is better to know a bad/failing relationship and call a spade a spade, than to grow up with lies – of which there are two kinds:

1. "The marriage is not working for us but we are staying together for the children"

    Have you asked them? If you have not, then this does not apply. The children have an opinion, even the young ones.

2. "Things are bad in the marriage but the children are protected because they don't know/see/hear about it."

    This is simply not true. Children are remarkably attuned to reality but they may be too afraid to speak to adults who don't want them to know the truth or desperate to believe the parents they love. Such lies enter relationships in the future. When a child has grown up denying their internal information providing radar (because acknowledging it is too painful or frightening), they take that malfunctioning/shut-down/self-doubting radar to their own life, their relationship to authority, at work, to their romantic lives, to their own children. It becomes inter-generational and in my clinical experience that is a very high price to pay.

Children who grow up with their parents having separated, may not know what a healthy working marital relationship looks like but they certainly know what a bad one looks like. That is a good-enough place to start.

Permission to Cry

'It is strange but true that people do need to be reminded that feelings matter. Our feelings are so much a part of us, and yet when it comes to the feelings of others we easily clock off, and pretend that all is well....Worst is the tendency we can find in ourselves to deny the fact of sadness or grief in others, to pretend to ourselves that things are all right really.

Perhaps we can be forgiven. We carry around with us, each of us to some degree, much sadness and confusion and even hopelessness, and we can only manage to get up in the morning and do our work on the basis of putting serious things aside....'[1]

We all defend ourselves from grief, our own and that of others. Even though, when shared, it has the capacity to strengthen relationships, it is what isolates us and creates walls between people, so we end up being lonely with our own sadness instead of together in it.

Children cry. Adults cry. But we learn not to as we get older, mainly because of the effect it has on significant others around us. They are embarrassed, don't know where to look or how to react or it irritates them or upsets them too and they want to cry. Slowly and systematically, crying, an expression of grief, frustration, anxiety, fear, anger or all of the above, becomes so loaded with 'What will others think?' or 'What will my mother feel?', that it is buried.

It has an early start, this practice and is repeated often enough for it to become an immovable structure within us. It is very common to see crying babies being jigged out of their sadness, distracted by flying birds or toys, food or smartphone screens, all because it distresses the care-giving adult, whether parent, nanny or other. Tiny nursery-going three-year-olds being told to stop being babies, to be 'a big boy/girl' and never mind that Mummy is leaving them with a stranger for what feels like forever and they are scared in this new overwhelming place. Children of all ages being told to not cry over scraped knees and bruised elbows and trained to dismiss their own pain, physical and otherwise.

How difficult it is for us as carers to bear the distress of the small person we are looking after and allow them the chance to feel their own feelings; because our distress is too much, because we feel their distress within us and because it reactivates our own early upsets, we clamp down on it all. Denied the chance to have a complete experience,[2] for an expression of sadness actually can lead to a spontaneous recovery, but few would wait long enough to discover that; from childhood onwards we begin to experience our feelings as dangerous and as something that others, especially adults, need to be protected from.

But this self-and-other protective-armour-building strategy often backfires.

'It is especially easy for us to belittle the effect of loss on the young. Young people are so distractible, and life comes bubbling up whether they like it or not. But loss of parent, or friend, or pet, or special toy, may take away the whole point of living, so that what we mistake for life is the child's enemy, a lifeline that deceives everyone except the child.'[3]

Twenty-one-year-old Reena came in to see me, exhausted, under-slept, unable to eat and unable to keep herself from crying. She explained that her long-time best friend and boyfriend had lost interest in her and she was devastated. It had been a few months but all she wanted was to get back with him and imagined that she would be happy ever after, that it could happen, if only she hoped hard enough. She found herself stalking him on social media, and though she was not proud of it, she really felt an intense need to believe that he still held her in his mind. That was enough to fuel her hopes of a shared future together.

The protracted length of time over which she had sustained an intense reaction to the loss of this relationship made me wonder what was fuelling it. I asked about previous losses and it turned out that Reena had suffered a series of sudden, traumatic losses from early childhood. Her father died in a car crash when she was five years old. This was followed by the loss of a grandparent. Soon after, a school friend drowned while on holiday and later as a teen, yet another friend died in more mysterious and tragic circumstances. Through all these losses, Reena had kept it together, starting with bearing the loss of her father with outward calm and inner turmoil. She recalled sitting on the top of the steps when her father was preparing to leave the house with a friend that night, and wishing that he would stay. With the particular combination of magical and concrete pre-operational thinking[4] that young children specialise in, five-year-old Reena had convinced herself that somehow she was responsible for the events which unfolded that night, even though the exact facts have been shrouded in secrecy for over 15 years, perhaps in order to protect people, relationships and money. She believed that she should have asked her father to stay, thrown a tantrum, done something. Anything. That wonderfully, the little girl at the top of the steps could have prevented him from leaving home that night, if only she had tried hard enough.

Trying hard was a bit of a theme in Reena's life. She was

constantly trying hard to not acknowledge her own feelings and constantly giving precedence to other people's opinions and feelings. She lived with the 'tyranny of the shoulds',[5] forever judging herself by the standards set by 'them'. As a result she constantly felt worthless, demotivated and unloved.

Over the next year, she talked about how she had in fact been burying all her feelings after losing her father. Sadness was not permitted; anger, which she felt toward him for abandoning her, was taboo; joy led to severe, self-punishing guilt. There was no way to be herself. All feelings were burdensome. After her father's sudden, traumatic death, in a way she had lost her mother too—to grief and to an overwhelming paralysing sense of responsibility of having to bring up two little girls by herself. She clearly recalls being taken out for a drive by an uncle and not being permitted to attend the prayer meeting that was being held for her father. However, she can also recall having had a sense that there was something big going on but not having a clear idea what it was. She recalls being asked by her aunt to not be sad, to be brave for her mother. So that is what she did. Between self-blame and a desire to protect the shadowy remains of the one parent she had left, Reena swallowed her feelings and went into her own lonely place. 'There was a tile in the bathroom that had a shape on it that looked like a face and I would talk to that face', she said. It was the only face, a ceramic, one-dimensional, unresponsive—unmoved and unmoving—face that she would allow herself to speak to about her feelings.

As she spoke, the loneliness and intense sadness was palpable in the room. It hung in the air around us and I found myself with tears in my eyes. With tears in her own eyes, where for once she was focusing on her own feelings and not protecting another, she only noticed mine when I moved to wipe them away and in a shocked tone said, 'Are you crying?' Trying to be as matter-of-fact as possible, I replied saying that it was very sad, that I was crying for the lonely and sad little girl she had been and still carried within her. Reena said that she too felt very sad for that little girl inside her and cried for several minutes. In fact, she cried for the entire year. All the uncried tears she had held within her for 15 years. She expressed genuine surprise that someone else was crying for her, as if it was difficult for her to imagine her grief being taken seriously. Yet, this very 'being taken seriously' gave her the permission to cry.

After a few months of work together, Reena told me of a bookshelf in her living room which held the family photographs that included her father. For years, she said, she had avoided looking at the photographs and bookshelf, in fact that entire section of the room. This was a preamble to letting me know that not only had she approached that section of the living room, she had also been looking at pictures of her father, of her parents as a couple and of them as a young family. It had been extremely difficult for her to do so and she had spent days crying over what she had lost and would never get back.

Noticing the toys in my consulting room she expressed surprise that I see young children. 'Parents bring their small kids?' she asked.

'You would like to have someone to talk to as a kid', I replied, linking the question back to her, doing my work as the meticulous (and also caricatured) psychotherapist.

She nodded.

Painfully, she acknowledged that as a child she had gone un-noticed; that in her photos from age six onwards she looks like an '*ujra hua baccha*', switching to Hindi in an otherwise English conversation and using an adjective usually used to describe land—a barren, desolate, impoverished child. She wishes her mother would notice her pain for itself, without guilt, without defensiveness, without mixing it with her own sorrow. She says to me:

It is strange to know that there is something that would never ever change.

Whatever amount of feelings I would have nothing will ever get him back.

He wasn't here to see me grow up, and he'd never ever see me grow up.

He'll not see me make a decision like settling for a man, or I won't get them to meet.

Never.

I will never have him to accept or reject, or discuss, or just know him.

And I can't even tell myself or remind myself about this unchangeable absence because I don't want sympathy from even myself. But I also need someone to hear that, and not tell me how Ma has played both roles and that I should be happy that she is there. I am thankful about that, but that won't change the missing part....

It will always be missing.

For Reena, her father's loss is what Stephen Grosz calls a 'living grief'.[6] She wrote the passage above seven months into our work together. After more than 18 months of work, she continues to acknowledge and live her grief over her loss. Ironically, it gives her the space to also appreciate what she does have. Though dealing with the usual uncertainties that come with being 21—of choice of career, partner, identity, relationship with parent—she will herself say that she is stronger than she was a year ago and mostly because she was given the permission to cry.

'When we find a child unhappy and withdrawn we can surely do more by a sympathetic holding operation than by jogging the child into a state of false liveliness and forgetfulness. If we stand by and wait and wait we shall often be rewarded by real changes in the child that indicate a natural tendency to recover from loss, and from the sense of guilt that the child feels even when it can truly be said that the child did not contribute to the tragic happening.'[7]

Fifteen years too late, Reena and I were doing exactly this together.

If a child had been physically hurt and lay bleeding steadily on the floor, would we stand about watching? Would we leave the child there and gently tiptoe around the blood and the child, lest we disturb the process? Would we politely request the child to bleed elsewhere so as to not soil the carpet, because 'you know my dear, then it creates a lot of work for us, cleaning up the mess, and all that... I am sure you understand, you are such a good little one who loves your family, we know you don't mean to soil the carpet with your blood and pain, so please do it elsewhere'. Would we pretend that the injury never happened? Would we ignore the child lying there and never talk about it?

This is exactly what happened with six-year-old Tia whose father died during a heart operation. She had not been told that he was going for a surgery. She sat in her room waiting for him to return. In the days and weeks after his non-return, she remembers 'politely' being told by an aunt to not cry because it would upset her mother. Blood on the carpet; too messy; too much work for the adults.

What is most moving is the reality that little children actually comply with this request. They do move out of the way. They do it out of love for the surviving parent and for the rest of the family. They take their pain elsewhere or swallow it, bleed somewhere else or bleed internally.

The blood = emotional pain analogy may sound ridiculously far-fetched to some but it is a well-acknowledged truth that when emotional pain is not addressed as emotional, it becomes lodged in the body; it becomes embedded in us at the level of biochemistry; stress hormones, endocrine changes—whatever terminology we prefer.[8] Grief changes us from within. And when it happens early, there is structural damage during construction.

At 21 years of age, Reena had suffered a lot of damage already. In our attempts to hide our feelings from view, we forget that our inner worlds are both mind and body. That which begins as emotional, if not attended to in the world of feelings, will make its presence felt in more concrete ways, in the body. It tends to become somatic (i.e., in the body) and then will be harder to ignore. Reena developed an auto-immune disorder that affected her endocrine system and led to hypothyroidism, the symptoms of which are often strikingly similar to depression. Thirty years later, Tia was diagnosed with hypothyroidism, after struggling with low energy, depression and mucus membrane sensitivity (allergies) and weight gain. So many years later, the knot of emotions, which are now housed in the body, become extremely difficult to unpick. How does one untangle this knot? Which thread do we pull first?

Recent research[9] has further underlined the central defining nature of parental loss on children under the age of 18 and how the effects persist into adulthood. On the list of most damaging effects, are the following:

- discontinuity (or continuity that does not meet the child's needs). After the death of a parent, the child's life often changes; whether it is school and peer networks, financial security, emotional availability of the surviving parent and family connections;
- a lack of appropriate social support for both the child and surviving parent; and
- a failure to provide clear and honest information at appropriate time points relevant to the child's level of

understanding. This gap in communication with children leaves them scared and wondering if they could have saved their parent. Magic and wishing takes over because reality is so painful and included in the failed magic is the punishment for having failed.

Adults often look back at the suffering of their child selves in poignant detail, making it clear that the pain of losing a parent in childhood was still fresh and etched into their memory. In this research they were clear that these missing ingredients had a negative impact on them for all their following years by affecting trust, relationships, self-esteem, feeling of self-worth, and the ability to express feelings.

What grieving kids value is normal kid activities with people who understand that they are struggling, by receiving attention from loved ones and friends who encourage them to talk about their feelings. Looking at old photos and videos together with the surviving family, listening to their favourite music and writing down memories of their parents in journals may be more valuable to some kids than talking to therapists.[10]

As I write this, I recall how 10-year-old Surajit refused to enter my consulting room where his mother was trying to get him to express his feelings, months after his father had died of cancer. He sat in the car and refused to come out, saying he was fine and playing video games instead. 'Fine' was far from the truth; he had been hiding his emotions (the video games were not helping), and the strain was beginning to tell. He had admitted to his mother that he was seeing things that other kids in school could not see. In other words, he was hallucinating.

In a way it was true. He had had experiences others had not had and he could not bring himself to share them. He had seen things others had not and his inner world was leaking out of him despite his desperate attempts at control.

He never did come into the room.

NOTES

1. D.W. Winnicott. 1968. 'The Effect of Loss on the Young'. In R. Shepherd, J. Johns & H.T. Robinson (eds), *Thinking About Children* (1996). London: Karnac, p. 46.
2. Ibid.
3. Ibid., p. 47; also see Oliver Jeffers. 2010. *Heart in a Bottle.* New York: Philomel Books.
4. J. Piaget. 1971. 'The Theory of Stages in Cognitive Development'. In D.R. Green, M.P. Ford, & G.B. Flamer. *Measurement and Piaget.* New York: McGraw-Hill.
5. Karen Horney. 1950. *Neurosis and Human Growth: The Struggle Toward Self-Realization.* New York: W. W. Norton & Company, Inc. (1991 edition).
6. Stephen Grosz. 2013. *The Examined Life: How we Lose and Find Ourselves.* New York: Norton.
7. D.W. Winnicott. 1968. 'The Effect of Loss on the Young', p. 47.
8. S. Gerhardt. 2003. *Why Love Matters: How Affection Shapes a Baby's Brain.* London: Routledge.
9. Jackie Ellis, Chris Dowrick, Mari Lloyd-Williams. 2013. 'The Long-Term Impact of Early Parental Death: Lessons from a Narrative Study'. *Journal of the Royal Society of Medicine*, 06: 57–67. DOI 10.1177/0141076812472623
10. J. Zaslow. 2010. 'Families with a Missing Piece. A New Look at How a Parent's Early Death Can Reverberate Decades Later'. *Wall Street Journal.* http://www.wsj.com/articles/SB10001424 05274870487560457528040059625 7236
    Also see www.Hellogrief.org for more information on children coping with grief.

Take Care of Yourself

A young person of 16 came in one day and immediately
winced while sitting. I asked about his leg, which had been
bothering him the previous week as well. He said it did not
matter.

I repeated his words to him as a question: the pain does not
matter?

I am used to it, he said, dismissing his pain.

Not letting him dismiss my line of questioning and not
colluding in his neglect of himself, I brought to his notice that
he had dismissed his pain as unimportant and I wondered if
by doing this repeatedly he may be causing his body more
harm. After all, pain in our bodies has a purpose. It alerts us
to the fact that something is wrong. Or at the very least, that
something is happening.[1]

I could see he was having trouble with this conversation,
becoming visibly anxious; hands were wrung, a leg jigged and
shoulders stiffened.

I asked what would make his leg more comfortable.

'Being able to put it up,' he said

'So which piece of furniture in this room would be useful to
you to make your leg more comfortable?' I asked.

'That chair,' he said, pointing.

'So, what do you need to do next?'

'I need to ask you for that chair.'

I was aware of his anxiety rising as I pushed him to go out of his comfort zone of neglect and dismissal. I remained silent but I raised my eyebrows and nodded, as if to give permission and simultaneously ask a question.

He finally asked me for the chair for his leg.

'Thank you', he said as I brought it over.

'You are welcome.'

We had gone through that slowly, deliberately, and for him, painfully. It was painful for him to acknowledge his own needs and more so to ask for them to be fulfilled. It was worse than bearing the physical pain in his leg. The pain, he was 'used to' but the discomfort of experiencing his need was far greater. Asking for help, he said, felt like he was being 'high maintenance' and a burden to me. Dismissing his own needs was a well-practised pattern of how he treated himself.

During that same conversation I could see that his mouth was getting dry, another sign of anxiety, but he did not ask for water. However, when I asked if he would like water, he said yes he would, and added that he would not have asked for it. He felt embarrassed to do so. In an interesting way he was turning me into the maternal figure who would know his needs without his needing to say so. (Not a good recipe for an adult relationship but then this was psychotherapy, an essentially asymmetrical situation. And anyway, this is a path we all need to tread before we can do it for ourselves. We need to have an experience of having been attended to before we can learn to attend to ourselves[2]). He recalled that he had not asked his previous therapist for water. Ever. Over six years, even though the bottle would be next to him and he would be thirsty since he went for his session after school. All he had to do was to help himself.

Often he does not eat even when hungry, he told me. He

does not sleep because he tells himself that he should not need to. He neglects pains in his body and tells himself that it does not matter.

He really did not know how to take care of himself.

Then again, he did drink four glasses of water in that hour.

We had made a start.

'He is just being a wus'[3]; or he is just lazy, some may say, but this is not about being weak or having no will power. For a body or psyche that is battered, survival depends on developing a thick skin, a kind of defence mechanism; letting hurt wash over them, ignoring pain[4]—as we saw in this young man. We get programmed very early on, in the first few years of our lives, in what to expect from our relationships, how to treat ourselves and how to respond to stress. Our responses to new stuff/scary stuff, threats/challenges, separations and other anxieties become hardwired in our bodies through the workings of the autonomic nervous system.[5] It becomes our wiring, and changing this wiring is very hard work.

Thinking and feeling are the two manifestations of this wiring that psychological interventions focus on but it is not enough because we are not separate minds and bodies, as Cartesian dualism would have us believe (well-educated, well-read intellectuals are the largest group of people suffering from the implications of this philosophical mirror-trick). Our minds and bodies entwine in ways that science has not really looked at or has preferred to ignore because it does not make as much money as the standard practice of giving pharmacological drugs. After all, which drug company wants to fund research on people getting better by themselves and using fewer drugs?

Most of us treat our bodies as taxis for our heads. To take

us around, where the 'us' is the thinking, searching, analytic, interpreting, sense-making mind. Thinking, is what we do in the absence of what we need. So if we were to 'catch our (own) drift' it may help us know what we really need. Where do we go off to in our heads? What thoughts, activities or day dreams occupy us? When we live in our heads, we are living the life that we are not living.[6] 'Thought is what makes frustration bearable, and frustration makes thought possible'.[7] Thinking fills the gulf between wanting and actually doing something about it. It is the link, the bridge and not an end in itself. Not a day-dream. Thinking is a means to modify the reality of feeling frustrated, to figuring out what we are going to do about it, and doing it. It is in the region of *doing* that taking care of ourselves lives. But for many of us, this journey to the other end of the bridge, to the region of doing, is fraught with obstacles; with conflicting thoughts that battle and where eventually the rest of us, our bodies and relationships, lose.

Don't get me wrong, I am all for thinking; thinking is great but it is not everything. Our feelings are not just words, they have a complete, complex, physiological retinue attached. Fear, love, anger, excitement do different things to us internally, chemically and repeated over years, they create furrows in the substrate of our bodies through which our emotional responses tend to flow. The effects of chronic stress, such as a bad early attachment relationship or early loss, make for a good example. Cortisol, along with adrenaline and other hormones instruct our emergency response system—the fight-or-flight reaction—to kick in. Evolutionarily speaking, this emergency response evolved as a response to physical injury, predator attack exhaustion or starvation but in today's world, we are more likely to be emotionally attacked by people in our family than physically by wild animals. Psychological traumas too trigger the fight-or-flight reaction. Our bodies become alert as soon as we see, smell, hear or *even imagine* a threat. Unlike other animals, our sophisticated brain lets us learn from mistakes and plan ahead and therefore by the same mechanism, also helps us worry about threats and problems when they are not actually there. This is why zebras don't get ulcers and we do.[8] During fight-or-flight reactions, our bodies ready the heart, the blood sugar levels and the immune system. When the stressful event is over, levels of these hormones quickly return to normal. When the threats are perceived to be continuous, like an absent or frightening parent or a dangerous neighbourhood, cortisol is released into the bloodstream all the time. This has an effect on our blood pressure, blood sugar levels and immune system, to say the least. It is, we are, an incredibly complex system and we are nowhere near understanding the nuances of how we function. Putting stress into words has been found to be an effective way of coping with it in many circumstances[9]—but this is not an option for a small child and with nowhere else to go, it goes into the body.

For much of my life, I have been this person, living in my head, retreating either from the unpredictability and harshness of people on the outside or their predictable absence, thinking a lot and doing a lot to avoid feeling. I was small-built, quiet, shy and uncertain of myself, which also made me undemanding, restrained and self-effacing. Not a good recipe for valuing myself. I could make do with little—food, water, company and attention. I read, I day-dreamed, I could spend time by myself but quietly I suffered; anxiety, for as far back as I can remember, was constant. It affected me inside-out—gut-wrenching, stomach-churning, immunity-killing, breath-stifling, word-erasing, self-throttling anxiety. As an adult, I read, I wrote, I worked hard and designed myself a mind and an effective manic-defence. I had an exterior that often appeared calm, collected, even wise, though sometimes cold and aloof and occasionally frazzled. I was resourceful, productive and very competent but only I knew how doubt and anxiety drove that. Having been forged out of pain, resourcefulness is exacting, harsh on self and other. Born out of frustration, resourcefulness and productivity are more grit and less love. It is the phoenix out of the fire. It is a fortitude that emerges from a resistance to collapse and it is ironic, since resistance is not freeing. It binds us to that which we are fighting. It is still not about spontaneity, creativity, and growth for ourselves. It is still about the other or about that-which-was-not-optimal. This resourcefulness and resilience are also neglectful in some ways. To forgive those who looked after us, less-than-optimally, we make our wants into wishes and begin to treat ourselves as we were treated, with less-than-optimal gentleness. It is a gift of love to our parents, that at best, we treat ourselves as they treated us and 'at worst, we hate our needs'.[10]

There are always pressures that take parents' attention away from their children's needs, money being one. Vivek's mother worked as a nanny looking after the children of a rich family. His own family adored him and his mother felt awfully guilty that she could not be with him more. When he was a few months old, she started taking him to work with her, keeping him in another room, a basement, away from her employers and from her work. She would come in regularly to feed him and that was that. Temperamentally, he was a peaceful, undemanding baby, who trusted his mother to come and feed him. But he had to wait, a lot. He waited to have his diaper changed. He waited to be held, he waited for some company and stimulation, conversation. In his inner world, it became a struggle between the will to live and the pull of death; to collapse from neglect or to fill something of his own into that emptiness. His solution was to enliven dead things; to play with toys that *he* could move, something *he* could control. Seen from the outside, he continued to be peaceful and got very good at waiting; at making his needs wait while he played by himself with his toys, for hours. On the inside, he was battling a deathly emptiness;

in order to survive, he made time meaningless. It was his way to control it; to bear its slow, painful passage and eventually to preserve his love for his mother.[11]

As a young man, Vivek was obsessed with vehicles of all kinds—bikes, cars, airplanes; he had trained as a mechanical engineer and would spend hours with his machines, recreating his early years, now with bigger toys that he could understand and control. Under a car, time ceased to matter, the way he had trained himself to deal with time; he would not remember commitments he had made to other people (flatmates, friends, even his wife)—they could wait. Or the need for food, water, toilette, warmth or rest—that could wait too. Waiting was familiar to him and he recreated it in all his relationships, including the one to himself. Our solutions often do tell us a lot about what our problems are.[12]

This is the truth about our early relationships. They are our blueprints. We treat others and ourselves the way we were treated as children. All Unknowingly. All because it feels familiar. It is what we know. Good for us or not rarely enters the picture.

We are tempted to be self-satisfying, emotionally self-sustaining, to live in our minds but these fantasies are never satisfying because the 'only satisfactions available are the satisfactions of reality'.[13] An early shock is the realisation that we are not self-sustaining. We need others. Whether it is the milkman, delivery boy, cook, maid or friends, siblings, parents, teachers, guides. We need help to get something for ourselves, be it food, hugs or hand-holding. This adds another layer of complexity to the 'take care of yourself' project, our relationship to help. What do we feel about asking others to help us? To do so is to admit to being incomplete, to admit that we have needs that others are or are not meeting; that we need to depend on another. For many of us, turning off the need itself is preferable, less painful than emotionally connecting with another. Fighting our need to emotionally depend on another is often at the core of many interpersonal difficulties, and the conflict can begin very early in life when we are at our most dependent and when denying need or denying dependence seemed like a good solution to the problem of frustration.

Getting to know our needs and ourselves takes till about age 30, and a range of relationships, which are, if we are lucky, honest and internally watchful. Mostly there is so much noise around us—from the media, from our relationships and from the expectations of loved ones that it is hard to hear our own voice and to hear the answer. We could call this game 'Whose need is it anyway?' It can begin very early, even as early as babies being given the message that they are in the world to love mother, not the other way around; or babies being treated like they don't really deserve to have their needs attended to.[14] 'I exist to fulfil your needs, so I don't ever really know my own. I am very good at knowing yours and I live convinced, if I am lucky, that that is good enough for me.' This is an epidemic among our women[15] who often do not own their own soul.

'Take Care of yourself' entails listening to our internal messaging system and responding to it. Which, in turn, is only possible if we are aware of our needs—for food, rest, water, affection, companionship, stimulation, silence and who knows what else. It sounds straightforward enough. This simple 'Bye! Take care!' (hug & kiss) that we all enact as a routine parting endearment, we don't really know how nuanced and complex it is till it starts to fall apart. The capacity to take care of ourselves is truly tested when we are living alone. That is when we really discover whether we have the capacity to do so or not and what we need in order to look after ourselves. Most of us would only come upon this situation if we are studying or working in a city away from home, living with flatmates or by ourselves and for many young people this is one of the most difficult life-transitions to make, from being looked after (or not) to looking after themselves.

A year and a half later, the same young person, now 18, sits in front of me, helping himself to water from the bottle lying next to him. I smile to myself, noticing how much he has changed over this time. He has learnt a lot about his physical needs and now can go beyond them and consider his needs for friendship, affection, a father figure to look up to; his need for inspiration, for something to apply himself to; for a future ambition. It is as if once he could believe that he deserved better, he discovered so many unfulfilled needs and along with those, the pain of knowing that those nearest to him had neglected him.

Today, he feels stuck. It is the week before his exams and a paralysing anxiety he is only too familiar with, is welling up in him, creating an insurmountable wall. The only way to shrink the wall is to smoke marijuana. But that does not help him get his work done either.

Looking beneath the anxiety he finds memories from a long time ago, of being berated by his grandfather, told that he will never amount to anything; of being terrorised by his father, being hit and having his school books torn up. In one gut-wrenchingly painful memory, he is sitting in the living room, alone, waiting for someone to come to him and help him to feel loved, safer, better, anything other than scared and abandoned. No one did. He sat for hours.

I ask him how old he is in this memory; how old he feels as he tells me this. He says 'eight'.

'This is it' I think to myself. Here is this 18-year-old young man, 6 ft 3 in tall, slouching and shrinking into his chair, unable to feel effective and try out his capacities, still paralysed by self-doubt, loneliness and neglect—because in his mind he is eight. And at eight, he had needed a lot of looking after and received very little. 'All self-doubt is doubt about love.'[16] He had needed parents to open the world to him and him to the world, gradually. Instead he was either beaten back and terrorised or abandoned. Now he is doing it to himself.

Trying something new, wanting to be different from the men in his life, wanting to succeed for himself, working toward what he wanted, created huge anxieties in him.

'This is progress,' I said to him.

He looked at me as if to say 'you are being bizarre' and said only 'huh?'

'First there was only one set of voices in you,' I elaborated.

'The ones that said I was worthless,' he said.

'Yes. Then, you were okay with neglecting yourself, not bathing, smoking weed, lying in your bed for weeks,' I said, not exaggerating. 'But now, there is another voice, yours. One that says you have worked hard and changed things—lost weight, got back to school, made friends. And now you want more, so now there is a conflict and that is creating the anxiety. The question is which voice are you going to listen to? The one that holds you back or the one that propels you forward?'

'Mine,' he said.

Together, in a painful, slow and deliberate way, he and I were both learning[17] and teaching him how to take care of himself, from the outside-in. Eventually, a lot depends on what each of us makes of the too much and the too little we received as children and what we *do* about it.

Notes

1. R. Chauhan. 2016. *The Pain Handbook*. Penguin: New Delhi.
2. D.W. Winnicott. 1964. *The Child, the Family and the Outside World*, London: Penguin, p. 10.
3. Wus is defined as a 'person afraid to act or not up to the task

because of fear'. www.urbandictionary.com

4.   J. Mason, S. Wang, R. Yehuda, S. Riney, D. Charney and S. Southwick. 2001. 'Psychogenic Lowering of Urinary Cortisol Levels Linked to Increased Emotional Numbing and a Shame-Depressive Syndrome in Combat-Related Posttraumatic Stress Disorder'. *Psychosomatic Medicine* 63, 387–401.

5.   For easy to access reading on this topic, see Jo Marchant. 2016. *Cure: A Journey into the Science of Mind over Body*. London: Canongate.
      S. Gerhardt. 2004. *Why Love Matters*. London: Routledge.

6.   Adam Phillips. 2012. *Missing Out: In Praise of the Unlived Life*, Harmondsworth: Penguin.

7.   Ibid., p. 24.

8.   Robert M. Sapolsky. 1994. *Why Zebras Don't Get Ulcers*. New York: Holt Paperbacks.

9.   J. Pennebaker. 1993. 'Putting Stress into Words'. *Behaviour Research and Therapy*, 31 (6): 539–48.

10.   Adam Phillips. 2012. *Missing Out*.

11.   R. FairBairn. 1952. *Psychoanalytic Study of the Personality*. London: Routledge.

12.   Adam Phillips. 2012. *Missing Out*.

13.   Ibid., p. 25.

14.   S. Gerhardt. 2004. *Why Love Matters*, p. 109.
      H. Krystal. 1988. *Integration and Self Healing: Affect, Trauma, Alexithymia*. Hillsdale, NJ: Analytic Press.

15.   K. Lyons-Ruth. 1992. 'Maternal Depressive Symptoms, Disorganized Infant-mother Attachments and Hostile-aggressive Behaviour in the Preschool Classroom: A Prospective Longitudinal View from Infancy to Age Five'. *Rochester Symposium on Developmental Psychopathology*, 4: 131–71
      A. Schore. 1992. *Affect Regulation and the Origin of the Self.* Hillsdale NJ: Lawrence Erlbaum Associates Inc.

16.   Adam Phillips. 2012. *Missing Out*.

17.   Learning to take care of myself has been a slow, tear-stained journey about accessing my feelings, not thoughts, from deep down where I had buried them; attending to the small niggling pains and the entrenched chronic stuff. Once I began to listen

to more than my mind—to my 'gut' and involve my limbs for their own sake (yoga, zumba, dance, football), for the joy of it, not for the functional purpose of getting my mind from place A to B, many things changed. My anxiety reduced, my pains made sense and my health improved. Most importantly, it made me happy.

- I have found the following list very useful:
- Get enough sleep
- Pay attention to your feelings
- Spend time in nature
- Pursue a hobby
- Laugh often
- Grieve your loses
- Accept yourself, imperfections and all
- Only try to change yourself, not others
- Ask for help; you're not superman or superwoman
- Spend less time in front of electronics
- Connect with friends and family
- Try to do things because you want to, not out of obligation
- Practise gratitude daily
- Express your feelings
- Surround yourself with positive people
- Exercise
- Remember it's healthy to say 'no' sometimes
- Forgive yourself when you screw up
- Limit alcohol, caffeine, and other drugs
- Spend some time alone
- Get to know yourself
- Listen to your instincts

S. Martin Downloaded on 15th March 2017 from https://blogs.psychcentral.com/imperfect/2016/12/your-mental-health-is-just-as-important-as-your-physical-health/

Children and Emotions
Lesson 101

'Grown ups never understand anything by themselves and it is rather tedious for children to have to explain things to them time and again.
I have spent a lot of time with grown ups. I have seen them at very close quarters which I'm afraid has not greatly enhanced my opinion of them.'

The Little Prince
Antoine de Saint-Exupery, 1943, p. 11.

Childrearing myth #1: Children have no worries

Truth: children are anxious. Extremely or less, depends on their temperament and the way in which their specific environment responds to them from birth.[1] How they display their anxiety varies, because as we grow, we learn to build what are called defences against anxiety. As I have mentioned before, one of the jobs of a parent is to be a kind of emotion coach and to regulate in and for their children what feels like too much or too little.

Three-year-old Ria came into the consulting room and went speedily from toy to toy, repeatedly asking her mother, 'Yeh kya hai?' She did not explore anything and nothing seemed to hold her attention. It was as if she was on a fact-finding mission, not interested in imaginary play, she rejected all the toy animals, the dolls' house, vehicles and even a toy kitchen. Coloured felt pens made her pause for two minutes, but not more. Even in the small room of eighty square feet, she kept going back to her mother to ask her to leave. She was deeply uncomfortable. Her mother was there to tell me all about the many ways in which she and Ria were struggling. Mother worked full-time and Ria was with her grandparents and maid a lot. She slept poorly, ate poorly, fell ill a lot and was not settling into nursery. Now she has a two-month-old younger sibling to share the already-thinly-stretched line of attention from her mother. Ria had lots to worry about.

Myth #2: Children don't really know what is going on. They are involved in their own worlds.

Truth: Yes children are involved in their own worlds but they do so in order to make sense of what they know is going on around them and which they have intense feelings about. How the world, i.e., the people around the child, go forward to meet him/her, makes all the difference.

Three-year-old Adil was in an early years sports class along with five other children, approximately his age. Though he had not been explicitly told, the coach could tell that Adil was different from the other children. His physical features and responses to instructions suggested that he perhaps had some developmental delay. He was a silent child, who did not laugh or speak to the others. His voice was rarely heard during the lesson. It was clear to the coach that Adil needed to be communicated with differently. When the children were given instructions to run from the yellow cone to the blue cone, Adil seemed reluctant to leave the yellow cone, holding it with both hands as if protecting it. It may have been a confusion about colours, or about the instructions or perhaps the cone had become symbolic of something for Adil and it could easily have been interpreted as 'he has no idea what is going on here'. Any adult would have told him to 'get on with it' and do what the others were doing. The coach, however, decided to see the world from Adil's perspective instead of his own six-foot-high vantage point. He got down on his knees to be closer to the child's height, made eye contact and spoke to him about the cone—that it was okay, that no one would take it away, that perhaps he could run with the cone, take it along. Adil did what he could, along with the cone.

Towards the end of the hour, Adil and the coach found themselves on opposite ends of the play area with instructions on doing a duck-walk. Adil was still holding the yellow cone, clearly reluctant to part with it. The coach weighed the situation, realised Adil was anxious about something and sought first to calm him. Adil needed the adult world to understand him, to come forward to meet and encourage him. Speaking slowly, the coach duck-walked halfway down the path so he was closer to Adil. Seeing this, Adil came forward too. The coach reassured him and asked him to consider putting his cone down, that nothing would happen to it, and join the rest. Adil's eyes moved slowly from the coach, to the team to the cone, as if contemplating these possibilities in his mind. He returned the yellow cone to the coach and walked back to where the others stood. The other children cheered for Adil.

At the end of the session, as the coach was leaving, he heard other staff members calling out to him, 'Sir, Adil wants to say something'. There was Adil, smiling and waving to the coach who had understood him, who had joined him a little bit in his world and tried to make sense of his worries, and shouting 'Bye Sir!' This was most unusual for Adil whose voice was rarely heard and then, to add to everyone's shock, Adil put his fingers to his lips and blew his coach a kiss.

Myth #3: Everyone goes through it, so it's no big deal.

Truth: Everyone goes through it makes it even more of a big deal because it makes it fundamental. Whatever the 'it' is: separation from mother as weaning; separation from home to go to pre-school; birth of a sibling; puberty; transitions of any kind, the quality of these experiences and how we are helped through them become part of our character structures. Forever.

The over-the-hedge advice from neighbours, grandparents and others is usually of the 'don't make a big deal about it' variety. As if children won't notice their own feelings. They will certainly notice that you don't notice. It can lead to different outcomes, none of them good for relationships. Separation, pain and loss create anger, sadness and fear, whether the environment encourages it or not affects only the overt expression and the acceptance of these difficult feelings. Not their existence.

Myth #4: If you ignore it, it will go away.

Truth: Ignoring *feelings* teaches your child that you don't particularly care for his feelings, just his actions or his compliance. This only ensures that the feelings will reappear in a form that is harder to link to its source or origins. In other words, the child will use a defence in order to deal with a feeling and the anxiety its presence creates.

The entire process will go underground.

(Ignoring works for certain behaviours like a young child swearing. If your three-year-old says '*harami*', 'bitch' or 'fuck', it's best to ignore it and pretend nothing happened since he does not know what it means. At this age, many behaviours that do not want repeating can be ignored.[2] It is an effective pruning mechanism. In this case, reacting will let your child know that swearing has a fascinating, almost electric, effect on adults, who jump out of their skin, widen their eyes, draw in a sharp breath; you can almost see their hair stand on end. Reacting to an abusive word only ensure that your child learns that it is a word that gets a reaction from you. You may be interested to know where the child heard these words but there are many families where adults are quite free with their expletives).

Myth #5 or a corollary to Myth #4: If you don't see it or hear it, it's not there.

Truth: There is a reason it is called the inner world. It stays inside and is often chugging along outside of direct awareness therefore it is difficult to put into words. Things feel muddled, confused, messy and this creates internal distress, which in turn may emerge in unusual behaviour that symbolises the internal state in some way; in dreams, in tantrums, nail-biting, in mood swings, bedwetting, rejection of loved ones, in relationship dramas and self-sabotage—not eating, not sleeping, doing badly at school.

In fact, psychotherapists and many medical doctors would be out of work if #5 were true. Every decade we get 'scientific' evidence of things that we previously did not think existed or was measurable. If we insist on empirical evidence in order to believe, then we also need to realise that not everything is obvious or visible to the naked untrained eye. There is a lot more to us than what happens on the surface.

What psychotherapy does for children is to put words to complex, confused, muddled up, messy internal states and this acknowledgement, at the right time, is therapeutic in itself and prevents an ordinarily occurring distress from turning into a mental illness.[3] There is ample evidence of this in psychotherapy literature.

Childrearing myth #6: Good children listen to their parents

Truth: Of course, we adults would think so. But then what we end up with is a person who is good at listening.[4] To others. And while this may work well for a while, there comes a point, usually in early adulthood—at work or as a parent to a new baby—where we expect a person to be self-directed. But with little practice in this area of listening to one self, how is this capacity supposed to kick in after about 20 years of doing the opposite? Is it surprising then that many young people have no clue about what they want to choose as a career or what their personal goals are? Is it surprising that they come across as apathetic or easily swayed by peer groups? Or become so stubborn and obstinate that they disagree with their parents over everything, without thinking about the content?[5]

Be suspicious of the child who is always good. Because there is always the other side to all our personalities: the aggression and the negative feelings, and the good child is hiding that somewhere, sticking it down some hole. Compliance is comfortable for parents; we stop our children from doing things to stop them creating worry in us[6] but it is a huge price to pay and it will be the future of society and the child itself that will pay the cost some day. What does that mean exactly, you may wonder. It depends a lot on what kind of person we want to create at the other end of this process. 'Should we not be hoping to bring our infant up to be an adolescent who thinks and questions and then becomes an adult with a mind of his own rather than a replica of ourselves, however fine we may feel ourselves to be?'[7]

Helping your child to develop her own mind is extremely hard work because she will practise her new-found opinionated self on you, her parents. Yes, that is not fun for you. Tough luck. Unfortunately, there is no other route. Sparring makes for strength.

Truth #1: Be aware of how you treat your child's emotions because that is how they will learn to treat their own. That is how they will treat themselves.

How do you treat your own emotions and those of your child? Are you anxious and protective? Matter of fact? Indulgent? Avoidant? All of the above? Becoming aware of our attitude to feelings is crucial. 'If they are seen as dangerous enemies then they can only be managed through exerting social pressure and fear. Alternatively, if every impulse must be gratified, the relationships with others become only a means to your own ends. But if feelings are respected as valuable guides both to the state of your own organism as well as to that of others, then a very different culture arises in which others' feelings matter and you are motivated to respond.'[8]

Most of the time, my work is to make absences present, to acknowledge a child's feelings, and to help her parents acknowledge the feelings too. This strengthens the bond between parents and children. Twenty-three-year old Rakhi tells me that her mother finally acknowledged to her that there had been a struggle over money because of which she had not been able to fund Rakhi's dream of studying design. 'I was surprised', she said, 'I was relieved, not sad…just to hear her say it because it was the reality and she was not making excuses.'

Apparently, just calling a spade a spade is half the job.

Three-year-old Roma slips and falls on a stone floor and starts to cry loudly. Her mother comes over to her saying 'nothing happened!' She does not pick her up or hug her. She says 'nothing happened' and distracts her.

Really? Is it true that nothing happened?[9]

She did fall. On stone. She is only a little person. It probably did hurt her knees. So to hear her mother, the most significant person in her life, say 'nothing happened' puts little Roma in a really difficult place. Since her mother's response and Roma's own experience contradict each other, what is she to trust? Her physical and emotional experience or the interpretation given by her adored mother? What do you think she will choose? And what will be the long-term effect of many years of this kind of pushing aside of her own experience?

Unusually enough, I found one answer to this in a recent Hindi film where the character, a therapist, explains this to his patient:

> 'You know, in childhood when we want to cry,
> Adults tell us "Dry your tears. Laugh".
> When we are angry, adults tell us
> "Give us a smile".
> You know why?
> So that the home remains peaceful.
> When we want to hate, we don't get permission to,
> When we want to show love,
> we find that the entire emotional system is unregulated.
> It cannot function.
> Tears, anger, hate, nothing was allowed full expression
> So how shall we know how to express love?'

(Translated from Dear Zindagi, 2016.
Writer/Director Gauri Shinde)

THE MYTH OF A CAREFREE CHILDHOOD

Childhood is often idealised as carefree in the casual reports of most adults but ask again[10] and the surface cracks. Many of us, with some sustained pressure, can even manage to access unpleasant memories and feelings, significant anxieties, losses and difficult transitions. People work hard every day to fight off a sense of being ineffective at work or at relationships, of being unworthy of love—feelings that, unknown to them, have their origins in childhood and in the relationships of that time.

Most of us adults find it difficult to communicate our feelings. Most of us are running to stay still or running away. Yet, emotion is what relationships are made up of and in childhood, emotions are the fuel of everyday life. Children's fairy tales, replete with murder, envy, love, greed and rage give us a hint of the emotions that we experience as children. We have extremes of feeling towards people closest to us and we build special internal mechanisms—usually filters, compartments, separate mindscapes—to protect them from our hatred.

Children feel intensely. One has only to see a baby crying, a toddler throwing a tantrum or a child not wanting to separate from a parent at a school gate to realise that whatever it is, this energy underlying it all, is an intense one. Hunger is experienced as wild animals gnawing on the insides, and satisfaction makes the entire world beautiful. In children's realities, there are no half-measures; feelings are black and white; all or none, where one obliterates the other. Love and anger cannot exist beside each other and it is almost impossible to remember that the parent who shouted at me, actually also loves me. Anger and love are both intense: anger can destroy and love wants to eat up the loved one.

We are afraid of our own intensities.

It is strange but true that emotional development can side-step chronological age. In other words, just getting older is not a sufficient condition for emotional growth. It can proceed at a different pace from physical growth, the capacity to learn as well as chronological age. Parents may find it difficult to understand how their eight-year-old child who can speak in complex sentences and has an aptitude for math and music, becomes very anxious in social situations or weepy when his parents go out in the evening without him or angry when his father says 'no' for something. Inside every one of us is a version of ourselves at a younger age; sometimes a much younger age. Like the wooden Russian-doll toy, we carry them around inside a bigger, adult shell. When scared, tired or ill we can easily remember our need for a stronger, wiser parental figure who will make us feel better. Children are similar, only with better access to their need to be looked after at times of uncertainty, illness or fatigue. So it is entirely possible for this eight-year-old who sometimes speaks as though he could be fifteen, to be hanging onto his mother's sari, crying and behaving more like a three-year-old because he feels miserable at the thought of being left behind when she goes out. Children go backward and forward in their emotional age, many times even in a single day.

Twelve-year-old Shiv was a good example of this. His own mother described him as oscillating between behaving like a frightened, incapable two-year-old and an obnoxious, aggressive 18-year-old on any given day. In fact, the reality of his 12-year-old self was wobbly and rarely visible. Separating from his mother was a painful struggle for him—weaning, pre-school, school, holidays with dad—every one of these had been times when he had shrunk to the little boy inside him. Instead of broadening his world, these transitions frightened him. To compensate for the small scared child within, he developed a fondness for guns, knives and martial arts. 'It makes me feel safe,' he explained to me. However in his mother's experience, it was not about safety but power, because she was often at the receiving end of it. If helplessness is fundamentally what he was defending himself against, it is not surprising that the ways he had of doing this make him feel powerful. 'Our sense of power is a function of our helplessness, our games of autonomy are our self-cure for resourcelessness.'[11]

Children's emotional needs are unalterable. In other words, as children, we all have similar needs, for emotional bonds that provide security and space to grow. Their fulfilment forms the basis for health in their future relationships. These emotional needs, once attended to, leave the child fortified to move on with the business of living and learning.[12]

Emotions let us know about our inner selves and when attended to, they are an important source of clarity about who we are and what we need. Unfortunately, in the split between reason and emotion, the latter has been given the lower place and the training for this begins in childhood.

Many parents and teachers would like young children to communicate in words as early as possible so that the gap between children's communication styles and those of adults is reduced; so that children can be negotiated with in words and can explain themselves in words rather than through tantrums and disobedience.

By noticing that emotions and behaviours are communication, we can open our minds to the question of 'what is this child trying to tell me?'; 'what is her/my inner experience of this event?' and then start becoming curious. We can but we usually don't. We apply the common myths listed above and take a short cut. Or what we think is one. We pay for it in many other ways.

NOTES

1. S. Gerhardt. 2004. *Why Love Matters*. London: Routledge.
2. C. Webster-Stratton, *The Incredible Years* http://www.incredibleyears.com/team-view/carolyn-webster-stratton/

3.   Martha Harris. 1973. 'Complexity of Mental Pain Seen in a Six-year-old Following Sudden Bereavement'. *Journal of Child Psychotherapy*, vol. 3 (3), pp. 35–45.

4.   D. Pattanaik. 2014. *Fun in Devlok Omnibus*. London: Puffin Devdutt Pattanaik tells a story of a couple who wanted good obedient children. They learnt their lesson eventually.

5.   R.R. Greenson. 2016. 'The Fascination of Violence'. In *On Loving, Hating and Living Well*. Edited by Robert A. Nemiroff, Alan Sugarman and Alvin Robbins. London: Karnac.

6.   Martha Harris. 2011. *Thinking about Infants and Young Children*. London: Karnac.

7.   Ibid., p. 44.

8.   S. Gerhardt. 2004. *Why Love Matters*, p. 30

9.   Women in many communities in India have an early induction into disregarding pain and discomfort in their bodies. Staying hungry, thirsty, holding back urine till there is a safe place to use as a toilet, starts very early, encouraging a dissociation from the body. As if it and what happens to it, is not their experience at all. It then becomes easier to allow men and eventually children to use their bodies.

10. Dobara poocho is not just an ad gimmick.

11. Adam Phillips. 2010. *On Balance*, New York: Farrar, Straus & Giroux, p. 121.

12. It could be said that learning comes secondary to emotion, where the capacity to learn is freed up when the child's emotional world is stable. Having one's emotions attended to is the 'oil of learning'; it provides nourishment for the learning journey. Many a learning difficulty masks an underlying emotional problem.

Epilogue

Harry, there is never a perfect answer in this messy, emotional world. Perfection is beyond the reach of humankind, beyond the reach of magic. In every shining moment of happiness is that drop of poison: the knowledge that pain will come again. Be honest to those you love, show your pain. To suffer is as human as to breathe.

Dumbledore
Act four scene two
Harry Potter and the Cursed Child
JK Rowling, John Tiffany & Jack Thorne

Made in the USA
Monee, IL
08 July 2026